D0845173

QB
981
.N85

Numbers, Ronald L
    Creation by natural law : Laplace's nebular hypothesis in
American thought / by Ronald L. Numbers. — Seattle : University of Washington Press, c1977.

    xi, 184 p. : ill. ; 23 cm.

    Based on the author's thesis, University of California, Berkeley.
    Bibliography: p. 171-178.
    Includes index.
    ISBN 0-295-95439-6

    1. Laplace, Pierre Simon, marquis de, 1749-1827.   2. Nebular hypothesis.
3. Philosophy, American—19th century.   I. Title.

QB981.N85   521'.54   76-45810
                                                                MARC

CREATION BY NATURAL LAW

CREATION
BY NATURAL LAW

Laplace's Nebular Hypothesis
in American Thought

BY RONALD L. NUMBERS

University of Washington Press

Seattle and London

This book was published with the assistance of a grant from the Andrew W. Mellon Foundation.

Library of Congress Cataloging in Publication Data

Numbers, Ronald L
    Creation by natural law.

    Bibliography: p.
    Includes index.
    1. Laplace, Pierre Simon, marquis de, 1749-1827.
2. Nebular hypothesis.   3. Philosophy, American—19th century.   I. Title.
QB981.N85   521'.54   76-45810
ISBN 0-295-95439-6

FOR DIANE

Preface

One of the most significant developments in the history of modern Western thought is the decline of supernaturalism. Erosion of belief in divine activity is particularly evident in the nineteenth century, when scientific accounts of creation by natural law supplanted the religious myth of a world created by divine fiat. Traditionally the lion's share of credit—or blame—for this victory of naturalism has gone to Charles Darwin and the biologists who formulated theories of organic evolution, while cosmogonists have more often than not been relegated to historical obscurity. Certainly Darwinism deserves the spotlight, but it should not blind us to the important supporting role played by naturalistic cosmogonies, especially the nebular hypothesis proposed by Pierre Simon Laplace in 1796, which explained the origin of the solar system as a natural development over extended periods of time.

This study of the nebular hypothesis focuses on the American scene. The first six chapters trace the history of Laplace's cosmogony chronologically, from its European inception to its demise about 1900. They show, among other things, how this hypothesis came to enjoy widespread popularity with educated Americans, including the nation's most prominent scientists, well before the appearance of Darwin's *Origin of Species* in 1859. The last three chapters explore some of the theological and scientific consequences resulting from the acceptance of this cosmogony. They reveal how open warfare between the forces of science and religion was averted by reinterpreting natural and Biblical theology to accommodate the nebular hypothesis, and they suggest how this experience helped to pave the way for the surprisingly rapid assimilation of organic evolution in the 1860s and 1870s.

It is difficult, if not impossible, to determine precisely the impact of any idea on the thinking habits of a community. Our task is compounded by the fact that during the early nineteenth century several naturalistic theories were simultaneously impinging on the American mind. While astronomers were debating the validity of Laplace's cosmogony, geologists were imposing natural law on the earth's surface and paleontologists were proposing nonsupernatural explanations of the fossil record. Each of these ideas led to reinterpretations of traditional theology and extended the domain of natural law. Thus the influence of the nebular hypothesis was not entirely unique. The justification for singling it out in this volume is not that it was more important than other naturalistic theories, but rather that its history has not previously been told.

One conclusion does seem certain: the nebular hypothesis convinced many Americans that the solar system was a product of natural law rather than of divine miracle. For these individuals, its acceptance permanently erased all notions of supernaturally created planetary bodies. When the Laplacian theory failed at the turn of the century and a replacement was being sought, no one with any scientific pretentions gave the slightest thought to a miraculous explanation. No one even seemed to care any more whether or not the proposed substitutes harmonized with the Mosaic story of creation or the once-cherished doctrines of natural theology. The nebular hypothesis had established natural law in the heavens.

Acknowledgments

This study of the nebular hypothesis originated a decade ago as a paper in A. Hunter Dupree's graduate seminar in the history of American science at the University of California, Berkeley. Since that time Professor Dupree has patiently guided its evolution first into a doctoral dissertation and eventually into a book. My debt to him is immeasurable. I am equally indebted to Roger Hahn, whose encouragement and criticisms were a source of constant motivation and whose familiarity with Laplace and the nebular hypothesis saved me from many a needless error.

During the summer of 1969 the Office of Academic Programs of the Smithsonian Institution provided the financial assistance that enabled me to spend several months working in East Coast manuscript collections. Samuel T. Suratt, former archivist of the Smithsonian Institution, and the staff of the Smithsonian Institution Library were particularly helpful.

Both Michele Aldrich and Max H. Fisch directed my attention to documents I surely would have missed otherwise. Charlotte McGirr and Janet Schulze assisted with final preparations for publication. Dr. M. A. Hoskin, editor of the *Journal for the History of Astronomy*, kindly granted permission to reprint (in Chapters II and IV) portions of two articles that previously appeared in his journal. To all these individuals I am most grateful.

Finally, I owe many thanks to Maurice M. Vance, professor of history at The Florida State University, who introduced me to the pleasures of American science and guided my first hesitant steps as a historian.

Contents

CREATION BY NATURAL LAW

CHAPTER I

A Natural Cosmogony

.

Late in the seventeenth century a young English divine named William Whiston commented on the popular view of the Biblical account of creation. He criticized his contemporaries for habitually "stretching [the Six Days Work] beyond the Earth, either to the whole System of things, as the most do; or indeed to the Solar System, with which others are more modestly contented in the case."[1] In Whiston's day it was customary to accept the Mosaic story of creation found in the first chapter of the book of Genesis as a literal historical record. For most this meant that the entire cosmos, or at least the solar system, had been created by God's fiat in six successive twenty-four-hour periods, approximately four thousand years before the birth of Christ.[2] As long as natural philosophers were willing to tolerate supernatural explanations within the domain of science, there was little motivation to discard this traditional cosmogony. The desire for a natural history of creation became acute only after men of science began to view nature as "a law-bound system of matter in motion," virtually independent of any direct supernatural activity.[3]

Modern attempts to explain the origin of the solar system without recourse to divine intervention date from the mid-seventeenth century. As the new science resolved one after another of nature's mysteries, the temptation to formulate a purely naturalistic cosmogony became increasingly great. One of the first to yield to this temptation was the French philosopher René Descartes. His naturalistic theory of the origin of the solar system, sketched in the *Principia Philosophiae* as well as in his suppressed treatise *Le Monde*, followed logically from his twin beliefs in the constancy of the laws of nature and in the sufficiency of these laws to explain the phenomena of nature. Using vortices as a creative mechanism, he showed how the solar system could have been formed by the God-ordained laws of nature operating on a primitive chaos. Then, undoubtedly prompted by the recent experiences of Galileo, he cautiously added that he considered this hypothesis to be "absolutely false" and asserted his belief in the orthodox doctrine of the creation of the world in the beginning in a fully developed state.[4]

This thinly veiled attempt to eliminate God as a necessary element in the creation of the world brought Descartes considerable notoriety. In relegating God to the remote and seemingly minor task of establishing the laws of nature, he had overstepped the bounds of seventeenth-century tolerance. His fellow countryman Blaise Pascal could never forgive such blatant impiety. "In all his philosophy," wrote Pascal, Descartes "would have been quite willing to dispense with God. But he had to make Him give a fillip to set the world in motion; beyond this, he has no further need of God."[5]

Descartes fared no better with Isaac Newton, who consistently rejected suggestions that the solar system had been created by the "mere Laws of Nature." In the General Scholium at the end of the second edition of his *Principia* Newton summarized his reasons for believing in the necessity of divine action:

> The six primary planets are revolved about the sun in circles concentric with the sun, and with motions directed towards the same parts, and almost in the same plane. Ten moons are revolved about the earth, Jupiter, and Saturn, in circles concentric with them, with the same direction of motion, and nearly in the planes of the orbits of those planets; but it is not to be conceived that mere mechanical causes could give birth to so many regular motions, since the comets range over all parts of the heavens in very eccentric orbits. . . . This most beautiful system of the sun, planets, and comets, could only proceed from the counsel and dominion of an intelligent and powerful Being.[6]

Newton did not deny that natural causes had been employed in the production of the solar system. He only insisted that it could not have been made by the laws of nature alone. His position is stated clearly in a letter to Thomas Burnet: "Where natural causes are at hand God uses them as instruments in his works, but I do not think them alone sufficient for ye creation. . . ." In particular, he could discover no cause for the earth's diurnal motion other than divine action.[7]

Newton's own theory of the creation of the inanimate world, which he confided to Burnet, illustrates his preference for natural explanations. He regarded the Mosaic account as a description of "realities in a language artificially adapted to ye sense of ye vulgar," not as a scientifically accurate record of events. The Genesis story of creation related primarily to developments on this globe; thus, the creation of the sun, moon, and stars had been assigned to the fourth day because they first shone upon the earth at that time. Newton imagined that the entire solar system had been formed from a "common Chaos" and that the separation of the planets into individual "parcels" and their subsequent condensation into solid globes had been effected by gravitational attraction, though this possibly was the work of "ye spirit of God." Since the earth's diurnal motion probably had not begun until the end of the second day, at which time it had first become a terraqueous globe, it seemed as if the first two days of creation week could be made "as long as you please" without doing violence to the language of Genesis.[8]

Neither the private speculations of Newton nor the quasi-naturalistic cosmogonies offered by Burnet and Whiston succeeded in breaking the hold of a static creation on the collective mind of the seventeenth century.[9] Newton's widely circulated condemnation of hypothesizing about creation by natural law and his insistence on the necessity of divine intervention left the distinct impression that "Newtonianism and cosmogony were absolutely incompatible."[10] Meanwhile, the general public continued to follow "those Divines" who, in the words of Burnet, "insist upon ye hypothesis of 6 dayes as a physical reality."[11] And into the eighteenth century even enlightened men continued to view Newton as a Biblical literalist who "asserted that the immediate hand of God had instituted this arrangement [i.e., the solar system] without the intervention of the forces of nature."[12]

Although Newton and other English cosmogonists readily utilized natural laws to assist in understanding the events of creation, they always did so within the context of the Biblical record. They might speak of the days of creation as long periods of time and discuss the possible role of gravitational attraction in the formation of the solar system, but they were not at all interested in discarding the basic features of the Mosaic story. It was in France, among the scientific disciples of Newton and the spiritual heirs of Descartes, that totally secular cosmogonies, free from all Scriptural influence, first gained a foothold.

Georges Louis Leclerc, comte de Buffon, was one of the first French admirers of Newton; he was also one of the sternest critics of Newton's cosmogony. Whereas Newton actively encouraged the union of science and theology, Buffon demanded a complete separation. Those studying physical subjects, he argued, "ought, as much as possible, to avoid having recourse to supernatural causes." Philosophers "ought not to be affected by causes which seldom act, and whose action is always sudden and violent. These have no place in the ordinary course of nature. But operations uniformly repeated, motions which succeed one another without interruption, are the causes which alone ought to be the foundation of our reasoning."[13] Whether or not such explanations were true was of no consequence. What really mattered was that they appear probable. Buffon acknowledged, for example, that the planets had been set in motion originally by the Creator—but considered the fact of no value to the natural philosopher.[14]

Buffon's repudiation of the supernatural in science led him to search for a natural history of the solar system. He was far too good a Newtonian to consider the discredited Cartesian theory of vortices, and Newton's cosmogony was out of the question; so he had no choice but to formulate his own naturalistic hypothesis. The first description of it appeared in 1749 in his *Théorie de la terre*. Thirty years later he gave a somewhat modified version of his original ideas in *Les Époques de la nature*.

The numerous uniformities in the solar system persuaded Buffon that a common cause was responsible for all planetary motions. All the planets revolve around the sun in the same direction, and according to his calculations the probability is 64 to 1 that this was the product of one cause. In addition, the planes of the planetary orbits are inclined no more than 7½ degrees from the ecliptic, and the probability is 7,692,624 to 1 that this could not have been produced by accident. Such a high degree of probability, "which almost amounts to a certainty," seemed to be conclusive evidence "that all the planets have probably received their centrifugal motion by one single stroke."[15]

Though his calculations did not indicate whether the stroke had come from the hand of God, as Newton had assumed, or from some natural heavenly body, Buffon arbitrarily limited his search for an explanation to the latter type of cause. Since "nothing but comets [seemed] capable of communicating motion to such vast masses" as the planets, he confidently turned to them for the solution to his cosmogonical problem.[16] The hypothetical production of the solar system he described in the following way:

> The comet, by falling obliquely on the sun . . . must have forced off from his surface a quantity of matter equal to a 650th part of his body. This matter being in a liquid state, would at first form a torrent, of which the largest and rarest parts would fly to the greatest distances; the smaller and more dense, having received only an equal impulse, would remain nearer the sun; his power of attraction would operate upon all the parts detached from his body, and make them circulate round him; and, at the same time, the mutual attraction of the particles of matter would cause all the detached parts to take on the form of globes, at different distances from the sun, the nearer moving with greater rapidity in their orbits than the more remote.[17]

Buffon believed the diurnal motion of the planets to have resulted from the oblique blow of the comet, which would have caused the matter detached from the sun to rotate. And he imagined that a very oblique blow would have given the planets a rotation so great that small quantities of matter would have been thrown off to form the satellites. The fact that the satellites "all move in the same direction, and in concentric circles round their principal planets, and nearly in the plane of their orbits" appeared to be a striking confirmation of this theory.[18]

Although his cosmogony seemed "extremely probable" to him, Buffon fully realized that others might not be so easily convinced. Every man, he said, "has his own standard of estimating probabilities of this nature, and as this standard varies according to the different capacities of combining analogies more or less remote, I pretend not to convince those who are unwilling to believe."[19] Among the many disbelievers were those who accused him of reverting to prescientific speculations typical of the Cartesians. "I ask . . . why you undertake to explain such phenomena?" wrote A. R. J. Turgot, one of Buffon's fellow philosophes. "Do you wish to deprive Newtonian science of that simplicity and wise restraint which characterize it? By plunging us back into the obscurity of hypotheses, do you want to give justification to the Cartesians, with their three elements and their formation of the world?"[20] Surely Buffon could not have missed the irony of such criticism, for he had proposed his theory specifically to provide a scientific substitute for

Newton's metaphysical speculations. Much more deserved were the reproaches of Gautier d'Agoty and others for failing to consider final causes and theological traditions.[21]

Buffon's cosmogony failed to win general acceptance. Nevertheless, it remained, despite its scientific inadequacies, the most serious challenge to the Mosaic account of creation through the last half of the eighteenth century.[22] A few years before the outbreak of the French revolution the astronomer Jean Sylvain Bailly enthusiastically endorsed it in his *Histoire de l'astronomie moderne*, thus bestowing upon it a measure of scientific respectability. We know that Laplace read this particular history, and it seems likely that his attention was drawn to Buffon's cosmogony in this way.[23]

Pierre Simon Laplace was the leading Newtonian scientist in postrevolutionary France. Among the many similarities he shared with his illustrious English predecessor was the inclination to indulge in cosmogonical speculations.[24] In 1796 he sketched his ideas in a lengthy note appended to the *Exposition du système du monde* (see Appendix 2).[25] As far as Laplace could remember, Buffon was "the only one . . . who, since the discovery of the true system of the world, has endeavoured to investigate the origin of the planets, and of their satellites."[26] But on several counts Buffon's hypothesis was less than satisfactory. It could indeed account for the uniform direction of the revolutions of the planets around the sun and for their orbits lying nearly in the same plane, but it left many other phenomena totally unexplained. An oblique blow by a comet would not, as Buffon had assumed, necessarily impart a rotation to the planets in the same direction as their revolutions around the sun, nor would it ensure that the satellites revolved in their observed direction. Furthermore, Buffon's hypothesis did not explain why the orbits of the planets and their satellites are nearly circular, while the orbits of comets are very eccentric. If the planets had been formed from matter ejected from the sun, they would return close to that body during each revolution and would thus have orbits much more eccentric than they do. Since a comet clearly could not have produced the observed phenomena, Laplace looked for some other nonsupernatural explanation that would hold up under the strictest scientific scrutiny.[27]

As Buffon had done earlier, Laplace calculated the probability of the solar system's being a chance arrangement:

. . . the planetary system, such as we now consider it, is composed of seven planets, and fourteen satellites. We have observed the rotation of the Sun, of five planets, of the Moon, of Saturn's ring, and of his farthest satellite; these motions with those of revolution, form together thirty direct movements, in the prime direction. If we conceive the plane of any direct motion whatever, coinciding at first with that of the ecliptic, afterwards inclining itself towards this last plane, and passing over all the degrees of inclination, from zero to half the circumference; it is clear that the motion will be direct in all its inferior inclinations to a hundred degrees, and that it will be retrograde in its inclination beyond that; so that, by the change of inclination alone, the direct and retrograde motions of the solar sytem, can be represented. Beheld in this point of view, we may reckon twenty-nine motions, of which the planes are inclined to that of the Earth, at most 1/4th of the circumference; but, supposing their inclinations had been the effect of chance, they would have extended to half the circumference, and the probability that one of them would have exceeded the quarter, would be 1—1/29, or 536870911/536870912. It is then extremely probable, that the direction of the planetary motion is not the effect of chance, and this becomes still more probable, if we consider that the inclination of the greatest number of these motions to the ecliptic, is very small, and much less than a quarter of the circumference.[28]

The absence of any bodies in the solar system having orbits with eccentricities between the small ones of the planets and the large ones of the comets was an additional indication that planetary development had not occurred randomly.[29]

Having thus ruled out the possibility that the solar system was a product of chance, Laplace proposed a hypothesis capable of explaining the structure and motions of the system, of which only the briefest sketch was given in the first editions of the *Système du monde*. According to his hypothesis, the planets had been created from the atmosphere of the sun, which, because of its heat, had originally extended beyond the orbit of the most distant planet. As this atmosphere condensed, it abandoned a succession of rings—similar to those of Saturn—in the plane of the sun's equator, and these rings then coalesced to form the various planets. In a similar way the satellites developed from the planetary atmospheres.[30]

In the later editions of the *Système du monde* Laplace worked out this nebular hypothesis in greater detail, particularly those parts dealing with the formation of the rings and the breaking up of the rings into planets. During the years following the writing of the first edition he had become convinced that the primitive condition of the solar system closely resembled a slowly rotating hot nebula. As this body cooled and contracted, the speed of its rotation increased to such an extent that the centrifugal force acting on the particles in the plane of the nebula's equator equaled their gravitational attraction to the parent mass. Consequently, a large ring of nebulous matter was left behind to circle the central body. This process, repeated each time the centrifugal force became sufficiently great to counterbalance the effect of gravity, eventually produced a series of concentric rings rotating around the sun.[31]

The fate of these rings depended upon their individual constitutions. If they condensed so uniformly that no breaking up occurred, a solid ring would result. This extremely rare possibility had happened only once in the formation of the solar system, in the development of the rings of Saturn. More commonly, the rings would break up into a number of small rotating spheroids. Usually the largest of these bodies would attract the others to it and thus become a planet, but in the case of the asteroids the spheroids apparently had remained separate entities.[32]

Laplace's conviction about the nebular origin of the solar system rested largely upon William Herschel's recent telescopic observations of nebulae. Herschel, a German expatriate living in England, employed the most powerful telescopes in existence in a dedicated effort to determine the construction of the heavens. In 1791 he reported having discovered "*a star of about the 8th magnitude, surrounded with a faintly luminous atmosphere, of a considerable extent.*" Close comparison of this cloudy object with known clusters of stars indicated that the nebulous atmosphere about the star was nonstellar in nature. A truly new substance had been discovered in the heavens! Since this "shining fluid" appeared to be self-luminous and capable of existing independently of the central star, Herschel speculated that perhaps stars generally were produced from the condensation of this matter.[33]

The discovery of additional nebulae during the following years enabled Herschel ultimately to arrange his observations in a continuous series illustrating the various stages in the development of stars from nebulous matter. This evidence seemed to warrant the conclusion "that every succeeding state of the nebulous matter is the result of the action of gravitation upon it while in a foregoing one, and by such steps the successive condensation of it has been brought up to the planetary condition."[34] For some unknown reason

Herschel did not extrapolate his conclusions on the evolution of stellar systems to include the development of our solar system, leaving this for his more adventurous French colleague.

Apparently Laplace had not yet heard of Herschel's discoveries when he first conceived his cosmogony, for he made no mention of them in the first edition of the *Système du monde*. There is reason to believe, however, that he had become familiar with them by the summer of 1802, when Herschel visited Paris and became acquainted with Laplace. We do not know how much the two astronomers discussed their respective cosmogonies, but the subject did come up at least once—during Herschel's visit, with Laplace and Count Rumford, to the country estate of Napoleon. Herschel described the encounter in his diary, noting that his own comments on the construction of the heavens had given the First Consul great satisfaction, whereas Laplace's effort "to shew that a chain of natural causes would account for the construction and preservation of the wonderful system" disturbed Napoleon, who desired more emphasis on the role of God.[35]

But more important than how Laplace learned of Herschel's work is his recognition of the support it could give his hypothesis. Laplace's cosmogony was essentially a rational reconstruction of the history of the solar system based on a few hints provided by the present structure and motions of the system. It suggested merely how the planets and satellites might have been formed. It did not demonstrate that they had actually gone through the developmental process he proposed. Herschel's discoveries, on the other hand, showed that an analogous process was still going on in nature and that bodies like that postulated by Laplace as the primitive state of the solar system really existed. Here was the empirical evidence Laplace needed, and he did not fail to perceive its value:

> . . . by tracing the progress of condensation of the nebulous matter [as related by Herschel], we descend to the consideration of the Sun, formerly surrounded by an immense atmosphere, to which consideration we can also arrive, from an examination of the phenomena of the solar system as we see in our last note [which describes the nebular hypothesis]. Such a marked coincidence, arrived at by such different means, renders the existence of this anterior state of the Sun extremely probable.[36]

Laplace could not help feeling that his cosmogony possessed "a great degree of probability"; yet he was astute enough to realize that it lacked the certainty of proof. For this very reason, he presented the nebular hypothesis "with that diffidence which ought always to attach to whatever is not the result of observation and computation."[37] Unfortunately, this statement and the fact that the hypothesis, in its final version, was placed in a long "note" at the end of a popular work have led some scholars to suggest that Laplace was somewhat ashamed of his cosmogony.[38] Actually, he was rather proud of it and labored for years to improve it. In his monumental *Traité de mécanique céleste* he pointed with obvious pride to the successful way in which his nebular theory accounted for the rings of Saturn.[39] And among his scientific contemporaries it was well known that he took his cosmogony seriously. The German astronomer Wilhelm Olbers, for example, wrote in 1812 to his friend Friedrich Wilhelm Bessel that "La Place . . . has been exceptionally partial to his cosmogonical hypothesis and finds . . . much to support his conjecture in Herschel's new observations of nebulae."[40]

As Katherine Collier long ago pointed out, "the credit for having promulgated the theory which swayed the thought of the nineteenth century" belongs unreservedly to Laplace.[41] But his, though the most influential, was not the first nebular hypothesis to appear. Some forty years prior to the publication of the *Système du monde,* Immanuel Kant, in Germany, also reflected on the possibility of the solar system's having originated from a nebulalike mass. Frequently he is cited as a precursor of Laplace, but even a superficial examination will show that the two theories have little in common.

Although the direction and positions of the planetary orbits seemed unmistakably to indicate some sort of common origin, Kant was unwilling to assume an arbitrary hypothesis, like Buffon's comet or Laplace's extended solar atmosphere, to account for the phenomena. Beginning instead with matter distributed chaotically throughout the universe, he tried to show how the forces of attraction and repulsion alone would have produced our solar system and others like it. At some instant in the remote past, when gravitation first became a universal force, the largest particles of matter in space attracted the smaller bodies in their neighborhoods to form large masses or suns. Particles drawn from distant points were frequently deflected by the repulsive force of other particles; thus, instead of uniting with the central mass, they went into orbits around it. The largest of these orbiting bodies developed into planets by a process of accretion. Satellites were formed in a similar manner, except for Saturn's rings, which had developed anomalously from volatile matter thrown off by Saturn. In this explanation of Saturn's rings, a relatively minor part of his total cosmogony, Kant came his closest to anticipating Laplace.[42]

Kant's cosmogony first appeared in 1755 in a small, anonymous volume entitled *Universal Natural History and Theory of the Heavens*. Unluckily, bankruptcy prevented the publisher from distributing the book; so Kant failed to get his ideas before the public. In 1763 he tried again to obtain a hearing for his theory, this time in a philosophical work on *The Only Possible Argument for a Demonstration of the Existence of God*. But recognition still did not come, and his theory remained almost totally uninfluential until its "discovery" in the mid-nineteenth century.[43] Certainly Laplace was in no way indebted to the German philosopher. He probably never even heard of Kant's speculations. The roots of Laplace's nebular hypothesis are rather to be found in the writings of Descartes and Buffon, in their naturalistic approach to the cosmogonical problem.

CHAPTER II

The Nebular Hypothesis Comes to America

Throughout the eighteenth and early nineteenth centuries the advocates of natural cosmogonies won few converts in America, where there was a warm and persistent attachment to the familiar Genesis story and its six-thousand-year chronology. Buffon's collision theory, the best known of the pre-Laplacian cosmogonies, was universally condemned for being both theologically dangerous and scientifically unsound. In his *Brief Retrospect of the Eighteenth Century* Samuel Miller, Presbyterian minister and member of the American Philosophical Society, outlined Buffon's "bold and plausible" theory and then proceeded to enumerate its unacceptable features:

> Its manifest object is to exclude the agency of a Divine Architect, and to represent a world begun and perfected merely by the operation of natural, undesigning causes. That it cannot be reconciled with the sacred history, will appear evident on the slightest inspection; and that it involves the grossest philosophical absurdities has been clearly shown by succeeding geologists. It was embraced, however, by M. Bailly, of France, by the celebrated [Samuel Christian] Hollman[n], of Goettingen, and others; and continues to be respected and adopted by many to the present time.[1]

A similar denouncement appeared in William Paley's popular *Natural Theology*, a text used in schools throughout the United States. To ensure that the message got across, the editor of the American edition attached a note further condemning mechanical theories of the origin of the solar system.[2] An educated American could scarcely have escaped these warnings.

14

It should be pointed out that not all defenders of the Biblical story of creation believed that the formation of the solar system had occurred during one twenty-four-hour day. Some thought Genesis pertained only to this earth and that God had made the solar system prior to the week of creation. This interpretation proved to be especially useful in explaining the existence of light three days before the creation of the sun. In a 1798 oration on the Mosaic history of creation, Ebenezer Grant Marsh, a young instructor in Hebrew at Yale, argued that "it is certainly, much more rational to conclude, from the connexion between all the bodies in the solar system, that the sun and moon were in existence from the commencement of the creation, but could not be seen the three first days, on account of the vapours, and heterogeneous particles, with which the air was filled."[3] Though Marsh and his contemporaries were not at all inclined toward a naturalistic cosmogony, this exegesis, divorcing the formation of the solar system from the activities that took place on the six days of creation, gave freedom to succeeding generations to consider the origin of the solar system outside the context of revelation.

Even the deists, who were unrestrained by any particular allegiance to the Scriptures, generally supported the idea of a creation by divine fiat. As Daniel Boorstin has shown, their conception of God as Architect and Builder made it seem "axiomatic that the creation of the material universe was not a continuing process, but had been accomplished by a brief series of divine works at the very beginning."[4] To a deist like Thomas Jefferson, "dreams about the modes of creation, inquiries whether our globe has been formed by the agency of fire or water, how many millions of years it has cost Vulcan or Neptune to produce what the fiat of the Creator would effect by a single act of will [were] too idle to be worth a single hour of any man's life."[5]

Despite Jefferson's admonition, a few Americans did squander their time pondering the question of the earth's origin. Even the frugal Benjamin Franklin could not resist the temptation. Though he generally favored that "method of philosophizing, which proceeds upon actual observation, makes a collection of facts, and concludes no farther than those facts will warrant," he permitted himself "to wander a little in the wilds of fancy."[6] To support his contention that the center of the earth is fluid, he proposed the following hypothesis, vaguely reminiscent of Kant's cosmogony, in a letter to the Abbé Soulavie, dated 22 September 1782:

> If one might indulge imagination in supposing how such a globe [as the earth] was formed, I should conceive, that all the elements in separate particles being originally mixed in confusion and occupying a great space, they would as soon as the almighty fiat ordained gravity or the mutual attraction of certain parts, and the mutual repulsion of other parts to exist, all move towards their common centre: That the air being a fluid whose parts repel each other, though drawn to the common centre by their gravity, would be densest towards the centre, and rarer as more remote; consequently all matters lighter than the central part of that air and immersed in it, would recede from the centre and rise till they arrived at that region of the air which was of the same specific gravity with themselves, where they would rest; while other matter, mixed with the lighter air would descend, and the two meeting would form the shell of the first earth, leaving the upper atmosphere nearly clear. The original movement of the parts towards their common centre, would naturally form a whirl there; which would continue in the turning of the new formed globe upon its axis, and the greatest diameter of the shell would be in its equator.[7]

Several years after writing this letter Franklin read it before a meeting of the American Philosophical Society, and it subsequently appeared in the *Transactions* of that body. The popular *Columbian Magazine* printed it as well. Unfortunately for us, Franklin did not wish to trouble the abbé with his "fancies concerning the manner of forming the rest of our system," so his complete cosmogony remains unknown. We can only guess that it was no less naturalistic than his theory of the earth's origin.

Some decades after the death of Franklin another American effort to produce a scientific cosmogony ended in disappointment when the author, a minister named Isaac Orr, learned that he had been anticipated by Laplace himself. Orr graduated from Yale in 1818, studied theology, and then became a teacher in Thomas H. Gallaudet's Asylum for the Deaf and Dumb in Hartford, Connecticut. Later he served as an agent of the American Colonization Society and as secretary of the African Education Society. His fascination with cosmogonical problems undoubtedly stemmed from his close association with Yale's youthful professor of mathematics and natural philosophy, Alexander Metcalf Fisher, who assisted him in developing his cosmogony and promised to present it before the leading European scientists. Misfortune intervened, however. In 1822 Fisher drowned in the shipwreck of the *Albion* off the Irish coast.[8]

Bereft of his friend and collaborator, Orr turned for advice to America's foremost mathematician in the early nineteenth century, Nathaniel Bowditch of Salem, Massachusetts. When Bowditch saw the similarity between the ideas of Laplace and those of Orr, he sent the latter a copy of the passage in the *Système du monde* outlining the nebular hypothesis. From that extract Orr first learned that he had been anticipated. His initial reaction was "that it would be useless, and perhaps improper to publish [his speculations]. But on close examination and comparison, there appeared sufficient reasons to change that opinion."[9] In November 1822 he submitted his theory to the *American Journal of Science*, where it appeared the following year.

Like so many others before him, Orr was persuaded that various phenomena of the solar sytem—most obviously, the direction and positions of the orbits of the planets and satellites—"are much too regular to be considered the pure effects of accident, while on the other hand, they are not sufficiently so to be attributed to the immediate operations of an intelligent designing agent."[10] Very likely they indicated a common mode of development, which he set forth as follows:

> Suppose the component particles of the matter in the solar system to have never come together, but to be mixed indiscriminately, and distributed by means of light and heat, in a flat spheroid, having its greatest diameter some millions of miles longer than that of Herschel's [Uranus'] orbit, and revolving with such rapidity as to throw off portions from its circumference. As the heat and light abandoned it, its various parts would condense either by explosion or sudden combustion, according to the different forces of attraction among their component particles. Suppose that by some means or other its motion should be increased to such a degree, that by the time it had shrunk to about midway between the orbits of Saturn and Herschel, it would have thrown off from its circumference as much matter as is contained in Herschel and its satellites. Suppose that its motion should be still increased, so that by the time its circumference had arrived about midway between the orbits of Saturn and Jupiter, it would have thrown off as much matter as is contained in Saturn and its satellites. Make the same supposition for Jupiter, and so successively for all the planets below Jupiter. This ejected matter, unless the cause of motion were variable in its direction, would be left moving nearly in the same plane. Having lost its equilibrium the mutual attraction of its parts would unavoidably draw it together. It would first collect into small bodies, and these into greater.[11]

In this way the matter thrown off by the central mass or "solar wheel," as Orr called it, would form a "planetary wheel," which, if it acquired enough magnitude and motion, "would in its turn eject portions from its circumference . . . and these portions would form its satellites."[12]

Orr's cosmogony was a near duplicate of Laplace's, with two important exceptions. Laplace had made no effort to account for the rotation of his primitive solar atmosphere; he had simply postulated a rotating nebula as an initial condition. Orr, however, argued that the rotation of the solar wheel was a natural consequence of matter drawn to the center of the system by gravitational attraction.[13] The second difference concerned the extent and result of evolution in the universe. Whereas Laplace had believed that the development described by the nebular hypothesis ended in a permanent and stable arrangement and had limited his speculations to the solar system, Orr viewed the formation of the solar system as a characteristic but minor episode in the endless evolution of the universe.[14]

Being a clergyman, Orr naturally was concerned about the theological implications of his ideas. He was willing to allow that the solar system could have been formed "by the immediate agency of an intelligent spirit"; yet certain phenomena of the system seemed to be better explained by a natural cosmogony. For instance, "the relative diurnal motion of the various bodies in the system, present not the most distant indications of design; and yet they are about such as they must be, on the supposition that the system was produced by condensation from an aerial state."[15] He also readily acknowledged that if his opinions were "clearly and decidedly contrary to the meaning of scripture, it would be madness and disgrace as well as impiety and ruin to harbor them." But he was confident no such conflict with revelation existed and subtly suggested to potential critics that they would do well to remember the outcome of the Copernican debate and refrain from hasty condemnation. If atheists found his theory congenial, they had obviously failed to see that "it carries design through the whole of the universe, and stamps intelligence on all its departments."[16]

Orr's article did not create much of a stir among American scientists. His promise to provide additional demonstrations of his theory "if they should be demanded" was ignored. No one even bothered to accuse him of impiety, at least not in print. The very fact that his ideas were published in America's leading scientific periodical is evidence that in the early nineteenth century such unorthodox opinions were not considered too controversial to discuss openly.

Orr's and Fisher's ignorance of the Laplacian cosmogony suggests that the nebular hypothesis was still relatively unknown to Americans in the early 1820s.[17] Orr had read extensively in the current scientific literature, including William Herschel's papers in the *Philosophical Transactions* of the Royal Society;[18] and Fisher was a professor of mathematics and natural philosophy in one of the nation's best colleges. If Laplace's cosmogony had been even slightly familiar to Americans, these two almost certainly would have heard of it. Bowditch, of course, was in an exceptional position. Having translated Laplace's *Mécanique céleste*, he was better acquainted with the French astronomer's work than any other individual in the English-speaking world and was probably one of only a handful of Americans who knew of the nebular hypothesis.

Knowledge of Laplace's cosmogony came to America primarily by way of secondary sources rather than directly from the writings of Laplace. Little attention was given to the two English translations of the *Système du monde,* and even less to the section on the origin of the solar system. The British mathematician John Playfair, for example, failed even to mention the nebular hypothesis in his review of Pond's translation.[19] Fate cheated the nebular hypothesis out of additional publicity in America when the fifth volume of the *Mécanique céleste*—the only one in which Laplace discussed his cosmogony—came off the press too late in Bowditch's life for him to translate it.

Nevertheless, by the late 1820s and early 1830s scattered references to the nebular cosmogony began appearing in American periodicals. Bowditch alluded to it in his survey of modern astronomy for the *North American Review* in 1825, but refrained from elaborating on it. He did, however, challenge the common doctrines of the immutability of the heavens and the stability of the solar system, suggesting that the latter might be destroyed by the loss of light from the sun.[20] Five years later the *American Quarterly Review* carried an essay on the "Astronomy of Laplace," defending the Frenchman against certain charges of atheism that apparently had been made in response to his proposal of a natural history of the solar system. Such accusations were entirely unfair, declared the writer, "for, to proceed one step backwards towards the final cause of things, involves no denial of the omnipotence of that cause; nay, may in many cases lead to a more full exhibition of the wisdom with which the whole has been planned, and the power by which motions and properties, originally impressed upon inert and chaotic matter, have compelled it to assume a state, beautiful for its regularity, and admirable in its symmetry."[21]

In an exceptionally bold article written the following year—probably by Thomas Cooper, the freethinking president of South Carolina College—the *Southern Review* threw its support behind the nebular hypothesis. At the same time, it went out of its way to repudiate the Biblical account of creation. "We are surely bound by the common rules of philosophy," stated the author, "not to resort to the immediate agency of the Creator when events can be accounted for by secondary causes." If the Scriptures were contradicted as a result, so be it. No harm would come to its moral teachings.[22]

Such references to the nebular hypothesis, though generally favorable, were far too infrequent to be an effective means of popularization. Thus it was not until the publication in the 1830s of the eight Bridgewater Treatises and the separate works of John Pringle Nichol that widespread popular interest in the hypothesis was aroused. All these works were of British origin, but they circulated widely in the United States and exerted a notable influence upon American thinking.

The Bridgewater Treatises, dedicated to demonstrating "the Power, Wisdom, and Goodness of God, as manifested in the Creation," constitute the supreme effort of the nineteenth century to establish the design argument for God's existence on a firm foundation. No fewer than three of the eight eminent authors—William Whewell, William Buckland, and Thomas Chalmers—commented on Laplace's cosmogony. Whewell, fellow and tutor of Trinity College, Cambridge, devoted an entire chapter to "The Nebular Hypothesis" (apparently the first time this label was attached to Laplace's conjecture) in his *Astronomy and General Physics Considered with Reference to Natural Theology,* one of the most popular of the series. He did so "on account of the facts which it . . . presents, and the eminence of the person by whom it is propounded. . . . "[23] But since his sole purpose was to show that the hypothesis did not endanger the design argument, he passed no judgment on its scientific validity. The Oxford geologist Buckland, in his volumes on

Geology and Mineralogy Considered with Reference to Natural Theology, merely seconded Whewell's position and tried to show that the nebular hypothesis was consistent with the known geological evidence.[24]

Alone in expressing reservations about the nebular hypothesis was Chalmers, a Scottish divine and author of *On the Power, Wisdom, and Goodness of God as Manifested in the Adaptation of External Nature to the Moral and Intellectual Constitution of Man*. In good Newtonian tradition he denied that the world could have been produced by the mere laws of nature and strongly denounced Laplace for trying to prove otherwise. His greatest fear was that if the nebular hypothesis were ever to be demonstrated conclusively, the argument for atheism would be strengthened at the expense of the argument from design.[25]

These discussions in the Bridgewater Treatises rescued the nebular hypothesis from its previous obscurity, the remarkable sales of the series ensuring that the views of Laplace would be brought to the attention of a large audience.[26] Equally important was the encouragement given to other writers to take up the subject. The "nebulous theory" so impressed Buckland's reviewer in the *Knickerbocker*, for example, that he included a short description of it for the benefit of his uninformed readers.[27] And Chalmers' hostile remarks so provoked John Pringle Nichol that he took up his pen in defense of the nebular hypothesis and thus began a lifelong effort in its behalf.[28]

As a student at King's College, Aberdeen, Nichol had shown special promise in mathemetics and physics; nevertheless, upon graduation, he had entered divinity school. At an early age he was licensed to preach, but his unorthodox views soon caused him to abandon the ministry and turn instead to teaching and lecturing. In 1836 he was appointed professor of practical astronomy in the University of Glasgow.[29] The following year he published his widely read *Views of the Architecture of the Heavens*, which within seven years went through seven editions, including two American printings. Without a question it was the single book most responsible for bringing the nebular hypothesis to the attention of the American reading public.

The pages of *Views of the Architecture of the Heavens* overflowed with praise for the nebular hypothesis, reflecting the author's conviction that Laplace had at last put man virtually "in possession of that primeval Creative Thought which originated our system and planned and circumscribed its destiny."[30] The ecstatic Nichol could scarcely contain his enthusiasm for a theory "so beautiful and perfect." Contrasted with Buffon's "wild and reckless imagination," which failed to explain anything about the mechanism of the solar system, "Laplace's bold and brilliant *induction*" seemed to explain everything.[31] If, as some astronomers maintained, the satellites of Uranus had retrograde motions out of harmony with the rest of the system, Laplace's theory might need some modification, but it certainly would not be destroyed. Possibly, unknown forces in the remote regions of the solar system were producing the anomalous effects, suggested Nichol helpfully.[32]

A large segment of *Views of the Architecture of the Heavens* was devoted to the observations of nebulae made by William Herschel and his son John. Their studies seemed to Nichol to demonstrate the truth of the nebular hypothesis. "Its roots are seen in the Heavens," he wrote, "and [the nebulae] appear to go through every nook and alley of solar and planetary arrangements, not only explaining them, but comprehending their variety, and deducing the whole from one grand principle."[33] Nichol's failure to make an adequate distinction between the cosmogony of Laplace and the conjectures of the elder Herschel on the formation of stars from nebulae had a confusing effect. Partially as a result of his habit of lumping the two ideas together, they became so intertwined in the public mind that when the existence of nebulae was questioned a few years later, many believed Laplace's cosmogony was jeopardized as seriously as were Herschel's speculations.

Among the first of America's scientists to appreciate Nichol's book was the naturalist Constantine Samuel Rafinesque, a somewhat eccentric Philadelphian who had formerly been associated with Transylvania University in Lexington, Kentucky. In a little volume called *Celestial Wonders and Philosophy,* published in 1838, Rafinesque provided a résumé of *Views of the Architecture of the Heavens,* which, he complained, was so scarce in Philadelphia "that it is not to be found at our Booksellers of literary trash." The only copy available was in the Franklin Library. Though he no longer believed in the truth of the Genesis account of creation, he had misgivings about the nebular hypothesis. It was indeed "a bold and brilliant inductive conception, a beautiful and seemingly perfect theory," but "ocular demonstration and positive facts" were lacking.

Besides, the hypothesis was too mechanical for Rafinesque, who saw "LIGHT and MIND" at work in the skies. Nichol's optimism notwithstanding, mankind did not yet possess "the knowledge of the creative means employed by the DIVINE MIND and POWER."[34]

Two years passed after the writing of Rafinesque's book before anything was done to remedy the insufficient supply of Nichol's work. In the meantime three editions had appeared in Great Britain, and the few copies shipped across the Atlantic were eagerly bought up at $4.50 a volume, a high price in those days. To the New York publisher of the American edition "a more valuable and interesting volume [had] not been of late issued from either American or English press."[35]

The American press heartily concurred with the publisher's opinion. "A more remarkable, nay, astounding book, we have not read in a long time," exclaimed the *Knickerbocker*.[36] The *Princeton Review* reported they knew of "no recent work more fitted than this to startle the uninitiated by the novelty and surprising character of the truths it teaches." Then, relenting just a little, they admitted that the nebular hypothesis was still a conjecture and not one of the "positive truths of science." But, they went on, "let us remember that the theory of our solar system was a conjecture long before Newton proved it to be true. Even the conjectures of science are often found, in the progress of our knowledge, to have been the utterance of the first hints and surmises of the truth. And it may be that the hypothesis so eloquently explained and enforced by Dr. Nichol will hereafter be found to be the true theory of the universe."[37] In the minds of the reviewers, as in Nichol's book, Herschel's speculations on the origin of stars and Laplace's cosmogony were hopelessly intermingled.

In 1841 the *Christian Review* carried a lengthy article on *Views of the Architecture of the Heavens* written by a former Baptist minister, Alexis Caswell, who was then teaching mathematics and natural philosophy in Brown University. Several years earlier, in a review of Whewell's Bridgewater Treatise for the same periodical, he had singled out the chapter on the nebular hypothesis as one of the most interesting in the book but had refrained from commenting further on it.[38] This time, however, he gave his wholehearted approval to Laplace's cosmogony and cited abundant evidence in its favor. Geology testified that the earth had formerly been in a liquid state; celestial mechanics indicated that the solar system had originated

from a common cause; Laplace's cogent arguments demonstrated
that the system was "the direct and necessary consequence of a
condensing ethereal mass. . . . And, as if to lend invincible
confirmation to the hypothesis, one of the rings, that of Saturn,
remains unbroken."

"But the crowning argument," declared Caswell, "is one which
seems to paralyze all the powers of objection. An eminent French
geometer, M. Comte, conceived the idea of putting the question to
the rigid test of a *numerical verification,* which is regarded as the
final criterion of truth in every physical theory." When Comte
calculated the period of the earth's rotation with its matter extended
to the distance of the moon,

> much to his surprise, he found that [it] agreed to within less than a *tenth
> of a day* with the moon's actual periodic time! . . . Encouraged by the
> first application of his principle, Comte made similar calculations upon
> the sun, with regard to the primary planets, and found the agreement in
> every instance truly remarkable, though less exact than in the case of the
> moon. Severe and rigid in his analysis of facts, and cautious in his
> conclusions, he yet appears to regard the truth of the nebular cosmogony
> as resting upon a foundation, in point of security, second only to
> demonstration.[39]

Auguste Comte, who regarded the cosmogony of Laplace as "the
most plausible theory of any yet proposed," had first announced the
calculations described by Caswell in his astronomy course for the
workers of Paris, given in 1831, and had included them in the
second volume of his *Cours de philosophie positive.*[40] The Brown
professor was not alone in attaching great significance to this supposed verification. Among the British, David Brewster thought it
to be an "extremely remarkable" confirmation of the nebular hypothesis, and John Stuart Mill, a close friend of Nichol's,
agreed.[41] Later examination, however, showed Comte's calculations
to be inaccurate, and in the English translation of the *Positive
Philosophy* in 1853 they were deleted, on the recommendation of
Nichol.[42]

The evidence from geology mentioned by Caswell proved to be
more effective than Comte's computations in giving the nebular
hypothesis the appearance of truth. By the early nineteenth century
most geologists were convinced that the earth had originally been in
a fluid condition, and many wondered what cause had produced this
state. "The inquisitive mind," wrote Edward Hitchcock in 1829,
"does not rest satisfied with . . . insulated deductions from geologi-

cal facts, but is disposed to go farther back, and inquire into the origin of this internal ignition and fluidity of the globe."[43] When geologists learned about the nebular hypothesis in the 1830s, some saw it as a convincing solution to the problem of the earth's origin that accorded well with their own conclusions. Thus works like Gideon A. Mantell's popular *Wonders of Geology* and Henry de la Beche's *Researches in Theoretical Geology* presented the Laplacian cosmogony with approbation.[44]

By the early 1840s the nebular hypothesis was winning the endorsement of some of the leading members of America's small but influential scientific community and was beginning to appear more and more frequently in the curricula of the nation's colleges. On 8 March 1839, Eben Norton Horsford, a civil engineer only one year out of college, stood up before a class at the Rensselaer School in Troy, New York, to deliver the first lecture in a geology course he had been invited to give at his alma mater. The young instructor, who later went on to distinguish himself as a chemist, began by directing the attention of his students to "the one most prominent geological theory of the day," the nebular hypothesis of Laplace. Previous cosmogonies had "had their origin in the fancies of philosophers in times when few facts had been collected, and the science was in its infancy." But this one was different. It was not "a mere fiction of the imagination" nor a device serving "merely to gratify the curiosity, or absorb the powers of contemplation." Rather, "it was told in the prophetic language of perhaps the greatest astronomer that ever lived—and observation, comparatively recent, has developed the elements upon which as a basis his beautiful theory may now be established."[45] Detail by detail Horsford reconstructed the earth's early history, recapturing those scenes "the angels [had] watched with intense interest as [the earth] passed through the changes that were ultimately to fit it for the residence of man." To the devout, the nebular hypothesis posed no threat. Instead, it provided "food for a contemplative mind" that would nourish and sustain the spiritual life.[46]

Joseph Henry, who had recently made a name for himself in the field of electromagnetism, gave his students at Princeton a similar introduction to the nebular hypothesis. Beginning with the fall term of 1841 and continuing through 1847, Henry taught a geology course in the College of New Jersey in which the third lecture dealt with the Laplacian cosmogony and its connection with the history of the earth. Though "only an hypothesis," the cosmogony gave "such an exact account of the phenomena of the constitution of the solar system" that Henry felt "it should form a part of every course of geology." Those persons of self-proclaimed scientific ability who decried the use of such theories in science were obviously unaware of the value of theories—when "used with caution and a philosophical regard for truth"—in viewing the operations of nature. For without theories, no philosopher could expect "to extend in any degree the bounds of science." Henry explained to his students how splendidly the nebular hypothesis accounted for both the phenomena of the solar system and the geological fact of the earth's original state of intense heat. Surely, he told them, "it is one of the boldest and most sublime conceptions of the human mind."[47]

Harvard's Joseph Lovering and Benjamin Peirce also were openly supporting the nebular hypothesis by this time. In the short-lived *Cambridge Miscellany of Mathematics, Physics, and Astronomy,* jointly edited by the two professors, Lovering cited the Laplacian cosmogony as an example of the wonderful results obtained by applying the theory of probabilities to astronomical problems. The nebular hypothesis was, in the opinion of the Hollis professor, one of the great inductive generalizations of modern astronomy and was very likely to lead to other important discoveries. Future mathematicians might even "be able to settle with exactness the genealogy of our system according to Laplace's theory, and to assign the individual year when each of the outcast planets, from the grey Herschel and Saturn down to the infant Mercury, left its burning home and became an independent orb."[48]

Peirce, a brilliant young protégé of Bowditch's, thought the nebular hypothesis was "the most magnificent conception that was ever formed in the mind of a philosopher," for it undoubtedly revealed to man the very process adopted by the Deity in framing the universe. He was afraid, however, that many devout Christians, not realizing that "the character of the votary must not condemn the science," considered the nebular hypothesis suspect because Laplace had chosen "to diffuse around it the foul vapors of atheism." The narrow-minded followers of the Baconian philosophy, who judged all science according to its utility, were of equal concern because of their tendency to regard the nebular hypothesis as just another mathematical curiosity of no practical value. They failed to realize that mathemetics was the key to nature and that "the mere questions of curiosity, in which mathematicians have delighted, are the best possible preparation for the most serious contests of science, and have again and again led the way to the most brilliant investigations." The discovery of how the solar system had developed was alone "worthy of all the time, and all the genius, which have been devoted to mathematics."[49]

Peirce's fear that the nebular hypothesis would not receive a fair hearing because of its presumedly atheistic origin or its apparent uselessness was largely unfounded. During the early 1840s Laplace's cosmogony received little criticism, either in religious or secular periodicals, and its popularity steadily increased. College professors were discussing it in the classroom, while public speakers were describing it to eager audiences in the lecture hall. The period's most successful lecturer on scientific topics, the Cincinnati astronomer Ormsby MacKnight Mitchel, alone spread the news of Laplace's discovery to thousands throughout America. [50]

Even the literary thought of the day was beginning to reflect the influence of Laplace. His cosmogony played an important role in shaping Ralph Waldo Emerson's ideas on the history of nature,[51] and it inspired the unpredictable Edgar Allan Poe to create a universal cosmogony of his own. By 1841 Poe had somehow become convinced that the nebular hypothesis proved that the universe was perpetually undergoing change. Thus, according to his unique reasoning, it provided "the *only* irrefutable argument in support of the soul's immortality."[52] Later, in *Eureka*, published in 1848, he made the nebular hypothesis an essential part of his own cyclical theory of the universe. By that time serious questions were being raised about the validity of the nebular hypothesis, but Poe's belief in it never wavered. "It is by far too beautiful," he wrote, "*not* to possess Truth as its essentiality."[53]

Now and then concerned individuals did protest the hasty and uncritical acceptance of the nebular hypothesis. In 1841 Matthew Boyd Hope, a returned missionary from Singapore serving as an official of the Presbyterian church, called attention in the *Princeton Review* to the growing assumption "that the nebular hypothesis suggested by La Place is the true theory of the universe." This "is going too fast and too far," he complained.[54] Coming events would soon cause many others to express similar reservations about the nebular cosmogony, but in the early 1840s the Reverend Mr. Hope stood virtually alone.

CHAPTER III

The Nebular Hypothesis under Attack

Just as the nebular hypothesis was beginning to win acceptance and respectability in America, popular opinion suddenly turned against it. Two nearly simultaneous events were responsible for this dramatic shift in attitudes. First, the Laplacian cosmogony had the misfortune of being incorporated into a controversial scheme of evolution offensive to many pious persons. Then almost immediately thereafter British and American astronomers announced that improved telescopes were successfully resolving nebulae into stars. These resolutions deprived the nebular hypothesis of what was to many one of its most convincing evidences.

The vehicle for bringing notoriety to the nebular hypothesis was a book called *Vestiges of the Natural History of Creation,* a bold attempt to unite facts and speculations from the fields of astronomy, geology, and biology into a coherent history of creation by natural law. Knowing that his work would probably arouse the sympathy of few and the indignation of many, the author, Robert Chambers, a Scottish publisher and amateur geologist, prudently chose to remain anonymous. Nevertheless, within a year of its publication in 1844 the book had passed through several British and at least two American printings.

The nebular hypothesis had originally triggered Chambers' imagination to devise a universal system of evolution, and it provided a logical starting point for the resulting product.[1] The nebular theory of the *Vestiges,* however, differed substantially from that in the *Système du monde.* Instead of postulating the existence of a rotating solar atmosphere, as Laplace had done, Chambers began with nuclei of matter distributed throughout space and tried to show how these would become rotating nebulous stars. Two laws of nature guaranteed the desired result: agglomeration of matter at the nuclei would take place according to the law of gravitation, and rotation was ensured by another "well known law in physics that, when fluid matter collects towards or meets in a centre, it establishes a rotary motion."[2]

The *Vestiges* also contained a unique explanation of the formation of the solar rings. Laplace had said that rings would be abandoned by the primitive sun whenever its contraction produced a centrifugal force acting on the particles in the plane of its equator equal to their gravitational attraction to the central mass. But Chambers suggested that the rings were formed by a process of incrustation:

> If we suppose the agglomeration of a nebulous mass to be a process attended by refrigeration or cooling, which many facts render likely, we can easily understand why the outer parts, hardening under this process, might, by virtue of the greater solidity thence acquired, begin to present some resistance to the attractive force. As the solidification proceeded, this resistance would become greater, though there would still be a tendency to adhere. Meanwhile, the condensation of the central mass would be going on, tending to produce a separation from what may now be termed the *solidifying crust.* During the contention between the attractions of these two bodies, or parts of one body, there would probably be a ring of attenuation between the mass and its crust. At length, when the central mass had reached a certain stage in its advance towards solidification, a separation would take place, and the crust would become a detached ring.[3]

Chambers' differences with Laplace were probably more accidental than designed. Perhaps he was not even conscious of them. His primary aim was to promote, not revise, the nebular hypothesis. And the evidence in its favor, including Comte's calculations on the rotation of the solar mass when its surface had extended to the distances of the various planets, seemed to him overwhelming. Indeed, so many facts supported Laplace's cosmogony that he considered it "as verging upon the region of our ascertained truths."[4]

Wishing to have "as little vexatious collision as possible with existing beliefs," Chambers carefully avoided eliminating God from the universe altogether. Instead he bowed to the religious sentiments of the age and declared that the natural laws that had produced the solar system were "merely the mandates" of a First

Cause.[5] Had he not gone beyond describing the formation of the solar system and the earth's topography, he might have escaped the ire of the devout. But by suggesting that all life—including man— was the product of development, he assured himself a hostile reception.

Scarcely six months had passed after the embarrassing appearance of the *Vestiges* when the nebular hypothesis received an even more damaging setback. From Ireland came the disturbing yet exciting news of spectacular discoveries being made with a giant reflecting telescope recently completed by William Parsons, the third earl of Rosse. After three laborious years of grinding and polishing his six-foot speculum and constructing a suitable tube, Lord Rosse had finally turned the "leviathan of Parsonstown" heavenward on the evening of 5 March 1845. According to reports received by the *American Journal of Science*, the night "was very clear, and the sidereal pictures were glorious. Many nebulae were for the first time since their creation, seen as groups or clusters."[6] In announcing his discoveries, Lord Rosse observed "that now, as has always been the case, an increase of instrumental power has added to the number of the clusters at the expense of the nebulae, properly so called; still it would be very unsafe to conclude that such will always be the case, and thence to draw the obvious inference that all nebulosity is but the glare of stars too remote to be separated by the utmost power of our instruments."[7] Despite this warning, rumors that the existence of nebulae had been disproven continued to circulate.

Critics of the *Vestiges* saw in Lord Rosse's discoveries a ready weapon with which to demolish the very foundation of Chambers' work. They reasoned that the solar system could not possibly have developed from a nebula if no such objects existed and, therefore, that the nebular hypothesis must be false. By 1846 Chambers felt compelled to reply to this and other charges being leveled at his thesis. He did so in a second anonymous book, called *Explanations: A Sequel to "Vestiges of the Natural History of Creation."*

In the *Explanations* Chambers denied that the nebular hypothesis was essential to his basic argument for a natural history of creation. Since the evidence in favor of a natural origin of the solar system was so abundant, disproving Laplace's cosmogony would only necessitate finding a substitute hypothesis. Nevertheless, he admitted his position would be greatly strengthened if the nebular hypothesis could be retained. And he was confident it could. He certainly did not believe Lord Rosse's observations disproved it.

> The fact is, that the nebulae were always understood to be of two kinds: 1, nebulae which were only distant clusters, and which yielded, one after another, to the resolving powers of telescopes, as these powers were increased; 2, nebulae comparatively near, which no increase of telescopic power affected. Two classes of objects wholly different were, from their partial resemblance, recognized by one name, and hence the confusion which has arisen upon the subject. The resolution of a great quantity of the first kind of nebulae by Lord Rosse's telescope was of course expected, and it is a fact, though in itself interesting, of no consequence to the nebular hypothesis. It will only be in the event of the second class being also resolved, and its being thus shown that there is only one class of nebulae, that the hypothesis will suffer.[8]

Chambers went on to describe, with obvious relish, a remarkable experiment he had recently learned of that seemed to illustrate strikingly the nebular hypothesis. In the *Memoirs* of the Royal Academy of Brussels for 1842, Joseph Plateau, a blind professor in the University of Ghent, had announced a discovery he had made while investigating the properties of a globule of olive oil in a mixture of water and alcohol. When rotated, the sphere of oil first flattened at its poles and then abandoned rings, which ruptured and formed rotating globes circling the central mass. "The experiment," said Plateau, "presents . . . an image in miniature of the formation of the planets, according to the hypothesis of Laplace, by the rupture of the cosmical rings attributable to the condensation of the solar atmosphere." Even though he later retracted his support for the nebular hypothesis and pointed out that his results were the effect of molecular rather than gravitational attraction, his experiment greatly aided Chambers in defending the validity of the nebular cosmogony at a time when the resolutions of nebulae were making it appear increasingly untenable.[9]

While Chambers was busily trying to shore up the most vulnerable parts of his argument, his opponents were launching an intensive but diverse assault. Two lines of attack were open to them. Either they could charge the *Vestiges* with heresy, or they could impugn its science. Some critics—among them Francis Bowen, editor of the prestigious *North American Review*, and Tayler Lewis, professor of Greek in the University of the City of New York— resorted to both tactics.

The very plausibility of the creation story found in the *Vestiges* made Bowen treat the book with a measure of respect. "It is," he said, "a very pleasant hypothesis, set forth in a most agreeable manner; and though it contains many objectionable features, these are cautiously veiled and kept in the background, and the reader is seduced into accepting most of the conclusions, before he is aware of their true character and tendency." But behind the book's innocent façade Bowen saw nothing but a modern version of atheistic atomism, marred by a "gratuitous and arbitrary" attempt to assign to God the role of lawgiver. The science of the *Vestiges* was scarcely less offensive to the former academy mathematics teacher, who believed classification to be the only legitimate function of science and who regarded all theories of causation as unscientific. As for the nebular hypothesis, it was but a "*mere* guess, directly opposed by an obvious induction from those nebulae which are resolvable into perfect stars." To Bowen's satisfaction, Lord Rosse had come along just in time to guarantee that the *Vestiges* would receive no support from the field of astronomy.[10]

Lewis had no respect at all for the *Vestiges* or its author, and he made this quite clear in his comments on the book for the *American Review*. At least one reader of his review in the Whig journal found the occasional invective more than he could stomach. "A more rabid tirade," he exclaimed, "can scarcely be found this side of the Middle Ages, & the smell of roast heretic is truly overpowering throughout."[11] On most points Lewis differed little from Bowen; he was just more caustic in expressing himself. He, too, looked upon the nebular hypothesis with a skeptical eye and regarded the teachings of the *Vestiges* as nothing but "atheism—blank atheism, cold, cheerless, heartless, atheism." But whereas Bowen had been primarily concerned with the bearing of the *Vestiges* upon theism, Lewis was as greatly agitated over its tendency to undermine the Scriptural account of creation. His motivation, however, came not from any desire to defend the traditional six-day creation week, but solely from an honest conviction that the history of the world should be based upon a scholarly exegesis of the Biblical record.[12]

The scientists who reviewed the *Vestiges* and its sequel tended to be more tolerant of the nebular hypothesis and to have fewer theological axes to grind than Bowen and Lewis. For example, Harvard botanist Asa Gray doubted that the nebular hypothesis would survive the resolutions of nebulae; yet he thought it might "be less open to direct objection than the rest of the book." The brunt of his criticism was directed at the idea of the natural development of living things, and since the nebular hypothesis in no way increased the probability of events like man being " 'an advanced type' of the monkey race," he was content to ignore it. Moreover, he did not think Laplace's cosmogony eliminated the necessity of divine action in the creation of the world. For even if the solar system had developed in a manner analogous to Plateau's experiment, "an extrinsic agent, the stick or disk with which to stir the nebulous chaos about, and *the hand to move it*" were still needed.[13]

Chambers' unique adaptation of the nebular hypothesis naturally drew some criticism that was not applicable to Laplace's original theory. Writing in the *Methodist Quarterly Review*, William Henry Allen, professor of chemistry and natural history in Dickinson College, Carlisle, Pennsylvania, differentiated sharply between the well-reasoned cosmogony of Laplace and the absurd hypothesis of the *Vestiges*:

> In his solicitude to dispense with the agency of God, [the author of the *Vestiges*] goes back three steps behind the starting point of La Place, and, by so doing, proposes a problem which he not only fails to solve, but which is absolutely insolvable. The problem of La Place may be enunciated thus: *Given a solar nucleus with a nebulous atmosphere rotating on an axis, to demonstrate the possibility of forming a system of planets and satellites by dynamical laws.* The following is our author's problem: *Matter expanded by heat so as to fill space, and the laws of matter given, to develop the bodies of the universe.* The data of La Place leave room for the personal agency of God; our author leaves him nothing to do but to sit still and look on. La Place solved his problem; yet he called his hypothesis a *conjecture*, and published it with great diffidence, as possibly, rather than probably, true. Our author signally fails in his solution, yet takes his hypothesis as a fact on which to build his subsequent reasonings,—the cornerstone of his "great generalization."

Allen pointed out that even without the additional encumbrances of the *Vestiges*, the nebular hypothesis was far from certain. Various phenomena, like the retrograde motion of the satellites of Uranus, seemed inconsistent with it, and the resolutions of nebulae had greatly reduced the evidence in its favor. Plateau's experiment did not help, because it demonstrated only the effects of molecular attraction, not gravitation. If the nebular hypothesis were further burdened down with an unsuccessful explanation of the rotation of

the solar nebula and other unnecessary problems imposed by the
Vestiges, it had no chance whatsoever of being considered a valid
history of the solar system.[14]

The peculiarity of the nebular theory presented in the *Vestiges*
also disturbed Albert Baldwin Dod, Princeton's professor of
mathematics. Particularly upsetting to him was the method by
which the *Vestiges* explained "the *shelling off* of planets and satellites," that is, by the hardening of the nebula's outer surface rather
than by the accumulation of matter in the equatorial region, as
Laplace had suggested. In fact, the *Vestiges* had weighed down the
nebular hypothesis with so many "absurdities and contradictions"
that, lacking a better exposition, Dod would have dismissed "it at
once as one of the hasty, vague guesses so often made by unau-
thorized intruders upon the scientific domain." Instead, he gener-
ously offered "to substitute the sage conjecture of Laplace, for [the]
blundering guess" of the author of the *Vestiges*. Across the Atlantic
the Scottish scientist David Brewster similarly contrasted Laplace's
cosmogony with "the crude sun-making" of the *Vestiges*.[15]

Whatever tolerance Gray, Allen, and Dod may have had for the
nebular hypothesis, it did not mollify their opposition to the *Vestiges* as a whole. They all vigorously condemned it. Only rarely did
an intellectually daring person have the inclination and audacity
openly to defend its history of creation. Joseph Henry Allen, a
twenty-five-year-old Unitarian clergyman and Harvard graduate,
was such an individual. In reviewing the *Vestiges* for his church's
Christian Examiner, Allen astutely observed that even if every
statement in the book were disproved, the effort to explain creation
by natural law would not thereby be stopped. All of modern science
seemed to justify the endeavor, and as far as he could see there was
no obvious conflict with any cherished theological doctrines. The
nebular hypothesis he described as a "magnificent cosmogony,
which blends together the last results of almost the whole circle of
the sciences."[16]

Somewhat less openly, Henry Darwin Rogers, teacher of geology
and mineralogy in the University of Pennsylvania, indicated his
support of the *Vestiges*. Though he never published his opinion of
the book, he did write his brother William that it contained the
"loftiest speculative views in Astronomy and Geology and Natural
History, and singularly accords with views sketched by me at times
in my lectures."[17]

Any contribution the *Vestiges* made to the popularization of the nebular hypothesis was more than offset by its throwing "a dark suspicion" over the cosmogony, as Alexander Winchell described its effect.[18] To some Americans, the hypothesis was somehow tainted by its association with a book widely denounced as atheistic and unscientific. This attitude was strikingly exhibited in a review of the sequel to the *Vestiges* by James Davenport Whelpley, a physician and former associate of Henry Rogers on the geological survey of Pennsylvania. In rejecting the nebular hypothesis, Whelpley alleged that he would not have acted "so rudely, founded as it is upon excellent proofs, if it had not come attended by a load of false conclusions, as . . . of men originating by slow degrees from monkeys [and] with a crowd of like absurdities following, pell-mell, at the heels of a nebular hypothesis, and ending like that in mere vapor."[19]

While the controversy over the *Vestiges* raged on, the number of nebular resolutions continued to rise. In 1847 the Harvard College Observatory mounted an excellent new refractor, enabling Americans to join Lord Rosse in resolving nebulae. On 22 September of that year William Cranch Bond, the director of the observatory, sent the following letter to the president of the college, Edward Everett:

> Dear Sir:—You will rejoice with me, that the great nebula in Orion has yielded to the powers of our incomparable telescope!
>
> This morning, the atmosphere being in a favorable condition, at about three o'clock the telescope was set upon the Trapezium in the great nebula in Orion. Under a power of 200, the fifth star was immediately conspicuous; but our attention was very soon absorbed with the splendid revelations made in its immediate vicinity. This part of the nebula was resolved into bright points of light. The number of stars was too great to attempt counting them;—many however were readily located and mapped. . . .
>
> It should be borne in mind, that this nebula and that of Andromeda have been the last strong-holds of the nebular theory; that is, the idea first suggested by the elder Herschel of masses of nebulous matter in process of condensation into systems. The nebula in Orion yielded not to the unrivalled skill of both the Herschels, armed with their excellent reflectors. It even defied the powers of Lord Rosse's three-foot mirror, giving "*not the slightest trace of resolvability*"; by which term is understood the discerning *singly* a number of sparkling points. . . .
>
> I feel deeply sensible of the odiousness of comparison, but innumerable applications have been made to me, for evidence of the excellence of

the instrument, and I can see no other way in which the public are to be made acquainted with its merits.[20]

Bond's desire to present his discoveries in the best possible light led him to exaggerate the extent to which he had surpassed Lord Rosse. Actually, the British astronomer had announced over a year before Bond wrote his letter that he had plainly seen "that all about the trapezium [of Orion] is a mass of stars; the rest of the nebula also abounding with stars and exhibiting the characteristics of resolvability strongly marked."[21]

The resolutions, especially that of Orion, forced the supporters of the nebular cosmogony to reconsider its merits. Nichol, who lectured in the eastern United States during the winter of 1847-48 and who was regarded as the foremost champion of the nebular hypothesis, carefully redefined his position by treating the speculations of William Herschel and the hypothesis of Laplace as two separate entities instead of as parts of one great cosmogony, as he had previously tended to do. Only Herschel's ideas would have to be abandoned. Laplace's cosmogony, though weakened by being deprived of a "visible foundation in *fact*," could be salvaged. In addition to explaining the phenomena of the solar system, however, it now had to demonstrate that the system had once been in a nebulous condition. And, said Nichol, "to deduce the peculiarities of our system from a previous condition whose existence was recognized, and to demonstrate the reality of that previous condition, by remounting towards it from our existing epoch, are manifestly efforts of unequal difficulty, and very different ambitions." Still, he continued to believe in the essential truth of the Laplacian cosmogony, although the press sometimes reported otherwise.[22]

John Herschel was also beginning to urge the divorce of his father's conjectures from the hypothesis of Laplace, but his reason for wanting the separation was the opposite of Nichol's: he thought the nebular resolutions had left his father's views untouched while rendering Laplace's more doubtful. In his 1845 presidential address before the British Association for the Advancement of Science he discussed the significance of the resolutions for the two theories. Although a certain class of nebulae had been resolved into stars, other types had not yielded to the telescope and, in fact, seemed to be undergoing the very process of sidereal aggregation described by his father. However, in the "thousands of instances" in which sidereal aggregation appeared to have produced families of stars, no evidence indicated "its further result to be the surrounding of those stars with planetary attendants." The cosmogony of Laplace was thus "a matter of pure speculation," utterly unsupported by telescopic observations or, for that matter, by the circular calculations of Comte. By this time the younger Herschel was the leading English astronomer, and undoubtedly his opinions worked to retard the acceptance of the nebular hypothesis even.in America.[23]

Though enthusiasm flagged somewhat as a result of the discoveries of Lord Rosse and Bond, few American scientists went so far as to discard the nebular hypothesis entirely and some rallied to its defense. One of its most outspoken champions was the astronomer, Ormsby MacKnight Mitchel, who used his recently begun periodical, the *Sidereal Messenger,* to mount a spirited attack against the charge that the nebular hypothesis had been refuted by the resolutions of nebulae. He argued that since no one had ever claimed that nebulae like the one in Orion were composed of "*nebulous matter,*" their resolution was inconsequential for the nebular hypothesis. It had "neither lost nor gained by the discoveries thus far made." Mitchel's remarks circulated widely and were reprinted—without acknowledgment—in *Smith's Illustrated Astronomy,* a popular elementary text.[24]

Nonscientists, especially those who saw creation by natural law as a threat to certain theological doctrines, were generally more inclined than the scientifically trained to view the resolutions of nebulae as decisive evidence against the nebular cosmogony. James McCosh, the Scottish "common sense" philosopher who later became president of Princeton, expressed delight in the fact that there was no longer any evidence "of worlds being formed by natural law."[25] In Alabama an attorney named George Taylor praised the telescopic discoveries for helping to reunite science and religion by destroying the nebular hypothesis. With obvious relief, he penned these words: "The difficulty was removed, and all the strange appearances accounted for as the effects of varying distances. The stars of heaven are perfect: no rudimental or half-grown ones are found; the choir is full. The Nebular Hypothesis vanishes as a pleasant dream, profitable though we believe it has been; and with it various systems of cosmogony, the fears of timid Christians, and the hopes of Atheistical philosophers."[26] No less pleased was the conservative Andover theologian Austin Phelps, who saw the nebular resolutions as evidence that, if left alone, "the wise men themselves shall construct for us new instruments of science, like Lord Rosse's telescope, which shall refute many of their reasonings, and they shall come back to the believer, and shall say, 'we knew not that whereof we affirmed.' "[27]

Now and then a dissenting voice did speak out against the unfavorable consensus toward the nebular hypothesis developing in the popular and religious press. Perhaps the most remarkable example of such support was an anonymous article in the *Southern Quarterly Review* not only defending Laplace's cosmogony but maintaining that it was corroborated by the discoveries of Lord Rosse. "It is easy," said the author scornfully, "for those who have never read Dr. Nichol's work, or seen a paper of the Transactions of the Philosophical Societies of Europe" to pronounce the nebular hypothesis "exploded by the revelations of Lord Ross's telescope, and [to consign] it to oblivion, as a vain imagination of a few phantastic minds." But those familiar with "the laborious and long-continued observations and inductions of the Herschells, M. Compte, La Place, Struve, and a host of others" would never act so rashly, recognizing as they did that the nebular hypothesis was the most probable of all cosmogonies. The recent resolutions of nebulae had not decreased but increased this probability, the author ingeniously suggested, since the stars discovered by Lord Rosse had probably been formed from the same nebulous matter observed by William Herschel a half-century earlier![28]

Aside from occasional comments on the general implications of the telescopic resolutions of nebulae, American scientists said little in public about the nebular hypothesis in the last half of the 1840s. In private, however, some continued to think and write about it. And the more seriously they thought about it, the more their interest turned from religious and philosophical questions raised by a natural cosmogony to the detailed mechanical problems of producing a solar system from a rotating nebula.

In January 1846 Benjamin Peirce confided to his friend Elias Loomis that the nebular hypothesis had lately been troubling him. By this time Peirce had advanced from Bowditch's assistant to become Perkins Professor of Mathematics and Astronomy at Harvard, and Loomis was a professor of mathematics and natural philosophy in the University of the City of New York. "My mind has been dwelling of late upon Laplace's nebular hypothesis," wrote Peirce, "and the more I think of it, the less tangible does it become to me." Everywhere he looked he found difficulties. First, there was the nature of the rotating "sun" prior to the separation of the planets. It obviously could not have been solid, for then no rings would have been formed. Nor could it have been like Saturn's rings, with each particle apparently acting as an independently orbiting entity, "for in this case the separation is at once effected and the hypothesis is not needed to account for it while the cohesion into planets would be more mysterious than ever."

Second, he could not see how, after one planetary ring had been abandoned, the inner mass could continue to contract to the orbit of the next planet without leaving rings behind continually. And finally, some rough calculations he had made indicated that the diameter of the earth's original "shell" would have been less than one-third the distance to the moon—clearly much too small—and that the density of the moon's "shell" would have been greater than the earth's—another impossibility, according to the nebular hypothesis. He concluded his letter by imploring Loomis to think of these perplexing problems and either "realise them or set them aside" in his own way. [29]

A few months later Loomis sent him a brief and unenthusiastic reply: "My thoughts have repeatedly been turned to the nebular hypothesis, and I think some recent publications have given the impression that Astronomers attach more importance to the hypothesis than they really do. One of the difficulties you suggest might perhaps be obviated by supposing the solar mass to have been originally of very unequal density throughout. But I have not time to dwell upon the subject here." [30]

Notwithstanding this rather discouraging response from Loomis and the still unsolved problems, Peirce could not bring himself to abandon the nebular hypothesis, "for there were so many things in favor of that theory, that even when it was proved to be false, it was not easy to disbelieve it." [31] Evidence of his continued attachment to the Laplacian cosmogony can be seen in a paper he gave "On the Connection of Comets with the Solar System" at the second annual meeting of the American Association for the Advancement of Science (AAAS), in August 1849. As usually explained by the nebular hypothesis, comets were formed from nebulous matter originally left outside the sphere of solar attraction, and thus they were not true members of the solar system. Peirce had become convinced, however, that the absence of comets with decidedly hyperbolical orbits indicated these bodies were actually components of our system.[32] And even though the cosmogony of Laplace was then in disrepute, his fondness for it was so great that he felt compelled to try to reconcile it with his views on the origin of comets. Very likely he did not know, when he read his paper on the second day of the meetings, that just three days later his continued faith in the nebular hypothesis would seemingly be justified.

CHAPTER IV

Daniel Kirkwood's Analogy

The date 18 August 1849 marks a turning point in the history of the nebular hypothesis in America, for on that day, the fifth of the annual AAAS meetings in Cambridge, Sears Cook Walker announced the discovery of an extraordinary mathematical formula that gave "new plausibility to the presumption that [the nebular hypothesis] is a fact in the past history of the solar system."[1] Walker himself was not the discoverer, nor was any other prominent astronomer. The hero was an unknown academy principal from the backwoods of Pennsylvania.

Daniel Kirkwood was born on a Maryland farm and educated in a local country school. He had little inclination for farming and while still in his teens took a job teaching school in Pennsylvania. According to one report, his interest in mathematics was aroused during his first year of teaching by one of his pupils who wanted to study algebra. Since Kirkwood was not familiar with the subject, he and his student studied it together. After just one year of teaching he entered the York County Academy in Pennsylvania as a student, and four years later the school appointed him instructor in mathematics. In 1843 he became principal of the Lancaster High School, and a few years later he accepted a similar position in the Pottsville Academy.[2]

While still at the York County Academy Kirkwood became fascinated with the prospect of finding a law governing the axial rotations of the planets in the same way that Kepler's third law regulated their orbital revolutions around the sun. He made no systematic investigation of the problem, however, until the summer of 1839, when his attention was caught by a passage in Young's *Mechanics* suggesting "that both the progressive and rotary motions of the heavenly bodies were originally communicated by the same impulse."[3] For several years he spent his leisure hours comparing the masses, volumes, densities, and distances of the planets in a vain attempt to detect by trial and error some significant relationship, fully realizing that his limited scientific training would prevent him from solving his problem "by any direct process of mathematical reasoning."[4]

His persistence was eventually rewarded. In 1846, "as the only remaining source of hope," he began studying Laplace's nebular hypothesis and before long had identified two likely elements of his elusive law. The first, taken directly from the nebular hypothesis, he called "the diameter of a planet's sphere of attraction," the "diameter" being the width of the original nebulous ring or zone of rings from which the planet had developed. This quantity, represented by the letter D, he formally defined as the distance between two points, P and P', P being the point of equal attraction between any planet and the one next interior when the two bodies are in conjunction, and P' being that between the same planet and the one next exterior (see fig. 1). The second element of his law was simply the number of rotations, n, performed by a planet during its orbit around the sun. At last, on 12 August 1848, he obtained the following "simple analogy"—the term analogy here being used in its mathematical sense to signify an agreement of ratios—relating the elements D and n of one planet to D' and n' of another:

$$\frac{n^2}{n'^2} = \frac{D^3}{D'^3} \text{ or } n = n'\left(\frac{D}{D'}\right)^{3/2}$$

As he applied this formula, later known as Kirkwood's analogy, "to the different planets in succession and found its wonderful agreement with the known elements of the system," he was overcome with delight.[5]

Nevertheless, he was reluctant to disclose his discovery. Having heard that the nebular hypothesis had recently fallen into disrepute, he feared that his analogy would be rejected for being based upon a discredited hypothesis. He later described his plight in a letter to Benjamin Gould:

> Some time previous to the date of my discovery, I learned that the nebular hypothesis had been abandoned by some of its most distinguished advocates in consequence of the revelations of Lord Rosse's

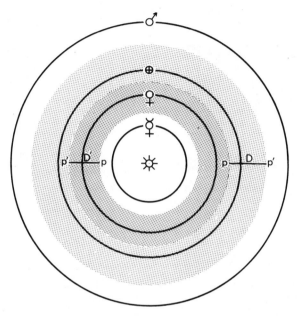

Fig. 1. Diameters of the spheres of attraction of Earth (D) and Venus (D′).

telescope. This fact, together with several other considerations, prevented me from at once making the result of my investigations public. Having, however, again and again revised my calculations, and having found that according to the theory of probabilities there are many millions of chances to one against the accidental coincidence of so many independent variable quantities, I ventured to submit the subject to the inspection of astronomers.[6]

Just what other considerations were involved besides the precarious status of the nebular hypothesis, we cannot determine. We do know, however, that it was late in September 1848 before he tried to establish contact with someone who could evaluate his analogy and present it to the scientific world.

The man chosen by Kirkwood was Edward C. Herrick, the librarian of Yale College, who had won scientific acclaim some years previous for his theory of the periodicity of the August meteoric showers (the Perseids). In his first letter to Herrick, Kirkwood made no mention of his analogy. He only asked for information regarding the masses of three planets, the period of rotation of Uranus, and the periods of revolution of some asteroids.[7] Herrick promptly sent the requested data, but it was the spring of the following year before he learned of the use to which they were put.

At the end of March 1849 Kirkwood sent Herrick a paper, "On the Law of the Planets' Rotations," describing his analogy. It was accompanied by the following note:

> Several months since[,] I took the liberty of troubling you with a few astronomical questions. . . . Supposing you might feel some curiosity to know my object in proposing these inquiries, I send you the enclosed paper which will speak for itself. It was written some time since with a view to publication, but I have not yet offered it for that purpose, nor do I design doing so for the present. You are the first to whom I have shown it. Perhaps it may be regarded by those better qualified for judging than myself, as a vagary not worthy of consideration. An author, you know, cannot be expected to form a proper estimate of his own production.
>
> Should you feel disposed to show my paper to any one, you are at liberty to do so, on the condition that you withhold my name. . . . [8]

Kirkwood, the small-town dilettante, was obviously reluctant to face the criticism of professional scientists. Perhaps this is why he had chosen Herrick, an amateur who had won the respect of the professionals, to be his first confidant.

Apparently Herrick did not feel qualified to judge the merit of Kirkwood's paper, for he suggested that it be sent instead to Sears Cook Walker, an astronomer on the staff of the United States Coast Survey who had recently achieved fame as a result of his determination of the orbit of the newly discovered planet Neptune. Kirkwood followed this advice and sent the paper to Walker, requesting him to ascertain whether or not the subject was "deserving of further investigation" and promising to abide by any decision he made.[9] Upon receiving this letter, Walker "proceeded at once to verify the numerical data and conclusions [it contained]. He found in them nothing requiring modification, except perhaps the substitution of some more recent values for the masses of Mercury and Uranus."[10]

Before relaying the good news to Kirkwood, Walker confidentially discussed the analogy with a few colleagues. On 20 July 1849, while visiting in Philadelphia, he attended a meeting of the American Philosophical Society where he "remarked at length on the nature of the analogy," giving his opinion that Kirkwood's discovery "deserves to rank at least with Kepler's harmonies, and that its close agreement with the elements of all the primary planets, justifies the remark [made by Kirkwood], 'that it is difficult to resist the conclusion that it is a law of nature.' " To the seven other members present he expressed his belief that the analogy would also throw new light on Laplace's nebular hypothesis. A few days later, upon returning to Washington, he likewise mentioned the analogy to Joseph Henry, secretary of the Smithsonian Institution.[11]

The day following his visit with Henry, Walker sent a letter to Kirkwood that could scarcely have failed to excite the young teacher. "I find your quantity $n/D^{3/2}$ to be nearly constant for the primary planets Venus, the Earth, and Saturn," he wrote. "Such a coincidence is hardly attributable to chance, and seems to indicate a law of nature." Walker went on to suggest that the constant might "be readily deduced from the nebular hypothesis, in which case both theories will strengthen each other." The letter closed with these encouraging words: "The subject is highly interesting to men of science [undoubtedly a reference to Henry and the members of the American Philosophical Society], and I shall be glad to make your discovery public, through the medium of some of our journals and scientific memoirs. Please let me hear from you at an early date."[12]

Kirkwood was indeed cheered by Walker's letter; yet he seems to have been somewhat puzzled by the remark about the nebular hypothesis. For some time he had worried that the abandonment of Laplace's cosmogony would jeopardize the acceptance of his analogy, but now Walker was suggesting that the two theories might even strengthen each other. Was it possible that the nebular hypothesis was not entirely discredited after all? Once again Kirkwood turned to Herrick for counsel. "Have you utterly abandoned the Nebular hypothesis of La Place, and has it been given up by scientific men generally?" he asked in a letter written soon after hearing from Walker. Kirkwood also had some lingering doubts about making his discovery public, despite Walker's eagerness to publish it, and he asked for Herrick's advice on this matter, too.[13]

Then, without waiting for a reply from Herrick, Kirkwood decided to grant Walker permission to take any action he thought best. "Allow me to leave the matter entirely in your hands," he wrote. "Anything I have written is at your disposal. Should you see proper to publish an article in your own name, giving me credit for suggesting the law itself, I should be highly gratified."[14] It is certainly to Walker's credit that he never abused this trust placed in him.

Walker's first opportunity to make a public announcement of Kirkwood's discovery came on the fifth day of the Cambridge AAAS meetings. After Gould, the secretary of the Section of Mathematics, Physics, and Astronomy, had read Kirkwood's letters describing the analogy, Walker commented on its importance and validity. In his praise for Kirkwood he never mentioned his own contributions. According to one who attended the meeting, Walker "ascribed the entire merit of the discovery to Mr. Kirkwood, claiming to himself nothing for the labor he had bestowed and the extension he had given to the imperfect conception. Yet it was clear to all present that without his aid the discovery would have continued to slumber in its obscurity."[15]

Kirkwood's analogy is "the most important harmony in the Solar System discovered since the time of Kepler, which, in after times, may place their names, side by side, in honorable association," Walker declared to the assemblage of scientists. He could envisage no sound objection to the analogy. It did seem to require the assumption—later rejected by Kirkwood—of a planet between Mars and Jupiter, in the region occupied by the asteroids, but, he said, "if the Geological Section was allowed the privilege of restoring fishes, lizards, and elephants, there was no reason why the Physical Section should not be permitted to restore a planet." In conclusion he asserted that "WHETHER KIRKWOOD'S ANALOGY IS OR IS NOT THE EXPRESSION OF A PHYSICAL LAW, IT IS AT LEAST THAT OF A PHYSICAL FACT IN THE MECHANISM OF THE UNIVERSE."[16]

In presenting Kirkwood's analogy, Walker emphasized its close relationship with the nebular hypothesis, pointing out that "the quantity D, on which the analogy is based, has such immediate dependence upon the nebular hypothesis, that it lends strength to the latter, and gives new plausibility to the presumption that this, also, is a fact in the past history of the solar system." Should the hypotheses of Laplace and Kirkwood be found to be true "laws of nature, they will throw new light on the internal organization of the planets, in their present, and in any more primitive state, through which they have passed."[17]

The members of the Physical Section of the AAAS responded warmly to the announcement of Kirkwood's analogy. S. W. Roberts, a prominent Philadelphia civil engineer, noted that few subjects of equal interest had been brought before the AAAS, and Joseph Henry said that he had "listened with admiration" to the story of

Kirkwood's discovery. But the most significant comment came from Benjamin Peirce. For several years he had been interested in determining whether or not the nebular hypothesis was a true history of the solar system. Recently the evidence seemed to be heavily against it; yet he had continued to hope it would eventually be vindicated. Kirkwood's analogy, based upon the diameters of the planets' spheres of attraction, seemed to do just that. This discovery, he said, "now for the first time gave an appearance of reality to Laplace's nebular hypothesis" and provided positive testimony in its favor that now outweighed whatever negative evidence there may have been. In his opinion, the analogy was "the only discovery of the kind since Kepler's time, that approached near to the character of his three physical laws."[18]

In a hastily prepared paper read on the seventh day of the meetings, Benjamin Gould, editor of the newly founded *Astronomical Journal*, re-emphasized the importance of the analogy in substantiating the nebular hypothesis. Since Walker's announcement of Kirkwood's discovery two days earlier, Gould had spent all his spare hours studying the analogy, and as the meetings came to a close he took a few minutes to report his conclusions, which closely paralleled those of Peirce. Kirkwood's theory, he said, would,

> if found to be true,—and the presumption seems to-day strongly in favor of its truth—furnish a remarkable and unexpected argument in support of the Nebular Hypothesis. The minds of many have been wavering of late with regard to this hypothesis; their doubts have been strengthened by the unqualified assertions that all nebulas are resolvable: but this analogy of Kirkwood tends most strikingly to confirm it—so much, indeed, that if this latter be true, I do not know how any one can resist the argument which it furnishes in favor of the former, in so far as it applies to our solar system. It is then no longer an hypothesis, but becomes a probable theory.

Briefly outlining the relationship of the nebular hypothesis to the analogy, he showed how the one would lead to the other. But he warned his colleagues not to expect an exact numerical verification of the analogy. Kirkwood had not discovered a physical law, which must be "precise and complete," but had found only an approximate relationship—"an analogy"— thus "the want of perfect accordance must not be considered to cast doubt upon the theory."[19]

Like Peirce and Walker, Gould could not resist comparing Kirkwood's achievement with Kepler's:

I do not wish to express myself strongly, but certainly when we look back upon the labors of Kepler, who strove so many years with results so unpromising, until he discovered the laws which underlie the whole fabric of our solar system, and then turn to Mr. Kirkwood, a teacher in the interior of Pennsylvania—who without the sympathies of kindred minds, or the use of any library of magnitude—without calling even upon the aid of strict mathematical analysis—has fixed his attention upon this one problem, and investigated it in all its bearings, until after ten years of patient thought and labor, he has arrived at such a result as this—we cannot but be struck with the similarity of the two cases; nor can we consider it as very derogatory to the former to speak hereafter of Kepler and Kirkwood together as the discoverers of great planetary harmonies.[20]

Almost singlehandedly Kirkwood's analogy restored the faith of American scientists in the nebular hypothesis. At the beginning of the AAAS meetings a widespread feeling of uncertainty about its truth had prevailed, caused largely by the resolutions of nebulae. But by the close of the meetings Laplace's cosmogony had regained a position of scientific respectability. According to one report, the members of the AAAS went home generally agreed "that Laplace's nebular hypothesis, from its furnishing one of the elements of Kirkwood's law, may now be regarded as an established fact in the past history of the solar system."[21] Three of America's most gifted astronomers—Gould, Peirce, and Walker—had testified publicly that Kirkwood's analogy lent strong support to the nebular hypothesis, and few of their countrymen were competent to challenge this judgment. Peirce's opinion alone, said the *Annual of Scientific Discovery*, "will probably be regarded as of more value on such a subject than that of any other man in this country."[22]

The American press quickly spread the news of Kirkwood's sensational discovery. Though the analogy was of no practical consequence, Americans appreciated its importance and prided themselves on having a Kepler in their midst. Newspapers, religious magazines, and scientific journals all proclaimed Kirkwood's achievement and informed their readers that the nebular hypothesis could once again be safely trusted.[23] The extent of Kirkwood's previous scientific isolation is illustrated by the fact that he first subscribed to the *American Journal of Science* in order to read about his own discovery.[24]

Across the Atlantic the analogy created a different response among men who derived no nationalistic pride from Kirkwood's accomplishment. Though some European scientists expressed admiration for what Kirkwood had done, they were often skeptical of its scientific value and its supposed support of the nebular hypothesis. Some, like the respected Cambridge geologist Adam Sedgwick, saw the analogy not as an empirical truth but only as "a hypothetical, and . . . very improbable, law of the Planetary System." Sedgwick loathed the *Vestiges* and was not inclined to surrender any ground that might prove advantageous to the enemy. Thus he denied that the analogy, even if completely verified, would have "any very obvious bearing" on the nebular hypothesis.[25]

Those more closely associated with astronomy than Sedgwick tended to be somewhat more appreciative of Kirkwood's work, though their appreciation usually fell short of the typical American response. C. Piazzi Smyth, the astronomer-royal for Scotland, looked upon Kirkwood's equation as "a mere arithmetical accident," like Bode's law. Yet he had to acknowledge that it did give fairly accurate results when applied to the three planets—Venus, Earth, and Saturn—for which there were adequate data to test it. The results were not always "so accordant as [he] had been led to expect, but still sufficiently so to give a certain probability of the approach to truth."[26]

David Brewster was even more approving of Kirkwood's analogy, though he questioned its ability to substantiate the nebular hypothesis. In his 1850 presidential address to the British Association for the Advancement of Science he applauded Kirkwood's discovery as a work of genius that had provided astronomers with a means of determining the original size and period of the planet that had given birth to the asteroids. According to calculations based on Kirkwood's formula, which Brewster regarded as a verified law, "the broken planet [christened 'Kirkwood' by Walker] must have been a little larger than Mars, or about 5,000 miles in diameter, and . . . the length of its day must have been about 57½ hours." Solving the problem of the missing planet between Mars and Jupiter did not, however, entitle the analogy to be considered a proof of the nebular hypothesis, and Brewster predicted that the astronomers of England would not adopt the American opinion that the analogy demonstrated the truth of Laplace's cosmogony.[27]

Not surprisingly, the most enthusiastic of Kirkwood's British admirers was John Pringle Nichol, who welcomed the analogy as the savior of the nebular hypothesis. In addition to being mathematically accurate, the analogy had the great merit of flowing "out of a combination of the most important elements of the [solar] system," wrote Nichol in *The Planetary System*. Kirkwood's law was thus totally "unlike Bode's law, which is the result of a mere comparison of otherwise unmeaning numbers." But best of all, the analogy revealed "that the rotation of each planet is not a *separate* or *isolated* attribute, but a *consequence of the relations of that planet, in all its habitudes, with the general mechanism of the system;* and thus it impresses a view of that system, analogous in every important respect to that which characterises the philosophic speculation of LAPLACE." Kirkwood's discovery was, in short, a "virtual confirmation" of the nebular hypothesis.[28]

Continental scientists seem to have taken little interest in Kirkwood's analogy. The *Astronomische Nachrichten*, for example, treated its announcement with cool indifference. On the same day that he had reported Kirkwood's discovery to the members of the AAAS, Walker had written to H. C. Schumacher, editor of Germany's leading astronomical journal, describing the analogy and proposing that it be ranked with Kepler's laws in scientific importance. Schumacher printed the letter, together with a short postscript declining to criticize Walker's estimation of the significance of Kirkwood's work, since each reader could "judge for himself how much in [Walker's] summary is really factual and how much is simply hypothetical."[29]

Despite its chilly reception overseas, the analogy received nothing but praise at home for over a year after its announcement. On the surface it appeared as if all American scientists were agreed that the Pennsylvania schoolteacher had indeed made a genuinely important discovery. But beneath the calm, dissension was beginning to form; it broke into the open with the publication of Elias Loomis' survey of *The Recent Progress of Astronomy; Especially in the United States*.[30] Just before the manuscript went to press, Joseph Henry had written Loomis expressing his desire that the book would raise the morale of the American scientific community. "I hope," he wrote, "you have done especial justice to the labors of American Astronomers. It is time that we should have among us a scientific *esprit du corps*."[31] Unfortunately, the effect of the book was just the opposite of that hoped for by Henry. Loomis had deliberately snubbed Kirkwood's analogy.

Readers of *The Recent Progress of Astronomy* naturally raised their eyebrows when they realized that Kirkwood's name was not even mentioned. The omission was particularly strange since the book purported to emphasize developments in the United States. Herrick, Kirkwood's earliest scientific correspondent, could not fathom why Loomis had neglected so important a contribution to astronomy, and he asked Loomis' former teacher and associate, Denison Olmsted, for an explanation. Olmsted was at a loss to think of a reason for the omission; so in his next letter to Loomis he asked about it.[32]

Loomis' answer was blunt and to the point: "I did not notice Kirkwood's Law in my book because I have no faith in it." He made no attempt to explain his attitude, but did request Olmsted to provide him with an opportunity for stating his views publicly. "If you would have a brief notice of my book inserted in Silliman's Journal for November, incidentally mentioning the omission of any allusion to Kirkwood, it would afford me a plausible pretext for giving my views of the new 'Analogies' which I would not be unwilling to improve, in a subsequent number of the Journal."[33] Olmsted politely excused himself from the unsolicited and unwanted assignment by claiming that he "could not devise any good way of calling [Loomis] out in the Journal on Kirkwood's Law." He urged Loomis to "come out in the next number without calling."[34]

Having failed to persuade Olmsted to "call him out," Loomis next tried Herrick. This time he even specified the length and content of the notice he wanted to appear and explained why he felt such a device was necessary:

> I suppose a brief notice of my Volume on Astronomy, extending to a dozen lines or so, would not be inappropriate in the American Journal of Science. Would you oblige me by furnishing such a notice for the next number. . . . I wish you would also allude to the omission of any notice of Kirkwood, as I would like to make it the occasion of some remarks upon that subject in the succeeding number. I think Mr. Walker has committed himself too strongly in favor of this "Law", and I would like to give my opinion upon it—but without some good pretext it may look like an unprevoked [sic] attack. You know men of science are apt to be jealous of their reputation, and often construe a criticism upon their opinions into an attack upon their personal character. Still I think a new principle in science like that announced by Kirkwood should be open to the freeest [sic] criticism without giving offence—and I should hope to give no offence myself to any body. At the same time I want a plausible pretext for speaking on this subject at all—After enumerating the principal topics of the book—you may add, "we have looked in vain for any allusion to Kirkwood's celebrated Law connecting the rotations of the planets with their masses and distances from the sun."[35]

Herrick apparently obliged Loomis, for in the January 1850 issue of the *American Journal of Science* a short description of Loomis' book appeared, followed by this comment: "One omission should be noticed. We do not find in this volume any allusion to Kirkwood's celebrated law connecting the rotations of the planets with their masses and distances from the sun. In a history of American Astronomy especially, this discovery is entitled to an honorable mention."[36] Two months earlier the *Literary World* had similarly called attention to the lack of any mention of Kirkwood's analogy in *The Recent Progress of Astronomy*.[37] Whether this too was planted at Loomis' request cannot be determined. At any rate, he now had sufficient grounds for his planned attack.

"As the enquiry has been made from a great variety of sources, why I have omitted in my book to make any mention of Kirkwood's discovery, I seem called upon to assign a reason for this neglect." With this disingenuous remark Loomis opened his criticism of Kirkwood's analogy in the March number of the *American Journal of Science*. He then explained candidly that his reason for not noticing Kirkwood's law in his book was that he did not believe it to be true. The accordance of the analogy with current data regarding the masses and periods of rotation of the planets, especially of Uranus, was simply not close enough to be convincing.[38] Loomis demanded precisely what Gould had warned astronomers not to expect: an exact numerical verification of the analogy. The failure of the analogy to meet this requirement seems to have been the entire basis of his opposition. There is no evidence that he was motivated by any hostility toward the nebular hypothesis. In fact, he used the Laplacian cosmogony to compute the rotational velocity of Uranus in his refutations of Kirkwood. Also, in 1854 he published an article favoring the origin of the asteroids from a nebulous ring, and early in the following decade he defended the nebular hypothesis in his lectures on astronomy at Yale.[39]

To ensure hearing what others thought of his criticism of Kirkwood's law, Loomis distributed reprints of his article to a number of scientists. Olmsted, one of the recipients, was clearly pleased with the arguments of his former pupil and replied that he was waiting "impatiently to see what those will say who hastily ranked [Kirkwood's Law] with Kepler's 3d Law."[40] Olmsted, however, was not fully convinced that Kirkwood's discovery was entirely meaningless and in a second letter told Loomis that although he had "certainly made it appear quite evident that Kirkwood's Law does not reach all the exigencies of the case required in order to constitute it a law of nature, . . . the coincidences with many of the facts are quite remarkable." He hoped that the discussion stimulated by Loomis' article would "advance the cause of truth."[41]

In the May issue of the *American Journal of Science* Kirkwood himself replied to Loomis. He readily granted that the lack of accurate data on the rotation of Uranus and on the mass and period of the hypothetical planet between Mars and Jupiter made it impossible to check his analogy in the instances where this specific information was necessary. Nevertheless, he staunchly maintained that his formula harmonized "with the *known* elements of the solar system as exactly as even recent determinations of the masses of the planets by different astronomers agree with each other." It was inconceivable to him that the accordance of his analogy with seventeen independent variable quantities was purely accidental. "The conclusion seems irresistible," he wrote, "that my formula is the expression of a law of nature."[42]

Gould, too, was unwilling to accept Loomis' appraisal of the analogy and protested his use of questionable data in trying to disprove Kirkwood. His own position, he wrote in a letter to Loomis, had not changed since the AAAS meetings; he still thought the analogy, which proved correct in the three cases where it could be tested, was plausible and "a very beautiful thing," though it admittedly was not a conclusively demonstrated fact.[43]

Although Loomis failed to change the minds of Kirkwood and his most influential supporters, his arguments against Kirkwood's analogy appeared convincing to a few individuals of less stature. One such person was a Canadian mathematician, J. Bradford Cherriman, who published a note in the *American Journal of Science* calling attention to some alleged discrepancies that had compelled him "to reject Kirkwood's Analogy as 'the expression of a law of nature,' and [to] agree with Prof. Loomis in considering it *not* established as a 'physical fact.' "[44] Another who found Loomis' criticism of Kirkwood persuasive was Chester Dewey, the University of Rochester's sixty-six-year-old professor of chemistry and natural sciences who, as a Congregational minister, also "preached not a little."[45] For some reason, quite possibly religious in nature, Dewey disliked the nebular hypothesis. He had hoped that the resolutions of nebulae would give "a lasting quietus" to the Laplacian cosmogony, but lately American astronomers were again showing "an inkling after it." Loomis' neglect to speak out against the nebular hypothesis in *The Recent Progress of Astronomy* had greatly disappointed Dewey, but now that Loomis had attacked Kirkwood's analogy and indirectly struck a blow against the nebular hypothesis, he was satisfied.[46]

Kirkwood's analogy successfully weathered the storm created by Loomis, retaining the respect of the majority of American astronomers and continuing to be taken by them as significant evidence in favor of the nebular origin of the solar system. The analogy, however, remained a purely empirical formula, much like Kepler's third law before Newton, and thirty-five years after its announcement the retiring president of the AAAS, Charles A. Young, cited its establishment as one of the "Pending Problems in Astronomy."[47] By this time the analogy no longer captivated the popular imagination, and most individuals had long forgotten the important role it had played in confirming the nebular hypothesis. Kirkwood himself had become a respected member of the American scientific establishment, having served from 1851 to 1856 as professor of mathematics in Delaware College and since then—with the exception of two years at Washington and Jefferson College—in a similar position in Indiana University.[48]

CHAPTER V

Acceptance

Thanks in large part to Kirkwood's analogy, the cloud of suspicion that had been hanging over the nebular hypothesis since the resolutions of nebulae and the appearance of the *Vestiges* finally showed signs of dissipating. Consequently, more and more educated Americans came to regard the nebular cosmogony as the most reasonable history of the solar system available, until by the end of the 1850s relatively little opposition to Laplace's theory remained. Among nonscientists, for whom one visual demonstration of the hypothesis was worth more than all the proofs of the mathematicians, Plateau's experiment had special appeal. Despite the Belgian professor's belated reminder that the physical forces operating in his experiment were different from those that had formed the solar system, the miniature reproduction of the nebular development of the planets was not easy to set aside. Such visual demonstrations, however, carried little weight with the professional scientist. More often than not he was attracted to the nebular hypothesis by its usefulness in explaining astronomical phenomena.

The origin of the asteroids is typical of the problems on which the nebular hypothesis was able to shed some light. Since the discovery of the first of these bodies at the beginning of the nineteenth century, astronomers had generally accepted Olbers' hypothesis that the asteroids were fragments of an exploded planet. As early as 1812 the French astronomer Joseph Louis Lagrange had indicated the compatibility of this explanation with Laplace's cosmogony, and in 1850 Brewster, using Kirkwood's analogy, had even calculated the approximate size of the lost planet. But as Kirkwood pointed out in 1852, his analogy did not require the assumption of a previously united planet; it merely indicated "what *would have been* the mass, mean distance, and time of rotation of the resulting planet, had all the matter in the primitive ring collected about a single nucleus." It seemed more probable to him that the asteroids had developed individually from nebulous matter than in the manner suggested by Olbers.[1]

In a study of the asteroids published in the Smithsonian Institution's *Annual Report* for 1854, Elias Loomis reached the same conclusion. Upon examining the orbits of the asteroids, he had found that they did not have a common point of intersection, as they should have had if Olbers' conjecture were correct. Although he could not be certain that the orbits had never intersected, he was sure that they had not done so in the recent past. If a planetary explosion had produced the asteroids, it "must have occurred *myriads of years ago.*" The plausibility of Olbers' hypothesis was further lessened by the increasing number of asteroids being discovered. It was, said Loomis, "hardly less reasonable to suppose that the earth and Venus originally constituted but one body, than to admit the same for the thirty-three asteroids." Like Kirkwood, he thought the nebular hypothesis provided a more probable explanation of the origin of the asteroids, for if the solar system had been formed in the manner proposed by Laplace, the asteroids were simply the offspring of an anomalous ring that had failed to coalesce into a single planet.[2]

Because the secular variations of each of the asteroids had not yet been computed at the time Loomis made his study, he was unable to refute Olbers' hypothesis with mathematical certainty. The task of delivering the *coup de grâce* to Olbers' theory was thus left to Simon Newcomb, a promising student of Benjamin Peirce's who had just graduated from the Lawrence Scientific School at Harvard. Newcomb's refutation of Olbers' hypothesis, presented in 1859 in his initial appearance before the American Academy of Arts and Sciences in Boston, was his first important scientific accomplishment.

His paper began with a description of the two hypotheses that seemed most capable of explaining the origin of the asteroids: the theory of Olbers and the nebulous ring theory. Olbers' hypothesis had two counts against it: no known natural cause was capable of breaking up a planet, and the orbits of the asteroids lacked a common point of intersection. It was difficult to determine how much weight should be assigned to the first objection, "since the limits of our knowledge are not necessarily the limits of possibility"; but the second objection could be evaluated objectively and precisely. In computing the secular variations of eight of the asteroids, Newcomb had discovered several instances where the orbit of a particular asteroid could not possibly have intersected the orbits of others—at least, it could not have done so if the present orbits of the asteroids had not been unduly disturbed by mutual attraction. Though prevented by this possibility from absolutely disproving Olbers' hypothesis, he nevertheless showed it to be so unlikely as to be undeserving of any further recognition.[3]

The second hypothesis was clearly superior, for a somewhat eccentric nebulous ring, inclined to the plane of the ecliptic and not revolving in its own plane, would very likely have produced a phenomenon like the asteroids. To be sure, this explanation was dependent upon the truth of the nebular hypothesis, which had not been demonstrated, and it was "not equally susceptible with that of Olbers of *a posteriori* tests"; but these weaknesses were slight compared with the objections to the theory of Olbers.[4] This capacity to suggest solutions to astronomical problems like that of the origin of the asteroids made the nebular hypothesis appear increasingly credible in the eyes of American astronomers.

It was during the 1850s that Daniel Kirkwood entered upon his career as America's leading defender and critic of the nebular hypothesis. From his pen there issued the first of a stream of articles on the history of the solar system and its constituents that flowed until his death near the close of the century. Aside from a note elucidating his analogy,[5] his earliest publication on the Laplacian cosmogony was an effort to determine the relative age of Saturn and the possible fate of its ring. Early in the previous decade Joseph Lovering had prophesied of a time when mathematicians would "be able to settle with exactness the genealogy of our system according to Laplace's theory, and to assign the individual year when each of the outcast planets, from the grey Herschel and Saturn down to the infant Mercury, left its burning home and became an independent orb."[6]

The Hollis Professor had assumed as obvious that the ages of the planets were directly proportional to their distances from the sun, but Kirkwood now questioned this assumption on the grounds that the giant rings farthest from the sun would have taken the longest time to consolidate into planets and that the planets having the greatest spheres of attraction would have been the slowest to condense. Therefore, Saturn, with the largest sphere of attraction of the major planets, was probably the youngest member of the solar family. And if this were true, it seemed likely that Saturn's ring would eventually collect about a nucleus and become a satellite like its older cousins.[7]

Writing anonymously for the *Presbyterian Quarterly Review* in 1854, Kirkwood evaluated the arguments for and against the nebular hypothesis. "No modern theory of cosmogony has been more favorably received by the scientific world than that of the celebrated Laplace," he said. Lately even the man in the street was showing a fascination for the idea, and well he might, since there was never a time when the hypothesis was held in higher esteem by men of science. Baron von Humboldt and Benjamin Peirce were only two of "an imposing array of illustrious names" that could be cited in support of this claim.[8] Why Kirkwood singled out Humboldt is difficult to understand, for though the German scientist did accept the general idea of the development of the solar system from a nebulous mass, he had reservations about the Laplacian cosmogony, which drew "conclusions from the present state of things, as to the entire series of conditions which have been passed through from their commencement."[9] Perhaps Kirkwood was only taking advantage of von Humboldt's outstanding reputation in America.

For those who required more than an appeal to scientific authority, Kirkwood provided an impressive list of arguments from astronomy and geology in favor of the nebular hypothesis. The motions and arrangement of the solar system are just what one would expect if the hypothesis were correct; in fact, Saturn's rings look as if they "had been left by the Architect of Nature as an index to the creative process." The hypothesis could be extended to binary and multiple star systems, and whatever "leads us higher in the process of generalization may be presumed to have some foundation in truth." Geological evidence indicates that the earth developed from a primitive state of igneous fluidity, and the other members of our system show signs of having gone through a similar process. "The spheroidal figure of the planets points to a great and significant fact in regard to their primitive constitution—the fact that they have *all*, at former epochs in their history, been in a liquid, if not in a gaseous state." Finally, the nebular hypothesis could explain the origin of comets and the zodiacal light from remnant nebulous matter and could also account for the fact that the periods of axial rotation and orbital revolution of many of the system's satellites are equal.[10]

"Such are some of the evidences by which this theory is supported," he said. "Adopting it, we derive all the motions of the solar system from a SINGLE IMPULSE communicated by the Creator to the primitive nebula: rejecting it, each motion of every member demands the *separate* operation of his power." It seemed preposterous that God would have chosen the latter course, that He would have adopted any means but the simplest to accomplish His ends. God was not prodigal; therefore, the nebular hypothesis must be true.[11]

Against such overwhelming evidence, continued Kirkwood, detractors of the nebular cosmogony had been able to muster only three principal criticisms: "(1), that [the nebular hypothesis] can not be reconciled with the retrograde motions of the satellites of Uranus; (2), that its main support has been removed by the revelations of Lord Rosse's telescope; and, (3), that its tendency is atheistical." Each of these he dismissed as invalid. The retrograde motions of the satellites of Uranus were not irreconcilable with the nebular hypothesis, for they could easily be explained by assuming either that the moons had developed anomalously, or as Laplace had proposed, that collisions with comets had deranged their orbits. The second objection was not true, because the hypothesis was supported primarily by the phenomena of the solar system. Besides, comets and the zodiacal light proved that nebulous matter did actually exist.

The charge of atheism was more serious—but illogical. The existence of a law plainly implied the existence of a lawgiver; thus the substitution of "natural law for the direct agency of the Deity" in no way eliminated the necessity for divine action. "Moreover," said Kirkwood, "if the power of the Deity is manifested in accordance with a uniform system . . . in *sustaining* and *governing* the material universe," it should not "be regarded as derogating from his perfections, to suppose the same power to have been exerted in a similar way in the process of its formation." Since much of the misunderstanding of the theological implications of the nebular hypothesis had been fostered by the *Vestiges*, he made a point of emphasizing that there was no connection between Laplace's cosmogony and Lamarck's theory of organic development.[12]

During the years following the writing of this summary Kirkwood continued collecting all the evidence he could find that might possibly corroborate the nebular hypothesis, and in 1860 he reprinted the article, somewhat revised and expanded, in the *American Journal of Science*. To the list of phenomena explained by the Laplacian cosmogony, he now added the heat of the sun, the asteroids, and the distribution of satellites around the planets. This time he also included his own analogy, which strangely had been omitted earlier.[13]

Second only to Kirkwood, the American most concerned with the implications of the nebular hypothesis was Stephen Alexander, Joseph Henry's cousin and brother-in-law. After graduating from Union College at the age of eighteen, Alexander taught school at Chittenango, New York, and then joined the Henrys at the Albany Academy. When they went to Princeton in 1832, he tagged along and entered the Princeton Theological Seminary. The next year, however, he abandoned his theological studies to become a tutor in the College of New Jersey, where he taught mathematics and astronomy until his retirement in 1877.[14]

Alexander's scientific temperament was much like Kepler's and Kirkwood's. He was forever trying to discover some new harmony among the heavenly bodies. The nebular hypothesis played a central role in his thinking. His successor at Princeton, Charles A. Young, recalled that "Laplace's Nebular Hypothesis had always a powerful fascination for [Alexander]. He made it the basis of endless speculations as to the origin and genesis of the present state of things, and though he sometimes reached conclusions difficult to reconcile with it, as commonly understood, he was always persuaded of its essential verity."[15]

Alexander's lectures at Princeton on the nebular hypothesis, with which he traditionally concluded his astronomy course, attracted crowds of admiring auditors, both students and townspeople. According to one of his former pupils, these lectures

were characterized by a lofty and poetic eloquence, and drew to his class-room many others than the students to whom they were addressed. Even ladies from the village and elsewhere—so far did the traditional conservatism of Princeton give way before a wholesome pressure —invaded Philosophical Hall . . . and taxed to the utmost the gallantry of collegians. I vividly recall one of the occasions of which I speak—the hushed and expectant auditory; the shy, almost abashed, manner of the lecturer; the rapt look, the glowing countenance, the throbbing frame, which indicated how completely he was possessed by his theme; the magnificent sweep of his ideas concerning the formation of the material universe with its countless suns and systems; his happy application of Scripture phrase when, pointing to the drawings of certain nebulae of remarkable form, he would quote: "They all shall wax old as doth a garment, and as a vesture shalt thou change them, and they shall be changed;" the outburst of eloquence, seeming to our young minds akin to inspiration itself, with which he ascribed all the beauty and glory of creation to Him who is enthroned in majesty above all spheres, evermore controlling and guiding all, the Personal God, glorious in holiness, fearful in praises, doing wonders.[16]

The nebular hypothesis provided the inspiration for two of Alexander's most significant astronomical studies. One was a theory regarding the development of nebulae and star clusters; the other, a description of certain harmonies in the solar system. He began the first of these studies late in 1847 after reading about Lord Rosse's observations of the recently discovered spiral nebulae. It occurred to him that the shape of these nebulae—and perhaps others—might be accounted for by supposing them to be the products of enormous Plateau experiments. He immediately discussed this possibility with his brother-in-law but let several years pass before announcing it publicly at the 1851 meetings of the AAAS, held in Albany. The following year he published an exhaustive eight-part article in Gould's *Astronomical Journal* entitled "On the Origin of the Forms and the Present Conditions of Some of the Clusters of Stars, and Several of the Nebulae."[17] Alexander had become convinced that the spirals and some other nebulae were not stars in the process of being formed, as William Herschel had proposed for nebulae generally, but rather were stars in the process of disintegrating. In his paper for the *Astronomical Journal* he demonstrated how primitive spheroidal stars would break up to form various types of nebulae. If the same forces that had caused our sun to fragment into a planetary system also operated on huge spheroids rotating in a state of dynamical equilibrium, the "effects would be analogous to those supposed by the *nebular hypothesis* of Laplace to have occurred in the primitive state of the sun; and for similar reasons to those alleged by that eminent astronomer."[18]

Since the nebular hypothesis had "in some measure furnished the basis" for his generalizations concerning the development of nebulae and star clusters, Alexander gave some of the reasons why he believed that theory to be true. Besides "Kirkwood's beautiful analogy," he cited two investigations of his own that agreed favorably with the Laplacian cosmogony. In one (discussed below) he had attempted to show that the sun originally had been circled by two great rings, from which the planets had developed. In the other he had demonstrated the possibility of a common origin of the asteroids and comets of short period. If the planetary asteroids had formed one body with the nebulous comets at some time in the past, then they too must have been in a nebulous state, just as the nebular hypothesis required.[19]

Aside from the telescopic observations of stars seemingly decomposing into nebulae and the analogous development of the solar system, Alexander had a philosophical reason for believing in his hypothesis of disintegration: it harmonized with the Creator's known *modus operandi.*

> The growing leaf is fed by the exhalations which it finds in the atmosphere; and the leaf in its decay nourishes the vegetating tree; the roots of that tree are embedded in the *débris* of a comparatively ancient earth; the earth itself, in the view of the nebular hypothesis, has been detached from the sun; and the sun and other stars would now seem to be but the comparatively small fragments or drops of greater masses which *were* themselves but fragments of masses of even a higher order: the one great plan, pervading the *whole*, being, BY MEANS OF A SEEMING DESTRUCTION, TO PROVIDE FOR A MORE PERFECT ADAPTATION AND DEVELOPMENT.[20]

The second of Alexander's studies inspired by the nebular hypothesis, the one he considered to be his most important, occupied almost thirty years of his life. He began it in the late 1840s in an effort to save Bode's law from the contradiction posed by the newly found planet Neptune. That law, an empirical formula discovered by Johann Daniel Titius in the eighteenth century and popularized by Johann Bode, gave the distances of the planets from the sun as a mathematical progression. In July 1850 Alexander wrote Henry that the failure of Bode's law in the case of Neptune could be eliminated with the aid of a modified form of the nebular hypothesis. He had discovered that Bode's law worked if it were applied in two stages: from Mercury's orbit to Saturn, and from Saturn's orbit to Neptune. This, he wrote, "seems to say that not only is the Nebular Hypothesis in place; but that *the Sun was anciently surrounded by two systems of rings arranged like those of Saturn*—that the rupture of these furnished the planets; and the subdivision and rupture of one of them furnished the material for the asteroids." He reported this interesting finding to the AAAS at its 1850 meetings in New Haven.[21]

During the 1850s and into the following decades Alexander continued studying the ratios of the distances of the planets from the sun and even extended his inquiry to the satellite systems. Among his discoveries was the curious fact that the satellites of Saturn and Jupiter were arranged in the same pattern as the planets, an apparent confirmation of the validity of his approach. Always he based his work on the assumption that the planetary bodies had developed from nebulous rings.[22]

A typical problem he solved with the aid of the Laplacian cosmogony concerned the satellite system of Jupiter. According to his calculations, Jupiter was missing its most interior moon. He mentioned this to Gould, with whom he constantly corresponded about his research, and Gould in turn asked Bond at the Harvard Observatory to search for the body. When Bond was unable to find it, Alexander was forced to explain its absence. This he did by assuming that the ring that would have developed into Jupiter's innermost moon had failed to coalesce into a single body. As Benjamin Peirce had shown, a system with so few satellites could not sustain a ring, so the matter would have collapsed into Jupiter. "The bearings of this upon the nebular hypothesis are curious," Alexander wrote to Henry, "if indeed here was a *ring* just *where* a satellite ought now to be found."[23]

Over the years Henry encouraged his brother-in-law to persevere. "The field is a fertile one," he wrote in 1857, "and with the labor and ingenuity you are bestowing upon it, a valuable harvest may be reaped." The harvest, however, did not come soon. Alexander was sixty-eight years old when finally in 1875 he published his crowning achievement, a ninety-five-page treatise in the *Smithsonian Contributions to Knowledge* entitled "Statement and Exposition of Certain Harmonies of the Solar System."[24]

By the late 1850s the preponderance of educated Americans who expressed themselves on such issues believed the solar system had been created in the manner described by Laplace. According to the *Southern Quarterly Review* in 1856, more attention had been devoted to the nebular hypothesis in the popular literature than to any other astronomical theory. "Thousands of educated and intelligent people . . . have satisfied themselves of its truth," it reported.

"Its history, the facts on which it rests, the objections that are made to it, the affinities and relations which it has to other departments of acknowledged truth, the degree of confidence which it ought to have in the minds of wise and thoughtful men, are questions of general and popular interest." Despite the lack of absolute proof, the magazine recommended that Laplace's hypothesis be accepted. Only the nebular theory, it said, "explains the phenomena. Nothing that we know contradicts it. Having so many characteristics of a true theory, it claims to be received and believed."[25]

The *Southern Quarterly Review* implied that the nebular hypothesis had more popular than scientific support, but our study does not bear this out. By the end of the decade most of America's leading scientists were committed disciples of Laplace. Among the astronomers were Peirce, Harvard's Perkins Professor of Mathematics and Astronomy; Alexander, Princeton's professor of astronomy; Gould, editor of the *Astronomical Journal* and director of the Dudley Observatory in Albany from 1855 to 1859; Mitchel, director of the Cincinnati Observatory and successor to Gould at the Dudley Observatory; Loomis, professor of mathematics and natural philosophy in the University of the City of New York; and Kirkwood, professor of mathematics in Indiana University since 1856.[26] America's greatest physicist, Henry; its foremost botanist, Asa Gray; and its most prominent zoologist, Louis Agassiz, were also admirers of the nebular hypothesis. These men were the acknowledged leaders of the American scientific community. They controlled the country's important scientific institutions and influenced the scientific thought of the nation. Few of their colleagues had either the courage or the inclination to dispute their collective judgment.

Those who did—and there were some—almost always opposed the nebular hypothesis on scientific rather than theological grounds. Denison Olmsted, Yale's respected astronomer, is a good example of one who rejected Laplace's cosmogony for purely scientific reasons. In 1852 he decided it was time to include a lecture on the nebular hypothesis in his astronomy course. Not being well acquainted with the subject, he went directly to the original account in the *Système du monde* and perused it "with great care." On the fourth of March he delivered his newly prepared lecture, an outline of which is preserved among his notes. It is just as legitimate, he told his students, "to inquire for some physical cause of the phenomena unaccounted for by gravitation as of those that are so explained." Such inquiries are not atheistical because they do not eliminate the necessity of divine action. In the case of the nebular hypothesis, Laplace himself had been "obliged to admit a first cause" in order to explain the existence of the primitive rotating nebula. [27]

Nevertheless, Olmsted was "not a believer in the hypothesis." The fact that it explained so many characteristics of the solar system was of little consequence to him, since occasionally two different hypotheses could account for the same evidence equally well. Of far greater significance were the anomalies, because only one was necessary to discredit the entire theory. And he had found three. The nebular hypothesis demanded that all motions in the solar system be in the same direction, but the satellites of Uranus had a retrograde motion. The hypothesis required that the densities of the planets be directly proportional to their distances from the sun, but Uranus was more dense than Saturn. The hypothesis needed rings spaced at immense distances from one another, but he believed that a contracting nebula would abandon rings continuously. How could a hypothesis seemingly contradicted by so many facts possibly be true?[28]

As the furor created by the *Vestiges* began to subside in the 1850s, it became much easier to judge the nebular hypothesis on its scientific merits. An anecdote related by Mitchel during the discussion following Alexander's paper on spiral nebulae at the 1851 meetings of the AAAS illustrates this change. Several years earlier, when the Cincinnati astronomer was about to begin a similar investigation, a concerned friend had left a note on his desk "begging him to desist from such an 'atheistical' attempt!" Those days of religious hostility toward the nebular hypothesis had now passed, he said. [29] And to a significant extent, they had. In 1860 it was possible for Alexander Wilcocks to tell the Academy of Natural Sciences of Philadelphia that "the Nebular Hypothesis of La Place . . . having for a half a century stood the fire of the world's criticism, has passed that ordeal unscathed, and now holds an almost undisputed empire upon the minds of astronomers."[30]

Wilcocks would have been more accurate had he said "American astronomers," for his statement was not generally true of attitudes toward the nebular hypothesis outside the United States in countries like Great Britain. During the 1850s many of the most prominent British scientists were critical of the Laplacian cosmogony. William Whewell, who had helped to popularize the hypothesis in his Bridgewater Treatise, no longer liked the idea. David Brewster, who in the 1830s had considered the hypothesis to be verified, now thought it had "been overturned by arguments that have never been answered." John Herschel remained cool as ever. The ablest defense of the nebular cosmogony to appear in the British Isles during the decade was by the philosopher Herbert Spencer, not by an astronomer. It is easy to see why the British physician Henry Holland concluded—so differently from Wilcocks—that the most ardent advocates of the nebular hypothesis were those philosophers, undiscriminating in scientific matters, who espoused "the doctrine of progressive development."[31] Like Wilcocks, he had looked no further than his own scientific back yard.

CHAPTER VI

Confirmation and Rejection

The nebular hypothesis was already firmly entrenched in the minds of America's intellectual leaders when news reached the United States of a striking corroborating discovery. In 1865 the *American Journal of Science* announced that the English astronomer William Huggins had established beyond a doubt that not all nebulae were mere congeries of stars, as many had alleged since Lord Rosse's telescopic resolutions in the mid-1840s.[1] While investigating the spectra of nebulae on an August evening in 1864, Huggins had discovered to his great surprise that the spectrum of a certain planetary nebula in the constellation Draco consisted of only a few lines instead of the expected continuous bands of different colors characteristic of stars and all glowing solids and liquids. For a moment he suspected his apparatus was amiss, but then "the true interpretation flashed upon [him]." He suddenly realized he was looking not at a stellar spectrum but at the spectrum of a gaseous or vaporous body, distinguished by its lines.[2] Years afterward he recalled the effect this discovery had on cosmogonical thinking: "The riddle of the nebulae was solved. The answer, which had come to us in the light itself, read: Not an aggregation of stars, but a luminous gas. . . . There remained no room for doubt that the nebulae, which our telescopes reveal to us, are the early stages of long processions of cosmical events, which correspond broadly to those required by the nebular hypothesis in one or other of its forms."[3]

Continued observation revealed more nebulae with the telltale line spectra, and in each case the nebula had resisted resolution by Lord Rosse's telescope.[4] Thus was laid to rest the argument most frequently used to discredit the nebular hypothesis during the previous two decades, namely, that true nebulae, like that from which our solar system had supposedly developed, did not really exist.

With their spectroscopes astrophysicists were also able to detect nebular changes similar to those our solar system's progenitor might have undergone. The spectra of these nebulae were composed of continuous bands interrupted by bright lines, suggesting that condensation had already begun to produce solid or liquid nuclei. This discovery raised the hopes of some that eventually man would actually witness the process by which our system had been formed. "Can it be looked upon as impossible," asked one elated author, "that the truth of La Place's theory may yet be demonstrated by actual observation, and that our future physicists and astronomers, with their vastly improved means of observation, may watch the giant process of the formation of new worlds with the same ease with which the chemist, in his laboratory, watches the building of the beautiful and symmetrical crystal?"[5]

These unexpected spectroscopic corroborations of the nebular hypothesis seemed especially impressive because they were "not the results of investigations instituted for the purpose of thus confirming the theory."[6] For scientists and educated laymen alike, they successfully dispelled almost all lingering doubts about the validity of the hypothesis.[7] In 1874 Alexander Winchell commented on its nearly unanimous acceptance: "Occasionally we hear a dissenting voice; but it proceeds, almost always, from persons who, whatever their eminence in theology or letters, have little authority in matters of scientific opinion."[8]

Typical of the unscientific critics was George W. Eveleth, of Portland, Maine, who fought throughout his life against both the nebular hypothesis and the theory of gravitation. The former could not possibly be true, he argued, because matter thrown off from a rotating nebula would not "settle into an orbit and revolve round the Sun" but would sail off into space.[9] Apparently he had never bothered to read Laplace, or else he would have known that matter was not "thrown off" from the nebula but was simply abandoned whenever the centrifugal force acting on a particle equaled its gravitational attraction to the central mass.

But cranks and religious fundamentalists were not the only ones to find fault with Laplace's cosmogony. In the 1860s, at the height of its popularity, respectable scientists and philosophers finally began to give the nebular hyopthesis the careful examination it needed but had never received. They had come to realize, with Asaph Hall, that "Laplace did not wish to exempt his own theories from criticism, and neither should any one. In astronomy there is no final human authority, no synod or council, but simply an appeal to reason and observation. If a theory or a discovery be true, it will stand the test of observation and of calculation; if false, it must pass away to that Miltonian limbo where so many things have gone and are going."[10]

Led by Daniel Kirkwood, now at Indiana University, a number of American scientists participated in testing the nebular hypothesis and in trying to shore up the weakest parts. Among the most active were Simon Newcomb, of the United States Naval Observatory; Gustavus Hinrichs, a Danish-educated professor of physics and chemistry in the State University of Iowa; David Trowbridge, a self-educated mechanic and part-time teacher from Schuyler County, New York; Jacob Ennis, principal of the Scientific and Classical Institute in Philadelphia; and Pliny Earle Chase, a Quaker graduate of Harvard on the faculty of Haverford College.[11] These men were concerned almost exclusively with the scientific merits of the nebular hypothesis, and the American public—by this time thoroughly familiar with the idea of the solar system's natural origin—paid them little attention.

Laplace's cosmogony first ran into difficulty at the point where it sought to account for the formation of rings from the primitive sun. With the notable exception of Ennis, who thought it necessary to explain how the nebula had acquired its motion, virtually all cosmogonists simply assumed the existence of a rotating nebulous body as a given fact and went on from there, as Laplace had done.[12] They immediately encountered, however, two significant difficulties in Laplace's theory of ring formation. The first, noted by Kirkwood in 1864 and again in 1869, was that a shrinking nebula such as Laplace had imagined would not deposit a few large rings widely separated from each other but would, "after first reaching the point at which gravity was counterbalanced by the centrifugal force arising from the rotation of the contracting spheroid," leave a continuous succession of narrow rings in close proximity to each other.[13] A little later Newcomb reached a similar conclusion: that the nebula's contraction would have resulted in "a constant dropping-off of matter from the outer portions, so that, instead of a series of rings, there would have been a flat disk formed of an infinite number of concentrating rings all joined together."[14]

Kirkwood's modification of the nebular hypothesis seemed to be justified by his discovery in 1866 of the probable cause of gaps observed in the asteroids and the rings of Saturn. These intervals always occurred at distances where the periods of planetary bodies, had they existed, would have been commensurable with that of Jupiter or Saturn's largest satellite. In the instance of the asteroids, Kirkwood thought the disturbing effects of Jupiter at the distances where the gaps existed would have given rings or developing asteroids there such eccentric orbits that in perihelion they would have plunged back into the receding nebula, leaving these areas unoccupied. Saturn's satellite had apparently had the same effect in its system. Since this explanation was based on the assumption that the asteroids and small bodies constituting Saturn's rings had developed from "*an indefinite number of narrow annuli*," each having its distinct period of revolution, it gave credence to Kirkwood's supposition that throughout the solar system a continuous succession of small rings had been abandoned.[15]

In 1861 the French scientist Jacques Babinet found a second defect in Laplace's theory of ring formation, more consequential than that regarding the size and number of rings.[16] He showed, contrary to the Laplacian hypothesis, that a contracting homogeneous nebula would not produce rings having periods of revolution corresponding to those of the present planets. In the words of Kirkwood, "If the solar nebula . . . rotated once in 164.6 years when it filled the orbit of Neptune, its period when it had contracted to the orbit of Uranus ought to have been 67 years; at the orbit of Saturn, 16.7 years; at that of Jupiter, 4.94 years, &c., &c."[17] These values, varying greatly from the actual periods of revolution of the planets, were clearly inconsistent with Kepler's third law.

Various attempts were made to get around this difficulty. Trowbridge, for example, suggested that the nebula had not been homogeneous, that "even when the Neptunian ring was abandoned, the solar spheroid was very much condensed about the centre; and that probably more than half the mass was within the orbit of the earth as it now exists, and the major part of half of it was within the present orbit of Mercury."[18] This suggestion seemed to harmonize with Laplace's own description of the nebula as having a nucleus of greater density than the surrounding atmosphere; Laplace, however, had given no indication of being aware of the problem later discovered by Babinet.[19] Regardless of what the originator of the cosmogony might have thought, Kirkwood felt that arbitrary assumptions like Trowbridge's—"invented to sustain the hypothesis of Laplace"—could be of little help until they themselves had "been placed on a basis of facts."[20]

Laplace's theory of the formation of planets from the rings surrounding the sun also met with serious objections. He had assumed that in most instances a ring would divide into several parts, which would then coalesce by gravitational attraction to form a single body. At first glance this seemed like a reasonable explanation, but on close inspection it appeared quite improbable. Newcomb regarded it as perhaps the weakest part of the nebular hypothesis,[21] while the Californian George Davidson thought it was simply preposterous. When he read of it in Newcomb's *Popular Astronomy*, he jotted in the margin: "Just imagine if you can a ring with the circumference of Saturn's orbit resolving itself into a simple solid body!"[22]

In 1879 Kirkwood remarked that it was "obvious, on the slightest examination, that the mutual attraction of different portions of a zone could have very little influence in bringing its molecules together around a common nucleus." Besides, this method of development would consume more time than was commonly thought to be available and would be so slow that planets would be cold before they could give birth to satellites.[23] To avoid these difficulties, he proposed the following year "that each planet, at its origin, was separated from a very limited arc of the equatorial protuberance; or, in other words, that instead of the separation of a ring, the centrifugal force produced a rupture at the point of least resistance in the equatorial belt." The matter thus ejected would condense to form a planet, which, when in perihelion, would create a tidal wave on the surface of the central nebula, causing the separation of a second planet. This process would be repeated until the entire solar system had been formed.[24]

Defenders of the nebular hypothesis were also plagued by sundry phenomena in the solar system that seemed to be inconsistent with the mode of development proposed by Laplace. American friends of the hypothesis did their utmost to explain away these difficulties. Kirkwood, Hinrichs, and Trowbridge all suggested possible explanations of the fact that only Uranus and Neptune possessed retrograde rotations, in opposition to the requirement of the nebular hypothesis that every planet rotate in a retrograde direction.[25] These same men also sought to account for the retrograde revolutions of the satellites of Uranus, which, with the retrograde revolution of Neptune's satellite and other instances of deviations from the plane of rotation of the original nebula, contradicted one of Laplace's basic assumptions.[26] Chase and Kirkwood provided reasons why the inner moon of Mars, like the innermost ring of Saturn, had a period of revolution shorter than its primary's period of rotation.[27] But despite the good intentions, few of these proffered solutions were completely satisfactory, as were few of the efforts made by Europeans—notably the Frenchmen Édouard Roche, of Montpellier, and Charles Wolf, of Paris—to free the Laplacian cosmogony from its embarrassments.[28]

As the difficulties of the nebular hypothesis accumulated, its supporters became increasingly pessimistic about ever discovering the actual history of the solar system. Among the discouraged was Newcomb. At the beginning of his career he had brimmed with confidence that man would soon possess the true cosmogony, but by the late 1880s all such hope was gone. When a talented young American studying in Berlin expressed a special interest in cosmogonical problems, he received the following counsel from his country's most eminent astronomer: "Your interest in the formation of the heavenly bodies is very natural, but I have formerly given much attention to the question myself and have found it so unsatisfactory that I have entirely given it up. In the present state of our knowledge such investigations lead to nothing. I fear that nothing of a definite character along this line can be accomplished in our time."[29]

Dissatisfaction with the nebular hypothesis naturally prompted some scientists to search for a less objectionable cosmogony. Of the several substitutes proposed, only two became serious rivals of Laplace's theory: the meteoric (or meteoritic) hypothesis and the planetesimal hypothesis. The former cosmogony was an extrapolation of the meteoric theory of the conservation of solar energy, suggested by the German physician J. R. Mayer shortly after the discovery of the conservation of energy revealed that the sun's energy would have been exhausted after only a few thousand years had it not been replenished. In 1848 Mayer showed that the great amounts of energy released by the constant bombardment of meteors upon the sun were sufficient to sustain its ability to radiate. Though his views attracted little attention at first, by the 1860s several persons were extending his hypothesis to explain the origin of the solar system. They reasoned that the planets, no less than the sun, were subject to the continuous impact of falling meteors and, therefore, that the accumulation of these bodies had probably given birth to the planets.[30]

This cosmogony, however, failed to win widespread scientific support, for it was scarcely less objectionable than the nebular hypothesis. Critics pointed out that the earth's crust was not composed of meteoric ingredients and that there was no reason why aggregating planets would all revolve around the sun in the same direction, in almost circular orbits, and in nearly the same plane. Even more damaging was the demonstration that the meteoric hypothesis of the sustentation of solar energy was no longer tenable, on the grounds that the quantity of meteors needed to keep the sun shining was so great that their addition to the sun's mass would have significantly shortened the length of the day. In place of this hypothesis most scientists adopted Hermann von Helmholtz's theory, advanced in 1854, that the sun derives its energy from its own contraction as gravity draws the particles on its outer limits toward the center.[31] Since this theory and the nebular hypothesis both required a shrinking sun, they tended to reinforce each other. Both ideas, for example, benefited from Jonathan Homer Lane's seemingly paradoxical discovery in 1869 that gaseous bodies radiating heat as they cool compensate for this loss of energy by acquiring additional heat from the resulting contraction.[32]

For several decades the meteoric cosmogony was practically the only available alternative to the nebular hypothesis. Thus, despite its manifest imperfections, it found a few adherents. It seemed to appeal especially to those individuals, like Chauncey Wright, who opposed the Laplacian cosmogony primarily for philosophical rather than scientific reasons. Wright, better known as one of the founders of pragmatism, worked at the Harvard Observatory as a computer for the *American Ephemeris and Nautical Almanac*. Any theory that smacked of teleology aroused his suspicion and animosity, but none more so than Herbert Spencer's theory of universal evolution, of which the nebular hypothesis was an integral part.

Wright was unwilling to accept the history of the solar system so grandly portrayed by Laplace and Spencer as an "entirely regular development or . . . simple specimen of universal progress out of an original 'homogeneity' (as it is now the fashion to call the old nebula)." Science, he urged, "ought to free itself entirely from this unscientific prejudice which cannot be proven or tested any better than [a] miracle."[33] A truly scientific cosmogony would depend solely on the ordinary operations of nature and would show no more evidence of direction or progress than the ever-changing weather patterns. It would be based not on the principle of development but on "the principle of *counter-movements*,—a principle in accordance with which there is no action in nature to which there is not some counter-action, and no production in nature by which in infinite ages there can result an infinite product." Since the two chief agents of countermovements in the formation and destruction of solar systems are heat and gravitation—the former tending always to disperse matter and the latter tending always to concentrate it—he favored the theory that the planets had resulted from the aggregation of meteors formed at the outer edge of the solar system from gaseous matter dispersed by the sun's heat.[34]

J. B. Stallo, a Cincinnati attorney who had formerly taught chemistry and physics in Saint John's College, New York, shared many of Wright's objections to the nebular hypothesis. In his epistemological study of *The Concepts and Theories of Modern Physics*, first published in 1881, he was particularly critical of attempts to extend the hypothesis to the entire universe. It was absurd and unscientific to theorize about the beginning of the world, he argued. "The only question to which a series or group of phenomena gives legitimate rise relates to their filiation and interdependence; and the attempts to transcend the bases of this filiation and interdependence . . . are as futile as . . . the attempt of the eagle to outsoar the atmosphere in which he floats and by which alone he may be supported." Stallo ascribed the "ready and almost enthusiastic acceptance" of the nebular hypothesis to metaphysical rather than physical reasons, one being its conformation "to the assumption that, on any hypothesis respecting the mode of the world's formation, it must 'in the beginning' have been 'without form and void.' " Like Wright, he preferred the theory of meteoric aggregation to Laplace's theory, though he granted the latter was a legitimate scientific hypothesis when restricted to the formation of the solar system.[35]

Aside from an occasional maverick like Wright or Stallo, few Americans saw much merit in the meteoric cosmogony. But the same was not true for the planetesimal hypothesis of Thomas C. Chamberlin and F. R. Moulton. Chamberlin, head of the geology department in the newly founded University of Chicago, initially became interested in cosmogonical problems while studying the effects that past changes in the constitution of the atmosphere might have had on geological climates. These studies led him to investigate the nebular hypothesis, assisted by Moulton, a junior colleague in the astronomy department. By 1900 both men were convinced that the Laplacian cosmogony was hopelessly defective. Their principal criticisms concerned the solar nebula's moment of momentum, "a rock on which the ring theory breaks." In calculations similar to those earlier made by Babinet, Moulton determined that the solar system possessed nowhere near the amount of momentum necessary for the type of development described by Laplace. In fact, "if the solar system were converted into a gaseous nebula controlled by Boyle's law and given the existing moment of momentum and allowed to contract, the centrifugal force would not overtake the centripetal until long after the orbit of Mercury had been passed." The moment of momentum that would have been needed to bring about the separation of Neptune's ring alone was 213 times the total moment of momentum presently belonging to the entire system.

In another test of the nebular hypothesis Chamberlin compared the masses of the planets with their moments of momenta and discovered to his astonishment that *"the Jovian ring carried away less than one-thousandth of the mass of the nebula, while at the same time it took off 95% of the moment of momentum."* If only one nineteen-thousandth more of the mass had been abandoned with an equal proportion of momentum, the central nebula would have been left with none whatsoever![36] Obviously, a more tenable cosmogony had to be found, one in which *"the matter of the system must be so brought together as to give low mass, high momentum and irregular distribution to the outer part, and high mass, low momentum and sphericity to the central part."*

During the first years of the new century, after considering and rejecting several possible alternatives, including the meteoric hypothesis, Chamberlin and Moulton eventually adopted a variation of Buffon's cosmogony, ironically the very theory the nebular hypothesis had been designed to replace over a hundred years before. According to the Chicago scientists' theory, which they called the planetesimal hypothesis and which was largely Chamberlin's creation, the solar system owed its origin to matter drawn off from our ancestral sun when a passing star approached close enough to produce a large-scale tidal effect. During the encounter, solar matter was ejected in intermittent pulsations on opposite sides of the sun, resulting in a two-armed spiral nebula with irregularly spaced knots in its appendages and with diffuse nebulous matter in the intervening expanses. The knots became the nuclei of future planets (and perhaps satellites) and subsequently developed into the bodies we see today by agglomerating with planetesimals formed from the diffuse nebulous matter. The rotary motion originally imparted to the sun's projections by the attraction of the passing star explained why the planets all revolve in the same direction.[37] Within a short time of its announcement the planetesimal hypothesis superseded the nebular hypothesis as the most widely accepted cosmogony in America, and for several decades it went virtually unchallenged.[38]

The nebular hypothesis, however, escaped the usual fate of rejected scientific theories. Despite its repudiation as an accurate history of the solar system, it continued to serve as an aid in explaining other celestial phenomena. "Laplace's conception has been amazingly fruitful," wrote the English cosmogonist J. H. Jeans in the 1920s. "It would hardly be too much to say that it has either revealed or given a valuable clue to the origin of every normal formation in the sky, with the single exception of that of the solar system which it set out to seek."[39] In recent years, even this singular exception has been eliminated; for as encounter theories have been tried and found wanting, there has been a corresponding revival of interest in nebular theories of the solar system's origin.[40]

CHAPTER VII

Design and Providence

The nebular hypothesis owed its nineteenth-century popularity in part to the appealing way it accounted for various astronomical phenomena. But equally important was the fact that it could be harmonized with the prevailing theology. During the early nineteenth century there was no war between science and theology. Scientists and theologians alike generally regarded the investigation of the natural world as complementary to the study of the Scriptures, and it was not uncommon for individuals to engage in research in both fields. To preserve this concord, however, it was important for scientific theories not to violate any of the fundamental tenets of contemporary theology, among the most cherished of which were the doctrines of design and divine providence, and belief in the validity of the Biblical record.[1]

Orthodox Protestantism emerged from its eighteenth-century encounter with Enlightenment thought as strongly committed to natural theology—the study of the evidences of God's wisdom and power in nature—as to revealed theology.[2] According to the natural theologians, God's created works testified of His wisdom, His providence proclaimed His power. It was the duty of the Christian philosopher to provide specific examples illustrating these claims.

The doctrine of design, one of the classic arguments for the existence of God, was based on the observation that an object appearing to have been made for a particular purpose always has an intelligent and purposeful designer. If the solar system looked as if it were not the result of necessity or of accident, if it appeared to have been made with a special end in mind, then it must have had a designer, and that designer could only be God. Though the logical shortcomings of this argument had been pointed out in the eighteenth century by David Hume and Immanuel Kant, it nevertheless remained very convincing to most Americans in the early nineteenth century.

The doctrine of divine providence held that God ruled and controlled the operations of the universe. Traditionally, the greatest evidences of divine providence had been God's miraculous interventions in the natural world; but with man's increasing success in explaining naturally what had formerly been regarded as supernatural, it became necessary to assume that God usually chose to carry out His will indirectly and regularly through the medium of secondary causes—that is, in accordance with scientific laws. Thus, demonstrating that the solar system had been produced largely by secondary causes did not, for most Americans, indicate the absence of divine providence. And if special intervention had been needed to create the original rotating nebula, God's providence was beyond doubt.

The harmony of the nebular cosmogony with the dogma of natural theology was a key issue in even the earliest writings on Laplace's hypothesis. In the Bridgewater Treatises, which introduced many Americans to the cosmogony and influenced their attitudes toward it, the concerns of natural theology were paramount. William Whewell, writing on *Astronomy and General Physics Considered with Reference to Natural Theology,* stressed that the nebular hypothesis "by no means proves that the solar system was formed without the intervention of intelligence and design." Nothing but an intelligent and designing cause could have contrived a nebula that would "by its natural changes produce such an orderly system," he said. While the nebular hypothesis might force the natural theologian to modify his views of how the Creator worked, it would not "for a moment prevent [him from] looking beyond the hypothesis, to a First Cause, an Intelligent Author, an origin proceeding from free volition, not from material necessity." Whether true or false, the Laplacian cosmogony could not

> in sound reason, affect at all the view . . . of the universe as the work of a wise and good Creator. Let it be supposed that the point to which this hypothesis leads us, is the ultimate point of physical science: that the farthest glimpse we can obtain of the material universe by our natural faculties, shows it to us occupied by a boundless abyss of luminous matter: still we ask, how space came to be thus occupied, how matter

came to be thus luminous? If we establish by physical proofs, that the first fact which can be traced in the history of the world, is that "there was light;" we shall still be led, even by our natural reason, to suppose that before this could occur, "God said, let there be light."[3]

In his Bridgewater Treatise on geology and mineralogy William Buckland seconded Whewell's evaluation of the theological implications of the nebular theory. "Mr. Whewell," he wrote, "has shown how far this theory, supposing it to be established, would tend to exalt our conviction of the prior existence of some presiding Intelligence." In his own judgment, Laplace's theory was the most probable explanation of the origin of the solar system available.[4]

Among the Bridgewater authors, only the Scottish theologian Thomas Chalmers regarded the nebular hypothesis as a real threat to natural theology. Since evidence of design in the solar system came largely from "the dispositions of matter"—the arrangements and motions of the planetary bodies—rather than from the laws which governed matter, any attempt to explain the dispositions as necessary products of the laws was suspect. Atheistical writers, he had observed, tended "to reason exclusively on the laws of matter, and to overlook its dispositions," and Laplace's attempt to account for the solar system as a product of natural law looked like just another manifestation of this pernicious tendency. It seemed obvious that if "all the beauties and benefits of the astronomical system [could] be referred to the single law of gravitation, it would greatly reduce the strength of the argument for a designing cause." But all would not be lost; for even though the establishment of the nebular hypothesis as an accepted scientific theory would undoubtedly extenuate "the argument for a designing cause in the formation of the planetarium," it would "not annihilate that argument."[5]

Chalmers' fear of the nebular hypothesis was not widely shared. Some critics, like J. P. Nichol, went so far as to suggest that the views of the Edinburgh divine were a greater danger to sound theology than anything Laplace had proposed. Men like Chalmers, he wrote, "notwithstanding the stupendous and almost overwhelming representation [Laplace's theory] offers of the magnitude and solemnity of creation, . . . have strangely thought fit to launch at the nebular hypothesis the charge of impiety, and to regard all such speculations, in sober seriousness, as rebellion against the attributes and activity of God." But by affirming that "we can demonstrate the existence of a Deity more emphatically from that portion of creation of which we remain ignorant, than from any portion whose processes we have explored," they have revealed themselves to be the guilty ones.[6]

Nichol believed that religious antagonism toward the Laplacian cosmogony, toward the very idea of creation by natural law, had resulted from a misunderstanding of the meaning of the term "law." It was not, as some seemed to think, a substitute for divine providence:

> LAW of itself is no substantive or independent power; no causal influence sprung of blind necessity, which carries on events of its own will and energies without command. Separated from connection with an ARRANGER in reference to whose mind alone, and as expressive of the Creative Idea it can be connected with the notion of control—LAW is a mere name for a long order—an order unoriginated, unupheld, unsubstantial, whose floor sounds hollow beneath the tread, and whose spaces are all void; an order hanging tremblingly over nothingness, and of which every constituent—every thing and creature fails not to beseech incessantly for a substance and substratum in the idea of ONE—WHO LIVETH FOREVER!

Moreover, the nebular hypothesis was not a menace to the teleological argument. The evidence it gave of design in the solar system was so unmistakable that Nichol thought this to be one of the major reasons why Laplace's theory had been so well received.[7]

The majority of educated Americans agreed with Whewell, Buckland, and Nichol that the nebular hypothesis did not necessarily weaken the position of natural theology. They recognized, nonetheless, that the traditional doctrines would have to be modified in order to accommodate the idea of natural development. If, for example, the arrangement of the planetary bodies were the inevitable result of the operation of natural laws upon nebulous matter, the design of the solar system was not evidence of God and His wisdom; it was simply evidence of what happens to nebulous matter under the influence of natural laws. But whence came these laws that could produce such wondrous things, and what was their meaning? To most Americans, the obvious answers were that they had been instituted by God and were evidence of His existence and wisdom. In this way, as John LeConte pointed out in the early 1870s, the cosmogony of Laplace helped to bring about a transformation in the application of the principle of design "from the region of facts to that of laws."[8]

Supporters of Laplace's cosmogony recognized that if natural laws implied a designer just as strongly as tangible contrivances, the nebular hypothesis itself could be used to substantiate the argument from design. One advocate writing in the *Southern Quarterly Review* maintained that the nebular hypothesis opened "before the mind a stupendous and glorious field for meditation upon the works and character of the Great Architect of the Universe." Laplace's theory evinced "the handy work of a *creative intelligence,* with equal necessity and superior glory, to those [views of the origin of the solar system] usually entertained."[9]

The transformation of the design argument from the structure of the solar system to its mode of formation was curiously facilitated by Johann Franz Encke's discovery that the period of revolution of the comet bearing his name was progressively becoming shorter. The Berlin astronomer explained this phenomenon as an effect of the "resisting medium" or ether, which, according to the undulatory theory of light, was necessary for the propagation of light waves. This explanation implied that the planets, experiencing the same effect, would eventually collapse into the sun. Such a prospect was incompatible with the old design argument, which held that the permanency of the system was one of its greatest evidences of divine planning. It could no longer be argued, said one author, that the arrangements of the system "were intended by Deity to make our solar system permanent and everlasting," for surely God had not "given circular orbits to our planets, hurled them in the same direction and nearly in the same plane, to give everlasting duration to our system, when the resisting medium would interfere with the accomplishment of his purpose."[10]

Apologists were equally successful in modifying the doctrine of divine providence so that it, too, did not hinder the acceptance of the nebular hypothesis. Instead of pointing to the miraculous creation of the world by divine fiat, a "special" providential act, they emphasized God's "general" providence in creating the world by means of secondary causes. While the Creator's role in the formation of the solar system was thus changed, it was not reduced or eliminated, as some had feared. The nebular hypothesis left the doctrine of divine providence as strong as ever. As Daniel Kirkwood pointed out, if God's power is demonstrated in sustaining and governing the world through the agency of secondary causes, then it should not "be regarded as derogating from his perfections, to suppose the same power to have been exerted in a similar way in the process of its formation."[11]

God's reliance upon secondary causes in the daily operation of the world made it seem only reasonable to suppose that He had at least sometimes used the same means in creating it. "God generally effects his purposes . . . by intermediate agencies, and this is especially the case in dead, unorganized matter," wrote an anonymous author in a quarterly review. Special providences might be customary in the living world, but in the domain of nonliving matter natural law reigned supreme—except, of course, for those infrequent times when God temporarily suspended it.

> If, then, the rains of heaven, and the gentle dew, and the floods, and storms, and volcanoes, and earthquakes, are all products of material forces, exhibiting no evidence of miraculous intervention, there is nothing profane or impious in supposing that the planets and satellites of our system are not the immediate workmanship of the great First Cause. . . . God is still present; but it is in the operation of unchangeable laws; in the sustaining of efficient energies which he has imposed on the material world that he has created; in the preservation of powers, properties, and affinities, which he has transferred out of himself and given to the matter he has made. . . . It is therefore most idle to object to the nebular hypothesis, that it excludes the Creator and Governor of the world from the immediate generation of the circular motions of the planets, or of their daily rotation on their axes.[12]

The astronomer O. M. Mitchel expressed similar sentiments in his writings on the nebular hypothesis. Since the odds against the solar system's being a product of chance were "at least 100 millions to one," he was certain that "the Creator either spake the present system into being, or evolved it from chaotic matter by the operation of certain laws." Certainly God had "the power to bring such a system into being by the fiat of his will in one single instant, and without the intervention of any secondary laws or means," but "the analogy of God's creative providence" indicated that He had probably not employed this method to create the solar system. "We find nothing in nature starting instantly into full and mature being," he wrote. "So far . . . as we are able to trace the direct manifestations of God in the mineral, vegetable and animal kingdoms, He works by means, and according to a plan." The nebular hypothesis was just one more evidence of divine consistency.[13]

Some individuals saw in Laplace's cosmogony a demonstration of God's providence even more convincing than the traditional account of creation. One author vividly compared the two ideas:

> How much more sublime and exalted a view does it give us of the work of creation and of the Great Architect, to contemplate him evolving a system of worlds from a diffused mass of matter, by the establishment of certain laws and properties, than to consider him as taking a portion of that matter in his hand and moulding it as it were into a sphere, and then imparting to it an impulse of motion. In the former case the various attributes of Deity are all manifested—in the latter, scarcely any thing but Almighty power. In the former the grand principle of Divine appointment, by which every department of existence, whether inanimate or vegetable, instinct or reason, is required to put forth the utmost power with which it is endowed, is distinctly recognised—in the latter we have a total departure from everything known as the dispensation of His hand.[14]

Another who felt the nebular hypothesis commanded "a more intense admiration" than the idea of a special creation was Alexis Caswell, the Baptist minister–astronomer at Brown University. Caswell denied that the cosmogony of Laplace excluded "the agency of the Creator from the universe." Admittedly it removed "the immediate agency of the Divine Architect one step farther back in the order of events"; but this, he argued, only condensed God's power "into a narrower compass." It seemed to him that "to create the matter of a nebula and implant within its deep bosom the principle of organization, and make it, in pursuance of an appointed mechanism, the parent of suns and planets and circling stellar orbs 'of more than solar glory,' is as distinctively the province of Creative Power as any thing, which we can possibly conceive."[15]

Although many Americans had no trouble reconciling the nebular hypothesis with the teachings of natural theology, others could not easily forget that Laplace had apparently conceived the hypothesis primarily to eliminate God from the natural world and that his cosmogony had unquestionably been used to further the cause of atheism. Concern over these aspects of the nebular hypothesis was particularly noticeable in the years immediately after the publication of the *Vestiges* in 1844. Edward Hitchcock discussed these problems in his inaugural address as president of Amherst College in 1845 and again in his widely read work on *The Religion of Geology and Its Connected Sciences*, first published in 1851.

Hitchcock, whose primary interests were geology and natural theology, had paid little attention to the nebular hypothesis prior to the attempt by the author of the *Vestiges* to make it "a part of the foundation on which the doctrine of creation by law rests." This doctrine was anathema to the Amherst president, and he endeavored to discredit—scientifically and theologically—every theory that might possibly lend credence to it. Hypotheses like spontaneous generation and the transmutation of species could be handled without much difficulty, but the Laplacian cosmogony was too widely accepted to be treated lightly. Though the resolutions of nebulae had somewhat weakened its scientific appeal, Hitchcock had to admit that "even the Christian philosopher feels no difficulty in adopting this hypothesis, through fear of its irreligious tendency."

Being thus prevented from attacking the hypothesis for its atheism, he turned the tables and ridiculed Laplace for having "signally failed" in his avowedly atheistical effort "to dispense with an intelligent, personal Deity." Even if the noted French astronomer "could show how nebulous matter, placed in a certain position, and having a revolution, might be separated into sun and planets, by merely mechanical laws, yet where, save in an infinite Deity, lie the power and the wisdom to originate that matter, and to bring it into such a condition, that by blind laws alone, it would produce such a universe—so harmonious, so varied, so nicely adjusted in its parts and relations as the one we inhabit?" Hitchcock saw in Laplace's "failure" an instructive object lesson: "that a man may be a giant in mathematics, while he is only a pygmy in moral reasoning."[16]

Even Benjamin Peirce, who as early as 1839 had described the nebular hypothesis as a "grand but simple view of the process, which the Deity has adopted in framing the universe, [and which] bears upon its front the stamp of truth and of divinity,"[17] began to feel uneasy about the origin and implications of the Laplacian cosmogony after the publication of the *Vestiges*. At the 1851 meetings of the AAAS, as he closed a paper on the structure of Saturn's ring in which he had presented new evidence in favor of the nebular hypothesis, he gratuitously reminded his colleagues of Laplace's dubious motives in formulating the cosmogony. "The farther I extend my researches into the physical universe," he said, "the stronger appears to me the evidence that the process of creation was conducted by the divine geometer in a modified form of that very hypothesis, which was contrived by a shallow and wicked philosophy for the direct purpose of excluding the Deity from his own works."[18] Later, when he submitted an abstract of this paper to the *Astronomical Journal*, he attached a new ending, warning against speculating too much about God's method of creating the solar system:

> In approaching the forbidden limits of human knowledge, it is becoming to tread with caution and circumspection. Man's speculations should be subdued from all rashness and extravagance in the immediate presence of the Creator. And a wise philosophy will beware lest it strengthen the arms of atheism, by venturing too boldly into so remote and obscure a field of speculation as that of the mode of creation which was adopted by the Divine Geometer.[19]

In time, however, Peirce overcame with a vengeance his wariness "in approaching the forbidden limits of human knowledge." In a series of lectures given shortly before his death and published posthumously as *Ideality in the Physical Sciences* he proclaimed assuredly that the nebular theory was "the mode of growth adopted by the Creator to accomplish the plan of creation." Evidently forgetting that he, too, had once been apprehensive of the theological consequences of Laplace's cosmogonical ideas, he said:

> Certain wise and good men, jealous of their religious faith, have feared that the nebular theory is liable to the reproach of being an invention to relieve the Almighty from the incessant care of his creation. We cannot deny that some eyes have been dazzled by it, so as to become insensible to the more needed light of spiritual faith. But how could there be such brilliancy, except in an emanation from divine light? The intellectual force of the conception is consequent upon its verity. Any harm which it may have done is due, not to the impurity or dimness of the light, but to the weakness or disease of the eye.[20]

Since 1851 he had come to regard the nebular hypothesis as a virtual revelation from God Himself, designed to strengthen not "the arms of atheism" but man's faith in his Creator. He pleaded passionately with his listeners not to cast aside a truth so precious:

> O ye of little faith! Accept the divine record of the sidereal universe, or ye would not believe in God if his name were written in letters of fire upon the firmament! To reject the ideal history [i.e., the nebular theory] is to strengthen the stronghold of scepticism. It is to deny the celestial doctrine written upon the heavens and the earth. It is to reject the law of the Lord, which is perfect, converting the soul. Let the children be

faithful to the Father, and loyally receive the declaration that he made the light with which he shines through the stars, and that it is good.[21]

More than anything, the comments of Hitchcock and Peirce reveal that even individuals concerned about the theological implications of the nebular hypothesis usually did not see any incompatibility between the hypothesis and the doctrines of natural theology. Only a very few relatively uninfluential figures advocated rejecting the Laplacian cosmogony because of the harm it would do to those doctrines. One was George Taylor, a Virginia-born lawyer who served as a representative from New York in the United States Congress from 1857 to 1859. In 1851 Taylor published an attack on developmental theories that he thought were subverting the foundations of natural theology. The first sections of his book on *The Indications of the Creator; or, The Natural Evidences of Final Cause* advocated the repudiation of the nebular hypothesis on the grounds that it promoted atheism and was generally unscientific.[22]

Although Taylor's book undoubtedly influenced the thinking of some Americans—it went through four editions in eight years—the leaders of American thought were uniformly unimpressed by its arguments. *The Princeton Review*, in an article evidently written by its conservative editor, Charles Hodge, accused Taylor of being "too prone to admit inevitable and irreconcilable contradictions between scientific theories and the evidences or doctrines of natural or revealed religion." There were, said the author, "various and sufficient methods for harmonizing" the findings of science with the teachings of theology, and thus there was no reason for fearing the nebular hypothesis.[23] Kirkwood, writing in the *Presbyterian Quarterly Review*, expressed his appreciation of Taylor's "praiseworthy efforts to exhibit the 'natural evidences' of a designing, intelligent, personal Creator," while disapproving of Taylor's treatment of the nebular hypothesis. It required no reasoning, claimed the now-famous professor, to show that the hypothesis was "wholly independent" of speculations regarding organic development.[24]

Most mid-century Americans felt that one's attitude toward the nebular hypothesis should be determined by the use made of it. If the hypothesis were employed for atheistic purposes, as perhaps Laplace and the author of the *Vestiges* had done, then it should be condemned. If, however, it were used merely as a scientific explanation of the origin of the solar system illustrating God's design and providence—the way the majority of Americans used it—then it should be regarded with favor. As one writer in the *Princeton Review* put it, "very few scientific theories are essentially impious. They are made so by the spirit in which they are taught, rather than by their own intrinsic nature."[25] Stephen Alexander took a similar position. Laplace's cosmogony, he said, "has been, it is true, enormously abused and made use of for atheistic purposes; but we have yet to learn that what has been abused is thereby made untrue, and we shall be slow to take that lesson on the bare authority of those who, upon their own showing, are but the descendants of monkeys improved." He went on to state that he thought Laplace had died believing in a personal Deity, as if this fact would somehow increase the credibility of the nebular hypothesis.[26]

By 1859 the natural laws embodied in the nebular hypothesis had largely superseded divine fiat as the method educated Americans believed God had used in creating the solar system. The adaptability of the doctrines of design and providence to the new cosmogony had made this change possible. But harmony between the nebular hypothesis and the tenets of natural theology could not alone have prevented a clash between the forces of science and religion. It was also necessary to show that revealed theology was capable of accommodating the nebular hypothesis.

CHAPTER VIII

The Mosaic Story of Creation

Nineteenth-century Americans rejoiced in the belief that they possessed two revelations from God: one recorded in the Scriptures, the other written in the book of nature. The divine origin of both these revelations guaranteed their accuracy; so it was quite unthinkable that any contradiction could exist. Matthew Fontaine Maury, superintendent of the United States National Observatory, forcefully expressed this conviction in a letter written to a New York minister who had inquired about the harmony between science and revelation. One rule of conduct had always guided his scientific thinking,

> and that rule is never to forget who is the author of the great volume which nature spreads out before us, and always to remember that the same Being is also the author of the Book which Revelation holds up to us; and though the two worlds are entirely different their records are equally true, and when they bear upon the same point, as now and then they do, it is as impossible that they should contradict each other, as it is that either should contradict itself. If the two cannot be reconciled, the fault is ours, and because in our blindness and weakness we have not been able to interpret aright, either the one or the other or both. . . .[1]

The potential threat to scientific progress posed by the insistence on agreement between science and the Bible failed to materialize largely because pious and ingenious men repeatedly succeeded in devising new ways to reconcile the two revelations. They were much aided, of course, by the sometimes vague and seemingly contradictory language of the Bible, which allowed a great deal of latitude for theorizing. But whatever the tactics employed, the theological domination of science was successfully prevented. In fact, according to one recent scholar, "a good case might be made for the thesis that interpretation of Genesis generally reflected rather than determined prevailing currents of scientific thought."[2] Certainly this is true of the nebular hypothesis, which, in the words of Charles W. Shields, "had scarcely been formed before it was seized as the Biblical cosmogony or doctrine of creation."[3]

Contrary to popular opinion, Americans were widely divided over the correct interpretation of the first chapters of Genesis long before the arrival of Darwinism. Already by the second quarter of the century there were several versions of the creation story from which to choose. There was, of course, the traditional view that heaven and earth had been made in six literal days about six thousand years ago; that the sun, moon, and stars had been created on the fourth day; and that the earth's topographical features were largely a consequence of the universal Noachian flood. Though the adoption of this explanation meant rejecting virtually the entire body of historical geology and paleontology, which by the late 1820s included substantial evidence of the earth's great antiquity, many were willing to do so on the grounds that scientists were not correctly interpreting their data. As late as 1852 it was estimated that "perhaps one half of the Christian public" adhered to this position.[4] Of this number, few were among the nation's better-educated citizens.

As might be expected, alternative explanations of Genesis were not long in coming. In 1814 Thomas Chalmers, reacting to the work of the French zoologist Georges Cuvier, proposed allowing an indefinite period of time between an initial creation "in the beginning" and the relatively recent Adamic creation. Chalmers' proposal was widely popularized in Great Britain by William Buckland and in America by Edward Hitchcock.[5] As described by the latter in his influential textbook *Elementary Geology*, this explanation "supposed that Moses merely states that God created the world in the beginning, without fixing the date of that beginning; and that passing in silence an unknown period of its history, during which the extinct animals and plants found in the rocks might have lived and died, he describes only the present creation, which took place in six literal days, less than 6000 years ago."[6]

Without violating the Biblical story in any way, this theory gave geologists an unlimited amount of time prior to the week of creation for as many earlier creations and catastrophes as they wished. Those who accepted it generally held that the solar system had been created "in the beginning" but that dense vapors had obscured the sun and the moon until the fourth day of creation, at which time they had begun "to rule over the day and over the night, and to divide the light from the darkness." Of the various harmonizing schemes, this seems to have been the most popular from about the 1830s through the 1850s.[7]

An "extension of this interpretation," as Hitchcock phrased it, was advanced by the British theologian John Pye Smith in 1839. Like Chalmers before him, Smith believed Moses had described two separate creations, one "in the beginning" and the other about four thousand years before the birth of Christ. But here the two reconcilers parted company, Smith arguing that the more recent, six-day creation had been restricted to *the part of our world which God was adapting for the dwelling of man and the animals connected with him.* The precise portion of the earth involved was probably "a large part of Asia, lying between the Caucasian ridge, the Caspian Sea, and Tartary, on the north, the Persian and Indian seas on the south, and the high mountain ridges which run, at considerable distances, on the eastern and the western flank." Smith surmised that just prior to the week of creation volcanic activity had destroyed this entire area, saturating the atmosphere with ash and bringing near total darkness to the region. "By the fourth day," however, "the atmosphere over this district had become pellucid; and, had there been a human eye to have beheld, the brightness of the sun would have been seen, and the other heavenly bodies after the sun was set."[8]

This explanation, though widely publicized, gained few adherents. Most of Smith's American contemporaries looking for a scientifically respectable alternative to the traditional reading of Genesis turned to the seemingly less radical solution of Chalmers and Hitchcock, or to the quite different proposal commonly associated with the names of Benjamin Silliman, Yale's eminent professor of chemistry and natural history, and Hugh Miller, a Scottish geologist and author.[9]

According to the view of Silliman and Miller, the six days spoken of by Moses represented not twenty-four-hour periods but immense intervals of time. In his version of the creation story, given in an appendix to Robert Bakewell's *Introduction to Geology*, Silliman alleged that God in the beginning had instantaneously "created the heavens and the earth, and established the physical laws, the ordinances of heaven, by which the material world was to be governed." Subsequent to this act, our planet "was subjected to a long course of formation and arrangement, the object of which evidently was, to fit it for the reception, first of plants and animals, and finally of the human race."

Silliman divided the period of the earth's development into six epochs, each corresponding to a day of the creation week. During the fourth epoch the previously made sun and moon had begun to measure time, and at the end of the sixth epoch—approximately six thousand years ago—man had been created. Interpreting Genesis in this manner did not imply, for Silliman at least, that the Bible was in error. Geology and the Mosaic record are in full accordance, he said, "but more time is required for the necessary events of the creation than is consistent with the common understanding of the days. The history therefore is true, but it must be understood so as to be consistent with itself and with the facts."[10] Because Bakewell's *Geology* was a standard American textbook, Silliman's interpretation of Genesis came to the attention of a vast audience. Nevertheless, it does not seem to have attained the popularity of the view endorsed by Hitchcock.[11]

Among the four major interpretations of the Mosaic story of creation, not one made any reference to the nebular hypothesis. Even those that allowed for the earth's antiquity had been designed only to accommodate geological and paleontological evidence, the leading promoters of these views generally assuming that the solar system had been created by God's fiat at some time "in the beginning." Obviously it was not difficult for those who postulated two or more creations to admit the nebular development of the solar system during the interval between the original creation of matter and the Adamic creation—if they so wished. Likewise, those who believed the days of Genesis represented long periods of time could easily work in the nebular hypothesis prior to the first epoch. But there was no explicit recognition of the solar system's nebular history in any of the leading reconciling schemes. Clearly the time was ripe by the 1850s for a new version of the creation story that openly incorporated the now-accepted nebular cosmogony. By happy coincidence, America had just welcomed to its shores a man with such a plan: Arnold Guyot, a Swiss physical geographer.

Guyot was born in 1807 to a Swiss family of French Protestant background. In his early twenties he dedicated himself to the ministry and set off for Berlin to study theology. But after only a short time his deep love of nature overcame his devotion to the ministry, and he gave up his theological studies for science. In 1835 the University of Berlin awarded him a doctorate in philosophy for his research on "The Natural Classification of Lakes." Four years later, after working as a private tutor and making an important study of glaciers, he accepted the professorship of history and physical geography in the academy of Neuchâtel, Switzerland, where he was associated with Louis Agassiz, an acquaintance since youth.

When the academy closed its doors during the revolutionary turmoil of 1848, Agassiz, who had come to America two years earlier, urged his jobless friend to join him. Guyot accepted the invitation. His first six years in America were largely spent working for the Massachusetts Board of Education, lecturing prospective teachers on geography and methods of instruction. He quickly won recognition as the foremost geographer in the United States, and in 1854 the College of New Jersey installed him in a specially created chair in physical geography and geology. He remained at Princeton until his death thirty years later.[12]

During his student years at Berlin Guyot became imbued with the spirit of German *Naturphilosophie*. In the writings of Johann Wolfgang von Goethe and in the lectures of Henrik Steffens and Karl Ritter he discovered a philosophy of nature totally unlike his older mechanistic world view; he learned that nature was an ever-developing organism, not a ready-made machine. For the remainder of his life the idea of development dominated his thinking. The origin of the solar system, the formation of continents, the growth of human races and societies were all viewed as "a gradual specialization of parts and functions, comparable to the progress in germ development and having the same general formula; as beginning in a homogeneous unit, which has real but unmarked differences of parts, advancing through various changes and individualizations, and ending in the complex 'harmonic unit.' "[13]

Eventually this philosophy of nature led Guyot, in a roundabout way, to a new understanding of the Mosaic history of creation. Toward the end of his life he recalled how he had first arrived at a fresh interpretation of Genesis:

> In the beginning of the winter of 1840, having just finished writing a lecture on the Creation which was to be a part of a public course of Physical Geography that I was then delivering at Neuchâtel, Switzer-

land, it flashed upon my mind that the outlines I had been tracing, guided by the results of scientific inquiry, then available, were precisely those of the grand history given in the First Chapter of Genesis. In the same hour I explained this remarkable coincidence to the intelligent audience which it was my privilege to address.[14]

What had flashed upon Guyot's mind in 1840 was the close correspondence between the nebular hypothesis and the Mosaic narrative, when the days of the latter were taken to represent great epochs of creative activity. If the formless "waters" created by God in the beginning actually symbolized gaseous matter, then the light of the first day undoubtedly had been produced by the chemical action resulting from the concentration of this matter into nebulae. The dividing of the waters on the second day symbolized the breaking up of the nebulae into various planetary systems, of which ours was one. During the third epoch the earth had condensed to form a solid globe, and during the fourth, the nebulous vapors surrounding our planet had dispersed to allow the light of the sun to shine upon the earth. During the fifth and sixth epochs the earth had been populated with living creatures. "Such is the grand cosmogonic week described by Moses," declared Guyot. "To a sincere and unprejudiced mind it must be evident that these great outlines are the same as those which modern science enables us to trace, however imperfect and unsettled the data afforded by scientific researches may appear on many points."[15]

Guyot's version of the creation story first appeared in print in 1852. In March of that year the New York *Evening Post* carried lengthy abstracts of his series of lectures "on the Concordance of the Mosaic Account of the Creation with that given by Modern Science," delivered at the Spingler Institute in New York City. Since the *Evening Post* had only a limited readership, three years later the Reverend John O. Means, of East Medway, Massachusetts, published, with Guyot's approval and assistance, a summary of the Spingler Institute lectures in the *Bibliotheca Sacra,* an influential, orthodox journal put out by the Andover Theological Seminary. As his interpretation became generally known, Guyot frequently received requests to lecture on the harmony of Genesis with modern science. He spoke on this subject once at the College of New Jersey and for several years in succession at the Princeton Theological Seminary. In 1866 he presented his views in the Morse Foundation lectures sponsored by Union Theological Seminary, and in 1873 he

gave a condensed version of his views at the sixth general conference of the Evangelical Alliance, held in New York City.[16]

Guyot planned for years to publish his interpretation of Genesis
in book form, but he invariably postponed the unpleasant task of
writing. In 1858, shortly after James Dwight Dana had come out
with a 650-page tome, Guyot commented on his own tendency to
procrastinate:

> Meanwhile my restive pen does not start. Why is it so? It is because
> you are J. D. Dana, a strong mind to think & a strong arm to do, & I am
> A. G. your humble friend who thinks a good deal & delights in it, but is
> too easily satisfied with that selfish pleasure. But I acknowledge fully the
> duty for every one to give to others whatever he has received; for a pure
> gift, is every beam of truth granted to us. Thus don't despair of me, as
> many do: I shall come late, but *I shall come*.[17]

Over twenty years passed, and still there was no book. Again
Guyot wrote to Dana. "But it has been my lot all my life, perhaps by
my own fault, as well as by being overburden[ed], to fail to give in
print the results of my researches," he lamented. "Perhaps the
world has lost but little, but I have lost some legitimate influence
which I ought to have exerted."[18] Spurred on by the realization that
he had only a little time left, Guyot finally completed his long-
awaited volume on *Creation; or, The Biblical Cosmogony in the
Light of Modern Science*. He died the following year.

Guyot's aversion to writing did not prevent his interpretation of
Genesis from reaching the American public, for his ideas found a
well-known and able propagator in the person of the envied Dana.
By hard work—as geologist on the Wilkes expedition to the
Pacific—and by an advantageous marriage—to Silliman's daughter
Henrietta—Dana had climbed from humble beginnings to a position
of leadership in American science as an editor of the *American
Journal of Science* and, after 1856, as Yale's Silliman Professor of
Geology and Natural History. He and Guyot had struck up a
friendship soon after the Swiss geographer's arrival in the United
States, and one evening in August 1850, while visiting in Dana's
home, Guyot related his views on the first chapter of Genesis.[19]

Dana became an instant convert and immediately began pressing
his guest, without great success, to share his revelation with others.
The following January, in hopes of encouraging Guyot to speak out,
he sent a flattering message contrasting Guyot's sublime view of the

creation with a similar but less satisfactory account being presented by another scientist:

> I have recently endeavored to explain your views upon the harmony of Science and the Mosaic account of the Creation, before a few gentlemen, but wished much that you were here to do the subject justice. Professor Mitchell [*sic*] has also been lecturing on this point, and takes the same basis for his explanations—the nebular theory. But he is only an astronomer—no geologist, chemist, or zoölogist, and his views are therefore imperfect in detail and wanting in philosophical spirit. There is something exceedingly sublime in the command "Sit lux," when we consider that light is the first index of chemical combination and molecular change—and therefore the command is equivalent to "Let force act." The vivifying impulse thus given to the particles before inert would send a flash of light throughout the universe. This point, which you mention in your explanations, Professor Mitchell did not seem to comprehend in its full signification. I hope the time may come when you will speak for yourself here on the subject.[20]

Although Guyot did, as we have seen, make some attempt during the next several years to reach a wider audience with his views on Genesis, it was Dana who finally attracted the attention of America's intellectual community to what the Swiss immigrant was trying to say. The occasion for his entry into the debate over science and the Bible was the appearance in 1855 of a provocative work by Tayler Lewis, professor of Greek in Union College, challenging one of the most hallowed assumptions of the age: the inherent harmony between science and divine revelation.[21]

Independently of science, using philological methods alone, Lewis endeavored in *The Six Days of Creation* to establish the true meaning of the first chapter of Genesis. In spite of what appeared to some as a haughty contempt for science and scientists, he often found himself in the same camp with the opposition—he having followed the sure path of philology, they having stumbled along the treacherous trail of science. Much like Silliman and Guyot before him, he concluded that the Mosaic days of creation were intervals of indefinite length and that God, after starting each period of growth with a supernatural act, had allowed the world to develop naturally.[22] Nevertheless, he had nothing but disdain for those who insisted on harmony between science and the Biblical record. And though he saw the expression "without form and void" in Genesis 1:2 as signifying "a fluid or rarified condition with an absence of all solidity and cohesion, or [perhaps] a huge nebulosity that had been

floating through space for millions and millions of years," he
ridiculed the nebular hypothesis as a scientifically deduced cosmogony.[23]

But even so antiscientific a person as Lewis could not help being
impressed with the sometimes striking correspondence between
science and the Bible, and at times he succumbed to the temptation
to demonstrate the reasonableness of revelation by citing contemporary scientific knowledge. Regarding the Biblical teaching of the
nebular origin of the solar system, he wrote:

> Is not the telescope now revealing something of the same anomalous kind
> [of changes] as going on in parts of the universe which may be supposed
> to be as distant from us in space as the primaeval aspects of our own
> system are remote from us in time? In some quarters of the heavens,
> there would seem to be yet transpiring changes analogous, to say the
> least, to those that took place in our own earth's far-off infancy. . . .
> Adopting certain scientific theories as the ground of the fancy, we might
> imagine astronomers who lived at that remote day, in some other remote
> system of higher progress, turning their glasses towards the obscure
> nebulous cluster of bodies that may then have formed our condensing
> solar system, and speculating about their development.[24]

However eccentric his attitudes, Lewis was certainly no obscuran-
tist. Yet on one point he was adamant: if science conflicted with the
philologically determined meaning of the Scriptures, then science
would just have to give way.

It was in meeting this challenge to the integrity of the scientific
enterprise and to the harmonious union of science and religion that
Dana assumed the role of Guyot's spokesman on Genesis and the
Bible. Smoldering from Lewis' sneers at science and from his
insinuation that scientists generally were impious, he opened fire on
the Union College professor in the January 1856 issue of the
Bibliotheca Sacra. *The Six Days of Creation*, he wrote, contained
"much truth, well expressed and argued," but unfortunately also
"much arrogance and error." To a Christian scientist like Dana, the
study of nature was just as much a religious act as the study of the
Scriptures; and if anyone were guilty of impiety, it was Lewis—for
belittling science.

As for Lewis' exegesis of Genesis 1, Dana thought it showed "a
loose use of the Sacred Record, and a limited comprehension of the
grandeur of its truths." The best views on the subject were "those of
Prof. Arnold Guyot, a philosopher of enlarged comprehension of
nature and a truly christian spirit," traits Lewis obviously lacked, in

Dana's estimation. For those unfamiliar with Guyot's views, Dana provided a summary, carefully avoiding, however, any direct references to the nebular hypothesis and skipping over the second epoch of creation, during which nebulae had supposedly given birth to planetary systems. In a footnote he excused this omission on the grounds that "neither geology nor general science, apart from astronomy and general reasoning, afford much aid in interpreting the account." Whatever had occurred during this period had involved the separation of the earth from the "waters" or "fluid." Those interested in a more detailed explanation of the second day were referred to Means' earlier article on the subject.[25]

Dana's spirited defense of the integrity of his profession and his reaffirmation of the harmony between science and the Bible made him a hero in the eyes of many of his fellow scientists. Letters from throughout the nation poured into New Haven, thanking him for his efforts. From the Harvard College Observatory George Phillips Bond wrote to say how gratified he was with Dana's "decisive statement of facts in those departments of science, in Geology especially, having a bearing upon the question of the agreement of the scientific with the Mosaic cosmology." He professed to have found Dana's arguments "convincing."[26]

Several correspondents, evidently forgetting that the educated clergy in America were often among the best friends of science, or perhaps remembering some particularly unpleasant episode, took the opportunity to denounce ministers generally for their presumed hostility toward science. A professor in Columbia College, New York City, wrote: "I know not how it is with the clergymen of New England, but can testify that to the South of Connecticut, very many, probably the majority of Protestant divines have only crude notions of the relation of geology to Scripture, and many denounce that branch of Science & its followers."[27] Charles A. Joy, a Göttingen-trained chemist who taught with Lewis in Union College but who had little respect for his nonscientific associate, painted a similarly bleak picture of relations between clergy and scientists in the following note to Dana:

> I was glad to see from your Review of Dr. Lewis' book that you had taken up arms in defence of the orthodoxy of scientific men.—Humboldt stoutly maintained to a friend of mine last Summer that it was not safe for a man to pursue Geology in the United States for fear of falling within the ban of the Church.—He was not so very far out of the way—

As the times seemed to require that scientific men should make an example of someone, I am glad that you came to our college for the victim—. . . .[28]

Spurred on by the acclaim of his peers, Dana renewed his attack on Lewis with another article in the July number of the *Bibliotheca Sacra,* which, he boasted to Benjamin Peirce, charged Lewis with infidelity even more pointedly than his first paper.[29] Of course, Lewis could not let this go unanswered, but the editors of the *Bibliotheca Sacra* refused to let him use their journal for what they knew would be a vehement counterattack. He was thus forced to write a second book.[30] Upon hearing of this, Dana told Peirce: "Prof. Lewis is engaged in another book in which I look for a terrible flagellation: However it will not hurt."[31]

Dana's anticipated punishment came before the year was out. In a volume called *The Bible and Science* Lewis lashed out at Dana for fostering "a most one-sided error of the times,—the false position of Physical Science, and its naturalizing effect upon the theology and religion of the day." Strangely, Lewis felt that Dana had condemned his earlier work primarily "for some deficiency in not coming fully up to that nebular hypothesis of creation which has become so great a favorite with certain scientific writers, and with which they so please some of the religious people delighted as they are to be taught that Moses is so much more scientific than they had ever imagined, and still more delighted to find the Bible actually believed by such wonderfully clever men." Lewis charged that in constructing his scientific account of creation, Dana seemed to disregard completely the Mosaic record:

What he presents does not lean upon the Bible at all, and he takes no pains even to give it that appearance. In general it marches on independent of the Scriptures, all along assuming a harmony, but made out on no Bible grounds. . . . Now this is a peculiar feature of Professor Dana's articles; there are no difficulties in them, none whatever; everything is as easy as the latest geological theory. All he had to do was to weave in his nebular hypothesis in the way best adapted to show off this latest science in some of its more specious aspects. To look into the Bible, and to study the Bible with the hearty purpose of seeing how all this really agreed with the language of Moses, would have been troublesome. It would have been to meet with perplexities.[32]

Antipathy toward the nebular hypothesis, however, was not the motivation behind Lewis' opposition to Guyot and Dana. "Aside from any scientific knowledge on our own part," he said, "we could not help respecting what had been advocated by a Henry, a Peirce, and an Alexander among ourselves, to say nothing of distinguished names abroad." Still, he did not believe it could "be exegetically forced into any accommodation with the Mosaic creative history." It was preposterous to suppose that the first days of creation week pertained to nebular developments in the entire universe, but that the last days dealt only with changes on our small globe. And it was even more absurd that Dana had been unable to assign a specific work to the second day. "There are difficulties in the Scriptures, but none to be compared to this into which we get ourselves by departing from interpretation, and taking this pious talking science for our guide," he declared. Instead of manfully admitting the problem, Dana had cowardly sought "ease and refuge in a note."[33]

Stung by what he considered unduly harsh treatment for tacitly assuming the truth of the nebular hypothesis in a footnote, Dana prepared a final reply, which, thanks to editorial favoritism, appeared in the *Bibliotheca Sacra*.[34] "We purposely avoided discussing the nebular hypothesis," he explained, "and therefore gave an explanation (Prof. Guyot's) of the *second* day, in a note." Apparently his reason for doing this was to leave the subject for his friend Guyot. But now that he was pressed, he willingly confessed his attraction to the nebular hypothesis and to Guyot's interpretation of the days of creation. He saw two reasons for believing in the nebular hypothesis. The universal analogy of development suggested an evolution of the solar system similar to that proposed by Laplace; and certain scientific evidence, like Kirkwood's law, corresponded "so well with what would have been true in case of such an evolution from a universe chaos or deep, that the tendency is towards a belief in the nebular hypothesis, rather than against it." Should the hypothesis prove false, it would not affect the harmony between science and the Bible. It would only necessitate giving up Guyot's interpretation of Genesis and returning to the one advocated by Silliman.[35]

With these remarks the debate between Dana and Lewis came to an unhappy end. In terms of converts won, the philologist was unquestionably the loser.[36] For a long time he "felt a deep sense of injury" and for the rest of his life resented not having been allowed to defend himself in the *Bibliotheca Sacra*.[37] Few persons ever saw his answer to Dana, *The Bible and Science*, while many read Dana's articles and became disciples of Guyot. One of the more notable recruits was John William Dawson, principal of McGill College in Montreal, who during the heat of the dispute had written Dana promising to do all in his power to promote Guyot's views.[38] The Canadian, a competent geologist and a devout Christian, was true to his word. In 1860 he published a series of exegetical studies on the first chapter of Genesis, showing the perfect accord between the nebular hypothesis and the Bible and ably upholding the interpretation of Guyot.[39]

In the years following the Lewis-Dana controversy Guyot's reconciliation of science and the Bible soon became a favorite of Christian apologists in America. Young scientists learned it as a matter of course from Dana's celebrated *Manual of Geology*, much as their fathers had once learned Hitchcock's theory from his *Elementary Geology* or Silliman's scheme from Bakewell's *Geology*;[40] and members of the clergy were constantly exposed to it in the religious literature of the day, which often lionized the scientific defenders of the faith. Typical of the praise for Dana and Guyot was the comment by Joseph P. Thompson, a prominent Congregational minister and author, that these were "men whom Science recognizes among her wisest Interpreters, and Revelation among her ablest Defenders."[41] Similarly, President James McCosh of Princeton assured his readers that the accordance between Genesis and science had been demonstrated by "the three men on this continent who are most entitled to speak on the scientific question: Professor Dana, of Yale; Professor Dawson, of Montreal; and Dr. Guyot, of Princeton."[42]

Though Guyot did not escape all criticism—now and then he was charged with violating the language of Moses—virtually no one condemned him for his acceptance of the nebular cosmogony. A critic like Andover's professor of Hebrew, Elijah P. Barrows, might take issue with Guyot over the legitimacy of interpreting the words "water" and "deep" as a description of a nebulous condition, but even he had no quarrel with the nebular theory. "Of all existing hypotheses," wrote the Presbyterian minister, "we consider it best sustained by both present phenomena and the general analogy of God's proceedings." To avoid Guyot's "violent forcing of language," he proposed assigning the nebular development of the solar system to the period prior to creation week, the interval between the creation of matter and the creation of light.[43]

Surprisingly few articulate Americans expressed any desire to set aside the nebular hypothesis for Biblical reasons, and those who did were certainly not counted among the nation's intellectual elite. They were men like Thomas A. Davies, a West Point graduate in civil engineering, and Hiram Mattison, a self-educated pastor and teacher. Davies was a true believer. Inspired by an unquestioning faith in the literalness of all Scripture, he took time in mid-career to write an essay championing the creation of the world in "six diurnal days." This appeared in 1857 as *Cosmogony, or the Mysteries of Creation*. In this labor of love he defended his position by arguing that Moses surely had possessed the intelligence to know the meaning of the terms "day," "evening," and "morning," and the honesty not to deceive his readers intentionally. Besides, he said, it was "entirely inconsistent with the character of God" to make worlds from nebulae. "Planning and plodding belong to man. To God design is perfect, the Will is all-powerful, and the execution, as far as it can be without violating law, is immediate." Picturesquely he portrayed the events of the fourth day of creation week: "God touched with His finger these mighty worlds and systems, and at the same instant made effective the law of Gravity, and the journey of the Universe was begun in Equilibrium. Planets revolved around their suns, satellites around their planets, and solar systems around each other, till the vast vault of heaven was massive with worlds on worlds, wheeling in their majestic circles, and bound eternity-ward!"[44]

Mattison, a Methodist Episcopal minister, found it no easier than Davies to reconcile the nebular hypothesis with his understanding of revelation. Deprived of more than a modicum of formal education, he had acquired a working knowledge of astronomy during an extended illness. Before long he had authored an elementary astronomy textbook, liberally sprinkled with theological lessons. In his discussion of cosmogony he listed as the first of several objections to the nebular hypothesis its direct "variance with the Mosaic account of the creation of the sun, moon, and stars." To support his contention that cosmogonical questions lay outside the domain of science, he quoted Hebrews 11:3, adding appropriate comments in brackets: " 'Through faith we understand that the worlds were framed by the word of God [not by the law of gravitation], so that things which are seen were not made of things which do appear [or of pre-existing matter].' "[45] Despite the scattered use of his *As-*

tronomy by high schools in the 1850s, Mattison was helpless to turn
the tide of opinion against the nebular hypothesis. At this late hour
there was virtually nothing that he or Davies or anyone could do to
impede the steady advance of natural law.

Just as few educated Americans urged throwing out the nebular
hypothesis for conflicting with the Bible, so did few advocate
discarding the parts of the Bible that did not seem to harmonize
with science. The agreement of God's two revelations was too
thoroughly engrained to permit such action. When the English
layman Charles W. Goodwin suggested in his contribution to the
controversial *Essays and Reviews* that the Bible was intended for
religious instruction only and that "the erroneous views of nature
which it contains" should be frankly recognized, Americans reacted
with scorn.[46] "Such essays as this of Mr. Goodwin have long since
lost their interest to scholars on this side of the Atlantic," wrote one
American critic. A correct understanding of the language of
Genesis, he went on, has shown "that there is no discrepancy
between a just interpretation of the word of God and the revelations
of genuine science. Such an essay as this of Mr. Goodwin is,
therefore, behind the times, and reveals an unpardonable ignorance
of the present attitude of the subject."[47]

The Harvard professors Benjamin Peirce and Asa Gray were
clearly ahead of their time in denying that Genesis had scientific
meaning, but even they never accused Moses of teaching false
science. In a conversation in 1855 with the Reverend Thomas Hill,
later president of Harvard, Peirce disclosed his personal conviction
that Moses had not meant to give a scientific history of creation but
had intended only

> to assert in the strongest manner that God was the creator of all things.
> To do this he would assert him to be creator of six different classes,
> including all objects in nature, and he would state these classes in the
> natural order of thought, that is to say, in the order of their relative
> apparent importance. And this he does by the bold, figurative way of
> representing these as the work of six successive periods, using an order of
> time to express order of importance, or order of thought.

Thus, "if science could prove that no six periods of creation in time
ever existed, whether of a day's length or of ages', that would not
conflict with the account in the first of Genesis." Gray fully shared
this view of revelation, although both he and Peirce thought the

Biblical order of creation corresponded remarkably with the order Guyot had established using the nebular hypothesis.[48]

For even the very orthodox, revealed theology thus proved to be no greater an obstacle to the acceptance of the nebular hypothesis than natural theology. Three factors were primarily responsible for this. First, the Mosaic account of creation was vague enough to allow the most literalistic of readers to embrace the nebular cosmogony. As one author in the *Princeton Review* said, "Any old-fashioned Christian, beginning with the nebular hypothesis and resolving the fire-mist into chaos, might, if need be, proceed to the creation of the world in six ordinary days."[49] And of course the nebular development of the solar system presented no exegetical problems to the many who interpreted the days of Genesis as protracted periods of time, as eminent Biblical scholars assured them they could justifiably do.

Second, the opening words of Genesis seemed to be a veiled reference to the earth's former nebulous condition: "In the beginning God created the heaven and the earth. And the earth was without form, and void; and darkness was upon the face of the deep." According to one writer, Moses was simply describing "a phenomenon which the nebular theory reclaims from mysterious obscurity."[50] Another, in speaking of the nebular hypothesis, asked rhetorically, "If Moses had actually, in prophetic vision, seen the changes contemplated in this theory taking place, could he have described them more accurately, in popular language, free from the technicalities of science!"[51] And a third put it this way: "If one should seek to give a sketch in the fewest words of the Celestial Mechanism of Laplace, the Cosmos of Humboldt, and the geology of the latest and best authorities, he would do it in the very language of Moses."[52]

Third, Americans were so convinced of the harmony between science and the Bible that many naïvely assumed that the nebular hypothesis accorded with the first chapter of Genesis. A story told by Andrew Dickson White illustrates this attitude. A fashionable New York church once asked a noted professor of chemistry to demonstrate how modern science confirmed the Mosaic account of creation. He concluded his presentation with an exhibition of Plateau's experiment, which appeared to reproduce with a rotating globule of oil the formation of the solar system from a nebula. At the conclusion of the experiment the congregation voted unanimously to thank the professor for "this perfect demonstration of the exact and literal conformity of the statements given in Holy Scripture with the latest results of science."[53]

As we have seen in this and the previous chapter, the nebular hypothesis did not precipitate a conflict between science and theology in the United States.[54] To be sure, some persons opposed Laplace's cosmogony on theological grounds, but they were few in number and not very influential. The vast majority of articulate and educated Americans found the nebular hypothesis to be in perfect harmony with their theological beliefs. It illustrated God's benevolent providence; it gave evidence of His designing hand; it demonstrated the validity of His inspired Word.

CHAPTER IX

The Nebular Hypothesis
in the Darwinian Debate

No sooner had Americans adjusted their theology to accommodate a naturally developed physical world than Charles Darwin issued his monumental essay *On the Origin of Species,* seeking to extend the domain of natural law to the organic world.[1] Organic evolution was by no means a novel idea in 1859, but it had never before been supported by such a massive amount of evidence nor argued in such a convincing manner; and no person before Darwin had explained the origin of species so plausibly as he did with his theory of variation and natural selection. It was clear from the first that here was a challenge to the traditional account of creation far more serious than anything presented in the past by the author of the *Vestiges,* Lamarck, or Charles's own grandfather, Erasmus. Nevertheless, the nation's intellectual communities suffered surprisingly little trauma as they successfully and rapidly assimilated the new scientific doctrine. Much of the credit for making this possible should go, we think, to the nebular hypothesis and the other developmental theories that had already forced large numbers of Americans to resolve many of the issues raised by Darwin.

Despite the dogged opposition of the doyen of American science, Louis Agassiz, the concept of progressive development quickly captured the imagination of the scientific community, especially that portion working in the biological sciences. By 1872, less than thirteen years after the appearance of the *Origin,* the paleontologist E. D. Cope could say without fear of contradiction that "the modern theory of evolution has been spread everywhere with unexampled rapidity, thanks to our means of printing and transportation. It has met with remarkably rapid acceptance by those best qualified to judge of its merits, viz., the zoologists and botanists."[2] Even Agassiz, in his final statement on evolution just before his death in 1873, conceded that the idea of organic development had won "universal acceptance."[3]

The extent of the evolutionists' victory was spotlighted a few years later in a polemical war that broke out between two of New York's most popular religious weeklies, the somewhat liberal Congregational *Independent* and the staunchly conservative Presbyterian *Observer*. It began in 1879 when William Hayes Ward, managing editor of the *Independent*, informed his readers that "we are all taught in our best schools, by our scientific authorities, almost without exception . . . that man was, at least so far as his physical structure is concerned, evolved from irrational animals." The horrified editors of the *Observer* immediately contacted select college presidents for assurance that such was not the case. Most of the presidents, understandably reluctant to disclose to a conservative audience what was going on behind their ivy walls, denied that evolution was taught in their schools. But when Ward challenged the *Observer* to name just "three working naturalists of repute in the United States" who were not evolutionists, it could not do so.

Ward, on the other hand, was able to cite an imposing roll of scientists and institutions that had gone over to the side of the evolutionists. He began with schools included in the *Observer*'s survey. At Yale Othniel C. Marsh, James Dwight Dana, Addison E. Verrill, William H. Brewer, Sidney I. Smith, and "all the other teachers of the biological sciences" were evolutionists. At Princeton, where the geographer, Arnold Guyot, and the two clerics, L. H. Atwater and John T. Duffield, were still showing signs of resistance, the picture was not quite the same; but, significantly, the college's only naturalist, George Macloskie, its professor of astronomy, Charles A. Young, its physicist, C. F. Brackett, and its president, James McCosh, were defenders of the evolutionary point of view. At Amherst, Williams, and Brown the teachers of natural history, if not all evolutionists, were at least sympathizers. Elsewhere, in schools ignored by the *Observer*, the biologists were virtually unanimous in their support of evolution:

> Of all the younger brood of working naturalists whom Agassiz educated, every one—[Edward S.] Morse, [Nathaniel S.] Shaler, Verrill, [William H.] Niles, [Alpheus] Hyatt, [Samuel H.] Scudder, [Frederick Ward] Putnam, even his own son [Alexander]—has accepted evolution. Every

one of the Harvard professors whose departments have to do with biology—[Asa] Gray, [J. D.] Whitney, A. Agassiz, [Hermann] Hagen, [George Lincoln] Goodale, Shaler, [William] James, [William Gilson] Farlow, and [Walter] Faxon—is an evolutionist, and man's physical structure they regard as no real exception to the law. . . . At Johns Hopkins University, which aims to be the most advanced in the country, nothing but evolution is held or taught. In the excellent University of Pennsylvania all the biological professors are evolutionists—Professors [Joseph] Leidy and [Harrison] Allen in comparative anatomy, Professor [Joseph Trimble] Rothrock in botany, and Professor [J. P.] Lesley in geology. We might mention Michigan University, Cornell, Dartmouth, Bowdoin; but what is the use of going further? It would only be the same story. There can scarcely an exception be found. Wherever there is a working naturalist, he is sure to be an evolutionist.[4]

Ward, it should be noted, carefully avoided labeling the naturalists as Darwinians; he said only that they were evolutionists. And since probably the majority of the men on his list were more properly Neo-Lamarckians than strict Darwinians, the distinction was well worth making. The typical American evolutionist, as described by George Daniels, "assigned a relatively unimportant role to a struggle for existence and, instead, emphasized the direct action of the environment, the inheritance of acquired characteristics, the inherited effect of use and disuse of organs, and the purposeful adaptations of organisms in explaining evolutionary divergence."[5] But whether Darwinian or Neo-Lamarckian, the American scientists were evolutionists, and so far as the public was concerned that was what really mattered.

The scientific acceptance of evolution did not create nearly the furor in the religious community that many have imagined. As several recent studies have shown, American clergymen lagged only slightly behind their scientific brethren in embracing organic evolution. "Once a modified Darwinism became orthodox among American scientists," says Daniels, "most religious thinkers quickly accommodated themselves to the theory."[6] Michael McGiffert has similarly emphasized "the remarkably rapid adjustment of substantial sections of Protestant thought to evolution" in his study of "Christian Darwinism" in America.[7] Even the evangelicals were swept up in the Darwinian tide, although many, as William G. McLoughlin has noted, scarcely recognized the significance of their compromise with science.[8] To be sure, religious opposition did exist, but it was neither monolithic nor particularly effective.

The almost warm reception accorded the theory of organic evolution should lead us to suspect that the concept of development in
nature was no stranger to informed mid-century Americans.[9] And
when we look at the history of thought during the years leading up
to 1859, our suspicion is confirmed. What we see is a veritable
intellectual revolution taking place as "the static Renaissance view of
nature" steadily gives way to a "dynamic, developmental one," a
process so excellently described by Stephen Toulmin and June
Goodfield in *The Discovery of Time*. It is almost as if there is a
conspiracy to foster a consciousness of continuous development:
scholars studying the history of technology, science, and linguistics
become aware of the tremendous cultural advancement of the
human race; geologists discover the transformations undergone by
the earth's crust and use their discoveries to construct a greatly
extended time-scale; paleontologists disclose the temporal sequence
of organic forms; zoologists formulate crude theories of progressive
development; anthropologists speculate about the natural origin of
the races of men.[10]

To this impressive list we must add the often neglected contribution of Laplace, who so convincingly demonstrated to the
nineteenth century that the masterfully designed solar system was
simply the natural product of a cooling and rotating nebula. Hand in
hand with the other developmental theories, the nebular hypothesis
helped to create, in both the scientific and religious worlds, that
climate of opinion that made possible the rapid assimilation of
organic evolution. It is, of course, hazardous to attempt to assess the
relative contribution of the nebular cosmogony to the developmental revolution; nevertheless, by sifting through the records of the
Darwinian debate we shall pick up some valuable clues as to its
impact upon the thinking habits of the participants.

One of the strongest and most popular arguments in favor of the
evolutionary hypothesis was that it provided a scientific explanation
of the origin of species. It accorded, said the Congregational minister and sometime geologist George Frederick Wright, with the
fundamental principle of science which states that "we are to press
known secondary causes as far as they will go in explanation of facts.
We are not to resort to an unknown [i.e., supernatural] cause for
explanation of phenomena till the power of known causes has been
exhausted. If we cease to observe this rule there is an end to all
science and all sound sense."[11]

Belief in this principle had not sprung up overnight; the conviction had been growing with increasing vigor in the Christian West ever since the scientific awakening of the twelfth century when Adelard of Bath instructed his nephew on the virtues of natural causes. "So far as human knowledge has progressed it should be given a hearing," he said. "Only when it fails utterly should there be recourse to God."[12] During the ensuing centuries the repeated successes of natural law came to represent the very epitome of scientific progress, until by the nineteenth century there was scarcely a divine miracle that had not been weeded from the field of scientific thought. The unique, miraculous acts of creation were temporarily excepted, but only until satisfactory scientific substitutes, like Laplace's nebular hypothesis, could be found.

The successful accommodation of the nebular hypothesis tended to still whatever lingering fears Americans had about natural law and at the same time whetted their appetite for more of the same. They realized more than ever the desirability of nonsupernatural explanations. Thus when a respectable and thoroughly naturalistic hypothesis of organic development became available, they accepted it partially because, as one contemporary put it, there was "literally nothing deserving the name of Science to put in its place."[13] For a generation raised on the nebular hypothesis and natural law, this negative appeal was not to be taken lightly. Indeed, it helps to account for the ready acceptance of organic evolution. "The development hypothesis," wrote the radical theologian Francis E. Abbot in 1868, "is gaining ground every day with reflecting persons of all classes, simply because it is the *only* hypothesis anywhere presented that does not clash with the deep faith of the age in universal law."[14]

Beyond inspiring confidence in natural law, the nebular cosmogony encouraged Victorians to envision all creation as an evolutionary progression. In this respect, its influence may have outweighed that of any other single scientific theory, especially since uniformitarian geology was so decidedly nonevolutionary. Over thirty years ago the astronomer F. R. Moulton, one of the few twentieth-century scholars to appreciate the intellectual impact of the nebular cosmogony, called attention to the fact that this hypothesis had "accustomed scientists to thinking of change in long periods of time and thus prepared the way psychologically for the theory of organic evolution."[15]

American participants in the Darwinian debate, fond as they were of analogical arguments, frequently underscored the similarity between the nebular development of the solar system and the evolutionary origin of species. It seemed, said the Brown University biologist A. S. Packard, as if the acceptance of the nebular hypothesis led almost directly to the question of "whether plants and animals share in this process of evolution."[16] Or as Professor J. S. Stahr told the students of Franklin and Marshall College, "After it was found . . . that the creation of the world was not a mechanical work finished at one sitting, but rather brought about by the operation of Law during long periods, *ages* of time; it was natural to go a step farther and inquire whether it is not probable that living creatures were subject to a similar process."[17]

The evident parallels between the hypotheses of Laplace and Darwin helped to create the impression that the latter's extension of the domain of law to the origin of species was only "the finishing touch to a work which had long been building," rather than the beginning of a radically new structure.[18] To use Clarence King's metaphor, Darwinism was simply the last link in the chain of evolution that began with the nebular hypothesis.[19] This accordance with previously accepted theories undoubtedly forestalled much criticism and speeded up the process of assimilation. President E. O. Haven of Northwestern University proved to be a perceptive judge when he said that the "theory of Darwin would not probably have met with so much favor, had it not seemed to coincide with several other theories or hypotheses [like that of Laplace]."[20]

Besides helping to make Americans feel at home with creation by natural law and evolutionary development, the Laplacian cosmogony familiarized them with many of the theological problems generated by the *Origin of Species*. Thus, as Daniel S. Martin told his fellow Christian educators, the coming of Darwinism did not necessitate passing through a "new and strange ordeal."[21] Together with historical geology, the nebular hypothesis had so weakened the tradition of Biblical literalism that even the orthodox had no great difficulty reconciling the evolution of species with the Mosaic story of creation.[22] Their prior experience in successfully harmonizing the ages of geology and the nebular cosmogony with Genesis gave them confidence that, if required, they could do the same for Darwinism.

For this reason, relatively little opposition developed over the issue of inspiration.[23] From the *Baptist Quarterly* to the Unitarian

Religious Magazine and Monthly Review there was virtual unanimity that organic evolution posed no threat to God's written revelation (see Appendix 1 for a comparison of denominational attitudes toward the nebular and Darwinian hypotheses).[24] The common attitude of the educated was that expressed by Andrew Preston Peabody. "Let the lovers of the Bible wait without fear," he wrote in 1864. If the latest developmental theories should prove to be sound, "instead of making the Bible or any portion of it obsolete, they will only—as has already been the case with the established astronomical and geological truths which at the outset appalled timid believers—attach a profounder depth of meaning to the declaration, 'In the beginning God created the heaven and the earth.' "[25]

Evolutionists and nonevolutionists alike turned with relief to the nebular hypothesis for proof that Christianity had nothing to fear from theories of development. In his dissertation on "The Darwinian Theory of the Origin of Species" William North Rice, the twenty-one-year-old recipient of Yale's first doctorate in geology, examined Darwin's theory and found it scientifically untenable. Yet the young Methodist scholar did not find it theologically objectionable. Using the recent debate over the nebular origin of the solar system as "a sort of judicial precedent," he ruled that no "permanently disastrous consequences would ensue" should Darwinism be proved. "Let the lesson of the past be heeded," he urged in a summary of his thesis that appeared in the *New Englander* in 1867.

> As one theory after another, supposed to be inseparably connected with Christianity, has been swept away, Christianity has but risen from the shock stronger and purer. We may wait, then, without fear the issue of the scientific controversies of to-day. The foundations of our faith will remain unshaken in the future as in the past, whether the sun revolves around the earth, or the earth around the sun,—whether the universe was created by fiats, or moulded by the gradual operation of secondary causes,—whether the duration of man's existence be six thousand, or sixty thousand years,—whether all nations were "made of one blood" in a literal, or only in a spiritual or metaphorical sense,—whether "God formed man of the dust of the ground" immediately, or through a process of secondary causation.[26]

Among the leading disputants, there was little sympathy for what William Hayes Ward called "strict theories of inspiration."[27] Most either treated Genesis symbolically or took the position, earlier advocated by Benjamin Peirce and Asa Gray, that the Biblical record of creation was not a scientific document. Not surprisingly, this latter attitude began to seem more and more attractive. In reviewing Darwin's work for the *American Journal of Science*, Theophilus Parsons, Dane Professor of Law at Harvard, frankly confessed that he did not "believe that the first chapters of Genesis teach or were ever intended to teach natural scientific truth."[28] And at the Presbyterian Columbia Theological Seminary in South Carolina, James Woodrow touched off a heated controversy when he suggested that Genesis was not a description of how God made the world but solely a statement that he did create it. In his opinion and in the opinion of many of his contemporaries, the theory of organic evolution—rightly understood—no more contradicted "a single word of the Bible" than did the generally accepted nebular hypothesis.[29]

With Biblical literalism no longer the critical issue, the great theological debate over Darwinism centered on the question of whether or not it could be harmonized with the doctrine of design.[30] Here again, as in so many other instances, the nebular hypothesis had helped to smooth the way, this time by showing that God usually employed secondary causes in creating the world as well as in sustaining it and by demonstrating that objects formed in this manner were no less designed than had they been made instantaneously. Even before the appearance of the *Origin* the applicability of this lesson to the organic world was being noticed. We find Oliver Wendell Holmes, for example, writing in 1857 that "whatever part may be assigned to the physical forces in the production and phenomena of life, all being is not the less one perpetual miracle, in which the Infinite Creator, acting through what we often call secondary causes, is himself the moving principle of the universe he first framed and never ceases to sustain."[31]

History, the evolutionists loved to point out, seemed to be on their side. "It regularly happens," wrote John Fiske, "that the so-called atheistical theory becomes accepted as part and parcel of science, and yet men remain as firm theists as ever."[32] For evidence of this, one had only to look at Laplace's formerly suspect cosmogony that had now been baptized by the theologians. Even Darwin's critics derived comfort from the knowledge that, no matter what the outcome, natural theology would survive. Darwinism, "or any judicious modification of its principles," argued Edward Hitchcock's son Charles, may be used like the nebular hypothesis. The latter was devised by La Place to sustain atheism, but after being avoided by theologians as long as possible, has been generally adopted by them, and is turned against its original friends. Hence we say to the developmental school, go on with your investigations, and if you succeed in establishing your principles we will use your theory for illustrating the argument for the existence of God.[33]

Hitchcock was not alone in his conviction that no theory of modern science could destroy the treasured argument from design. For every Charles Hodge and Francis Bowen who saw Darwinism as a mortal enemy of natural theology, there was a James McCosh to declare that "the doctrine of development does not undermine or in any way interfere with the argument from design."[34] From the Darwinian George Frederick Wright to Williams' cautious President Paul A. Chadbourne to Agassiz's friend Samuel Atkins Eliot, there was complete agreement that the argument for the Creator's existence was invulnerable.[35] Though an accommodation between natural theology and the new scientific dogma was probably inevitable, it seems unlikely that it would have occurred so painlessly and so quickly for so many without the prior influence of theories like the nebular hypothesis in shifting the focus of the principle of design from the facts of nature to its laws.

Perhaps the best way to see the role played by the nebular hypothesis in the Darwinian debate is to look closely at the manner in which Darwin's American apologist Asa Gray utilized the hypothesis in making his case for organic evolution. Gray, the country's foremost botanist, had for several years carried on an extensive correspondence with Darwin and had early learned of the British scientist's ideas on evolution. When the *Origin* was published, he assumed responsibility for ensuring that his friend's views received a fair hearing in the United States. In the spring of 1860 he began a series of essays, later published collectively as *Darwiniana,* in which he explained and defended—and sometimes gently criticized—the Darwinian theory of evolution. Permeating these writings is the conviction that organic development is not inconsistent with teleology. Unlike Darwin, Gray was a theist, an orthodox Congregationalist; though Biblical problems were of little or no concern to him, he attached great value to the doctrines of natural theology and worked zealously to demonstrate their harmony with Darwin's new theory.[36]

Gray knew that Darwinism would never win American approval until it was shown that no harm would come to the design argument. If he could only convince the public that biological evolution was no greater a menace to teleology than the popular nebular cosmogony or the universally received theory of gravitation, half the battle would be won. It seemed to him that there was "scarcely any philosophical objection" to Darwin's theory to which the nebular hypothesis was not equally exposed, and he delighted in pointing out the inconsistency in accepting the nebular hypothesis—which he assumed most of his readers did—and yet rejecting Darwinism for theological reasons.[37]

His favorite target was his colleague Louis Agassiz. In an undisguised reference to the Harvard zoologist, Gray wrote that some scientific men, thinking that a material connection between species was "inconsistent with the idea of their being intellectually connected with one another through the Deity, i.e., as products of one mind, as indicating and realizing a preconceived plan," condemned the *Origin* as atheistical merely because it indicated how present species had developed sequentially and naturally from previously existing species. This reasoning, he argued, was as fallacious as saying that the nebular hypothesis undermined faith by showing that the solar system was an apparently fortuitous product, or that the theory of gravitation did so by demonstrating that the planetary orbits were the result of physical necessity. Darwinism, he went on,

> merely takes up a *particular, proximate* cause, or set of such causes, from which, it is argued, the present diversity of species has or may have *contingently* resulted. The author does not say *necessarily* resulted; that the actual results in mode and measure, and none other, must have taken place. On the other hand, the theory of gravitation and its extension in the nebular hypothesis assume a *universal and ultimate* physical cause, from which the effects in Nature must *necessarily* have resulted.[38]

The conclusion was obvious: if the nebular hypothesis and the theory of gravitation did not negate design in the solar system—and virtually nobody thought they did—then surely Darwinism did not negate design in the organic world.

Because of the random nature of many of the variations postulated by Darwin, it was necessary for Gray to show that "the accidental element may play its part in Nature without negativing design in the theist's view." To illustrate his assertion, he again turned to the nebular hypothesis and Agassiz. "No scientific person at this day doubts that our solar system is a progressive development," he said.

> What theist doubts that the actual results of the development in the inorganic worlds are not merely compatible with design, but are in the truest sense designed results? Not Mr. Agassiz, certainly, who adopts a remarkable illustration of design directly founded on the nebular hypothesis, drawing from the position and times of the revolution of the world, so originated, "direct evidence that the physical world has been ordained in conformity with laws which obtain also among living beings." But the reader of the interesting exposition will notice that the designed result has been brought to pass through what, speaking after the manner of men, might be called a chapter of accidents.[39]

Once more Gray's message was unmistakable: believers in the nebular hypothesis had no right to charge that Darwin had weakened the design argument by introducing random variations.

In evaluating the credibility of Darwinism as a scientific hypothesis, Gray continued to draw analogies with the Laplacian cosmogony. Though he believed it was "far easier to vindicate a theistic character for the derivative theory [of Darwin], than to establish the theory itself upon adequate scientific evidence," he nevertheless felt that the evidence favoring such development was just as convincing as that supporting the nebular origin of the solar system. Since neither Laplace's hypothesis nor Darwin's could be tested directly by experimentation, the acceptability of both depended solely on indirect evidence. The nebular hypothesis, said Gray, is accepted "not because it is proved—thus far it is incapable of *proof*—but because it is a natural theoretical deduction from accepted physical laws, is thoroughly congruous with the facts, and because its assumption serves to connect and harmonize these into one probable and consistent whole." If the same could be said for Darwinism, then it, too, was entitled to be regarded as "a tenable hypothesis."[40]

In Gray's opinion, the nebular hypothesis was partially to blame for the fact that a supernatural explanation of the origin of species no longer quenched modern man's curiosity. Together with other discoveries in the physical sciences—the conversion of forces, the periodicity of the elements, and the ultimate unity of matter—the nebular cosmogony had "largely and legitimately [extended] the domain of secondary causes" and had thereby whetted man's inherent thirst for new scientific knowledge. Surely, said Gray, "the mind of such an age cannot be expected to let the old belief about species pass unquestioned."[41]

Nor could the mind of such an age long reject the gift of knowledge offered by Darwin, thought Gray, who predicted that the Darwinian theory would continue to follow in the path cut out by the nebular cosmogony leading to eventual vindication. "It must not be forgotten," he wrote,

> that on former occasions very confident judgments have been pronounced by very competent persons, which have not been finally ratified. . . . The nebular hypothesis—a natural consequence of the theory of gravitation and of the subsequent progress of physical and astronomical discovery—has been denounced as atheistical even down to our own day. But it is now largely adopted by the most theistical natural philosophers as a tenable and perhaps sufficient hypothesis, and where not accepted is no longer objected to, so far as we know, on philosophical or religious grounds.[42]

He suspected that Darwin might even "enjoy a sort of satisfaction in hearing [his theory] denounced as sheer atheism by the inconsiderate, and afterward, when it takes its place with the nebular hypothesis and the like, see his judgment reversed."[43]

That the vindication of Darwinism Gray so confidently expected did not come sooner than it did was as much the fault of Darwin as it was the fault of the American people. Since he had not taken a stand in the *Origin* on the implications of his theory for natural theology, Darwin was still free in the months after publication to choose for or against a theistic interpretation. From America Gray pressed for the adoption of a teleological position, but his arguments failed to persuade Darwin or a majority of the circle of friends who advised him on strategy. Of the circle, only Charles Lyell sided with Gray. The others—Joseph Hooker and T. H. Huxley—joined Darwin in rejecting the design argument. Though this decision was reached in 1860, Darwin waited to announce it publicly until 1868, when he pointedly stated in concluding *Variations of Plants and Animals under Domestication* that he was unable to accept Gray's teleological version of his theory.[44]

The rejection of design by the Darwinian strategists had the unintended effect of linking Darwinism with atheistic materialism, and severely undercut the efforts of Gray. The reaction in America to these developments was diverse. For some, they merely confirmed what had been believed all along. Others resented having been duped into thinking that Darwinism was not inconsistent with Christianity and tried to save face by claiming that, despite Darwin's own opinion, the theory was not "necessarily" atheistic.[45] Still others, like Joseph LeConte, fought back to disentangle evolution from its "unnatural alliance with materialism."[46]

The net effect of the decision, however, was to strengthen the hand of the anti-Darwinians, of whom there was not an inconsiderable number. During his visit to the United States in 1874 the English astronomer Richard A. Proctor noted that "strangely enough many oppose the biological theories (not without anger), who readily admit that some form or other of the nebular hypothesis of the solar system must be adopted in order to explain the peculiarities of structure presented by that system."[47] Such persons, generally conservative Christians, saw a marked distinction between inorganic and organic development. The issue of biological evolution, wrote the fundamentalist Seventh-day Adventist editor Uriah Smith, "bears no comparison whatever to any that has ever been raised on the subject of astronomy or even of geology. There can be no adjustment here. It must be either teetotal denial or unconditional surrender; and the present outlook shows the religious world leaning rather to the surrender than to the denial." As he saw it, if Darwin were correct, "the record in Genesis is untrue; there has been no fall; the Bible is a fable, and Jesus Christ was an impostor."[48]

Darwinism was, in the eyes of many of its critics, "repugnant to the most cherished feelings and hopes of man."[49] Human vanity rebelled at the prospect of relinquishing an honored position at the head of created beings only to be herded together "with four-footed beasts and creeping things," over which man had formerly had dominion. Darwin's theory, complained one distraught evangelical, "tears the crowns from our heads; it treats us as bastards and not sons, and reveals the degrading fact that man in his best estate —even Mr. Darwin—is but a civilized, dressed up, educated monkey, who has lost his tail."[50] For those who believed they had been created in the image of God himself, the demotion was indeed humiliating.

The nineteenth-century fundamentalists, insisting on the literalness of Genesis and decrying man's kinship with the apes, represented, as even they recognized, a minority voice in America. But as they became more and more vocal, and the alliance between

Darwinism and materialism grew increasingly stronger, the Darwinian debate shifted ground. So long as the discussions had stayed on the familiar terrain of natural theology—and this, not the inspiration of the Bible nor the origin of man, was the focal point of the early American debate—recalling the recent experience with Laplace's cosmogony had seemed profitable. But to the fundamentalists and to the materialists, both of whom regarded Gray's teleological interpretation of the *Origin* as specious, drawing analogies with the nebular hypothesis was meaningless.[51] Thus, as the century drew to a close, the nebular hypothesis ceased to play its significant and constructive role in American thought.

Denominational Attitudes toward the Nebular and Darwinian Hypotheses

If the nebular hypothesis did play a role in the preparation of the American mind for the reception of Darwinism, as we have suggested, then we might reasonably expect to find some correlation between denominational responses to the two hypotheses. Unfortunately, there exists no entirely satisfactory study of the reaction of American Protestant churches to the Darwinian hypothesis. But the available studies do indicate that the religious bodies most sympathetic to organic evolution were ones that attracted large numbers of educated persons: the Unitarians, Congregationalists, and, to a lesser degree, Presbyterians.[1] An examination of representative periodicals reveals that these same denominations were among the most receptive to the nebular hypothesis.[2]

Of all the leading Protestant groups in America, the Unitarians were probably the least troubled by the developments of modern science. "We have no special interest in the subject of [evolution]," wrote the editor of the *Religious Magazine and Monthly Review* during the Darwinian debate. "So far as our philosophy of religion, or our faith in Christianity, is concerned, we are entirely impartial witnesses in the case. Nothing in the life or teachings of Jesus is involved in the controversy, so far as we can see."[3] Because of their disinterest, Unitarian journals had relatively little to say about the theological implications of the nebular hypothesis. Yet when Unitarian writers did comment on the subject, as they occasionally did in the Harvard-influenced *Christian Examiner* and in its successor, the *Unitarian Review*, they consistently treated Laplace's cosmogony favorably.[4]

Congregationalists *were* concerned with harmonizing science and theology—witness the names of Benjamin Silliman, Edward Hitchcock, James Dwight Dana, and Asa Gray—but they were no more antagonistic to the nebular hypothesis than the Unitarians. The *New Englander*, reflecting opinion at Yale, the *Bibliotheca Sacra*, representing the orthodox position of the Andover Theological Seminary, and the later *Congregational Review* all promoted the new cosmogony.[5] The resolutions of nebulae in the mid-1840s inspired a few anxious Congregational clergymen to make disparaging remarks, but criticism was only sporadic.[6] And no one writing in the Congregational periodicals ever branded the nebular hypothesis as an intrinsically atheistic idea. When one minister of that faith published a book describing Laplace's cosmogony as an unreliable servant of atheism, the *New Englander* promptly issued him a stern rebuke.[7]

The Presbyterians, like the doctrinally similar Congregationalists, responded to the nebular hypothesis with overwhelming approval. Neither the *Princeton Review*, of the Old School Presbyterians, nor the *Presbyterian Quarterly Review*, of the New School, ever attacked the cosmogony; indeed, both journals repeatedly endorsed it.[8] From time to time a writer would express mild reservations about its atheistic background or warn against embracing it too hastily,[9] but these weak protests made noticeably little impression on a church that produced the three most ardent scientific promoters of the nebular hypothesis: Daniel Kirkwood, Stephen Alexander, and Arnold Guyot.[10]

According to Windsor Hall Roberts, who several decades ago investigated the reaction of the various American Protestant churches to Darwinism, the nation's two largest denominations, the Methodists and the Baptists, which "drew the bulk of their people from the less intellectual elements of the population," generally opposed Darwinism but did not see it as a real threat to the impregnable teachings of Christianity that they espoused.[11] We have found that both denominations exhibited far less hostility toward Laplace's theory than toward Darwin's, but that they also showed less interest in the nebular hypothesis and were somewhat more suspicious of it than their better-educated brethren in the Unitarian, Congregational, and Presbyterian communions.

Prior to the coming of Darwinism the leading Methodist Episcopal periodical, the *Methodist Quarterly Review* (called the

Methodist Magazine until 1841), virtually ignored the cosmogony of Laplace. The reviewer of the *Vestiges* did point out in 1846 that the idea was harmless because Laplace had left "room for the personal agency of God," but that was about all that was written on the subject.[12] In the 1860s and 1870s, however, Methodist interest picked up, and the same journal carried five articles dealing with the nebular hypothesis, four for it and one against.[13] During the same time the *Southern Review*, after 1871 an organ of the Southern Methodist Episcopal church, took notice of the hypothesis only once—to condemn Laplace in an article on "Modern Atheism" for neglecting to credit God with imparting the original rotation to the primitive solar nebula.[14]

The Baptists followed a similar pattern, paying little attention to the cosmogony until the post-Darwinian period. There was the notable exception of Alexis Caswell's hearty endorsement of the nebular hypothesis in 1841 in the *Christian Review*, a Baptist quarterly; but over twenty years passed before the topic again attracted attention.[15] During the two decades after the appearance of the *Origin of Species*, opinion in the *Christian Review* and in the *Baptist Quarterly*, put out by the denomination's Publication Society in Philadelphia, was about evenly divided for and against the hypothesis, the argument against it being that it was sometimes enlisted in the cause of infidelity.[16]

Of the remaining Protestant churches, only the German Reformed made a significant contribution to the theological debate over evolution, reports Roberts, who attributes the denomination's liberality to the early influence of Philip Schaff.[17] A reading of the *Mercersburg Review*, the distinguished Reformed journal, shows that this church experienced little difficulty embracing the nebular cosmogony, which is mentioned favorably as early as 1852.[18] And if Tayler Lewis was representative of attitudes in the Dutch Reformed church, of which he was a member, the same is true for this body.[19]

Most of the other Protestant denominations bitterly but silently opposed Darwinism, says Roberts.[20] Whether or not this is an accurate appraisal, and we have some reservations about it, there does seem to have been less antipathy toward the nebular hypothesis than toward organic evolution. None of the three largest bodies in this category, the Evangelical Lutheran church, the Disciples of Christ, and the Protestant Episcopal church—ranking fifth, sixth, and seventh in membership among mid-century

Protestants—objected to the Laplacian cosmogony in their major publications, though they generally took little interest in it. The Lutherans' *Evangelical Review* (renamed the *Lutheran Quarterly* in 1878), the Disciples' liberal *Christian Quarterly*, and the *American Quarterly Church Review*, the leading quarterly of the Protestant Episcopalians, all found the cosmogony to be perfectly acceptable theologically.[21] We should bear in mind, of course, that these publications did not always reflect the sometimes great diversity of opinion among their readership. One of the most intransigent opponents of the nebular hypothesis, Martyn Paine, professor of therapeutics and materia medica in the medical college of the University of the City of New York, was a devout member of the Protestant Episcopal church.[22]

None of the mainline Protestant churches in nineteenth-century America ever tried to establish a united front against the nebular hypothesis. But some of the more unyielding fundamentalist sects did. The Seventh-day Adventists, for example, in their official paper the *Advent Review and Sabbath Herald*, repeatedly and emphatically insisted on the fiat creation of the heavens and earth in six literal days of twenty-fours hours each. To such a people, the nebular hypothesis stood in direct contradiction of the Word of God and was therefore to be condemned to perdition—along with the bulk of geology and all theories of organic development.[23] Undoubtedly many individuals of like mind remained in the more traditional churches, but outside the overtly fundamentalist groups they were—for the time being—virtually inaudible.[24]

Among Roman Catholics there was, for peculiar theological reasons, probably the least correlation between attitudes toward the nebular and Darwinian hypotheses. "The immediate Catholic reaction to evolution," states John L. Morrison in his historical study of American Catholic opinion on the theory of evolution, "varied from bitter hostility to friendly tolerance, but it rarely included outright acceptance." Not even those friendly toward evolution adopted Darwin's version of it, and for decades the antievolutionists in the church were more vocal and more influential than the evolutionists. In contrast to this, there was almost no opposition to the nebular hypothesis. In fact, says Morrison, the nebular cosmogony "was popular among Catholics who rejected with scorn the transformation of species."[25] Even Orestes A. Brownson, the most outspoken American Catholic critic of evolution, regarded the nebular hypothesis as a harmless speculation. The only opposition to the theory, claimed one writer in the highly respected *Catholic World*, was "neither scholarly nor intelligent."[26]

The primary cause of the differing attitudes toward organic and inorganic evolution was the impingement of the former, particularly Darwinism, upon a doctrine of faith. In 1863 Pope Pius IX affirmed that "doctrines which have been declared by all theologians at all times to be matters of faith must also be accepted without question by Catholics."[27] Since the supernatural origin of man's soul was one of these inviolable dogmas, orthodox Catholics could not accept Darwinism, which made no exception for the human soul. Theoretically they were free to admit the evolution of plants, animals, and even man's physical body, but many were reluctant to do so.[28]

There was no doctrine of faith, however, to discourage them from embracing the nebular hypothesis. "It does not come into collision in the slightest degree with any doctrine pertaining to faith, but is purely a matter for rational and scientific speculation," declared Augustine F. Hewit, assistant editor of the *Catholic World* and one of the most influential American Catholic apologists in the last quarter of the nineteenth century. As far as the nebular hypothesis was concerned, the only relevant doctrine of faith was "that God created all things from a beginning of time out of nothing." Since Laplace's hypothesis pertained "not to the *origin*, but the *formation* of the universe from matter already originated," this doctrine was not violated. In Hewit's opinion, the harmony of the nebular cosmogony with the teachings of the Church was "so plain and so universally admitted" that the subject scarcely merited serious consideration.[29]

It is clear from this summary that acceptance of the nebular hypothesis did not necessarily lead to acceptance of organic evolution. Nevertheless, attitudes toward the two ideas were not totally unrelated. The denominations most cordial to Laplace were often the most cordial to Darwin; those with mixed feelings toward the nebular cosmogony tended to display similar feelings toward organic development; and the groups that completely rejected the natural evolution of the solar system were equally adamant about the evolution of species. Just how great a role the nebular hypothesis played in molding attitudes toward Darwinism is impossible to determine. But certainly its influence was not negligible.

APPENDIX 2

Laplace's Nebular Hypothesis

However arbitrary the elements of the system of the planets may be, there exists between them some very remarkable relations, which may throw light on their origin. Considering it with attention, we are astonished to see all the planets move round the Sun from west to east, and nearly in the same plane, all the satellites moving round their respective planets in the same direction, and nearly in the same plane with the planets. Lastly, the Sun, the planets, and those satellites in which a motion of rotation have been observed, turn on their own axes, in the same direction, and nearly in the same plane as their motion of projection.

The satellites exhibit in this respect a remarkable peculiarity. Their motion of rotation is exactly equal to their motion of revolution; so that they always present the same hemisphere to their primary. At least, this has been observed for the Moon, for the four satellites of Jupiter, and for the last satellite of Saturn, the only satellites whose rotation has been hitherto recognized.

Phenomena so extraordinary, are not the effect of irregular causes. By subjecting their probability to computation, it is found that there is more than two thousand to one against the hypothesis that they are the effect of chance, which is a probability much greater than that on which most of the events of history, respecting which there does not exist doubt, depends. We ought therefore to be assured with the same confidence, that a primitive cause has directed the planetary motions.

This excerpt is from Laplace, *The System of the World*, trans. Henry H. Harte (Dublin: University Press, 1830), 2:326-29, 331-33, 336-37, 354-62.

Another phenomenon of the solar system equally remarkable, is the small excentricity of the orbits of the planets and their satellites, while those of comets are very much extended. The orbits of this system present no intermediate shades between a great and small excentricity. We are here again compelled to acknowledge the effect of a regular cause; chance alone could not have given a form nearly circular to the orbits of all planets. It is therefore necessary that the cause which determined the motions of these bodies, rendered them also nearly circular. This cause then must also have influenced the great excentricity of the orbits of comets, and their motion in every direction; for, considering the orbits of retrograde comets, as being inclined more than one hundred degrees to the ecliptic, we find that the mean inclination of the orbits of all the observed comets, approaches near to one hundred degrees, which would be the case if the bodies had been projected at random.

What is this primitive cause? In the concluding note of this work I will suggest an hypothesis which appears to me to result with a great degree of probability, from the preceding phenomena, which however I present with that diffidence, which ought always to attach to whatever is not the result of observation and computation.

Whatever be the true cause, it is certain that the elements of the planetary system are so arranged as to enjoy the greatest possible stability, unless it is deranged by the intervention of foreign causes. From the sole circumstance that the motions of the planets and satellites are performed in orbits nearly circular, in the same direction, and in planes which are inconsiderably inclined to each other, the system will always oscillate about a mean state, from which it will deviate but by very small quantities. The mean motions of rotation and of revolution of these different bodies are uniform, and their mean distances from the foci of the principal forces which actuate them are constant; all the secular inequalities are periodic.

. . . .

If the conjectures which I have proposed on the origin of the planetary system have any foundation, the stability of this system is also a consequence of the laws of motion. These phenomena, and some others which are explained in a similar manner, induce us to think that every thing depends on these laws by relations more or less concealed; but of which it is wiser to avow our ignorance than to substitute imaginary causes, for the sole purpose of dissipating our anxiety. I must here remark how Newton has erred on this point, from the method which he has otherwise so happily applied. Subsequently to the publication of his discoveries on the system of the world and on light, this great philosopher abandoned himself to speculations of another kind, and inquired what motives induced the author of nature to give to the solar system its present observed constitution. After detailing in the scholium which terminates the principles of natural philosophy, the remarkable phenomenon of the motions of the planets and of the satellites in the same direction, very nearly in the same plane, and in orbits Q. P. circular, he adds, all these motions, so very regular, do not arise from mechanical causes, because the comets move in all regions of the heavens, and in orbits very excentric. "This admirable arrangement of the Sun, of the planets, and of the comets, can only be the work of an intelligent and most powerful being." At the end of his optics he suggests the same thought, in which he would be still more confirmed, if he had known that all the conditions of the arrangement of the planets and of the satellites are precisely those which secure their stability. "A blind fate," says he, "could never make all the planets to move thus, with some irregularities hardly perceivable, which may arise from the mutual action of the planets and of the comets, and which, probably, in the course of time will become greater, till in fine the system may require to be restored by its author." But could not this arrangement of the planets be itself an effect of the laws of motion; and could not the supreme intelligence which Newton makes to interfere, make it to depend on a more general phenomenon? such as, according to us, a nebulous matter distributed in various masses throughout the immensity of the heavens. Can one even affirm that the preservation of the planetary system entered into the views of the Author of Nature? The mutual attraction of the bodies of this system cannot alter its stability, as Newton supposes; but may there not be in the heavenly regions another fluid besides light? Its resistance, and the diminution which its emission produces in the mass of the Sun, ought at length to destroy the arrangement of the planets, so that to maintain this, a renovation would become evidently necessary. And do not all those species of animals which are extinct, but whose existence Cuvier has ascertained with such singular sagacity, and also the organization in the numerous fossil bones which he has described, indicate a tendency to change in things, which are apparently the most permanent in their nature?

The magnitude and importance of the solar system ought not to except it from this general law; for they are relative to our smallness, and this system, extensive as it appears to be, is but an insensible point in the universe. If we trace the history of the progress of the human mind, and of its errors, we shall observe final causes perpetually receding, according as the boundaries of our knowledge are extended. These causes, which Newton transported to the limits of the solar system, were, in his time, placed in the atmosphere in order to explain the cause of meteors: in the view of the philosopher, they are therefore only an expression of our ignorance of the true causes.

....

Herschel, while observing the nebulae by means of his powerful telescopes, traced the progress of their condensation, not on one only, as their progress does not become sensible until after the lapse of ages, but on the whole of them, as in a vast forest we trace the growth of trees, in the individuals of different ages which it contains. He first observed the nebulous matter diffused in several masses, through various parts of the heavens, of which it occupied a great extent. In some of these masses he observed that this matter was fully condensed about one or more nuclei, a little more brilliant. In other nebulae, these nuclei shine brighter, relatively to the nebulosity which environs them. As the atmosphere of each nucleus separates itself by an ulterior condensation, there result several nebulae constituted of brilliant nuclei very near to each other, and each surrounded by its respective atmosphere; sometimes the nebulous matter being condensed in a uniform manner, produces the nebulae which are termed *planetary*. Finally, a greater degree of condensation transforms all these nebulae into stars. The nebulae, classed in a philosophic manner, indicate, with a great degree of probability, their future tranformation [*sic*] into stars, and the anterior state of the nebulosity of existing stars. Thus, by tracing the progress of condensation of the nebulous matter, we descend to the consideration of the Sun, formerly surrounded by an immense atmosphere, to which consideration we can also arrive, from an examination of the phenomena of the solar system, as we shall see in our last note. Such a marked coincidence, arrived at by such different means, renders the existence of this anterior state of the Sun extremely probable.

....

NOTE VII. AND LAST.

From the preceding chapter it appears, that we have the five following phenomena to assist us in investigating the cause of the primitive motions of the planetary system. The motions of the planets in the same direction, and very nearly in the same plane; the motions of the satellites in the same direction as those of the planets; the motions of rotation of these different bodies and also of the Sun, in the same direction as their motions of projection, and in planes very little inclined to each other; the small eccentricity of the orbits of the planets and satellites; finally, the great eccentricity of the orbits of the comets, their inclinations being at the same time entirely indeterminate.

Buffon is the only individual that I know of, who, since the discovery of the true system of the world, endeavoured to investigate the origin of the planets and satellites. He supposed that a comet, by impinging on the Sun, carried away a torrent of matter, which was reunited far off, into globes of different magnitudes and at different distances from this star. These globes, when they cool and become hardened, are the planets and their satellites. This hypothesis satisfies the first of the five preceding phenomena; for it is evident that all bodies thus formed should move very nearly in the plane which passes through the centre of the Sun, and through the direction of the torrent of matter which has produced them: but the four remaining phenomena appear to me inexplicable on this supposition. Indeed the absolute motion of the molecules of a planet ought to be in the same direction as the motion of its centre of gravity; but it by no means follows from this, that the motion of rotation of a planet should be also in the same direction. Thus the Earth may revolve from east to west, and yet the absolute motion of each of its molecules may be directed from west to east. This observation applied also to the revolution of the satellites, of which the direction in the same hypothesis, is not necessarily the same as that of the motion of projection of the planets.

The small eccentricity of the planetary orbits is a phenomenon, not only difficult to explain on this hypothesis, but altogether inconsistent with it. We know from the theory of central forces, that if a body which moves in a re-entrant orbit about the Sun, passes very near the body of the Sun, it will return constantly to it, at the end of each revolution. Hence it follows that if the planets were originally detached from the Sun, they would touch it, at each return to this star; and their orbits, instead of being nearly circular, would be very eccentric. Indeed it must be admitted that a torrent of matter detached from the Sun, cannot be compared to a globe which just skims by its surface: from the impulsions which the parts of this torrent receive from each other, combined with their mutual attraction, they may, by changing the direction of their motions, increase the distances of their perihelions from the Sun. But their orbits should be extremely eccentric, or at least all the orbits would not be *q.p.* circular, except by the most extraordinary chance. Finally, no reason can be assigned on the hypothesis of Buffon, why the orbits of more than one hundred comets, which have been already observed, should be all very eccentric. This hypothesis, therefore, is far from satisfying the preceding phenomena. Let us consider whether we can assign the true cause.

Whatever may be its nature, since it has produced or influenced the direction of the planetary motions, it must have embraced them all within the sphere of its action; and considering the immense distance which intervenes between them, nothing could have effected this but·a fluid of almost indefinite extent. In order to have impressed on them all a motion *q.p.* circular and in the same direction about the sun, this fluid must environ this star, like an atmosphere. From a consideration of the planetary motions, we are therefore brought to the conclusion, that in consequence of an excessive heat, the solar atmosphere originally extended beyond the orbits of all the planets, and that it has successively contracted itself within its present limits.

In the primitive state in which we have supposed the Sun to be, it resembles those substances which are termed nebulae, which, when seen through telescopes, appear to be composed of a nucleus, more or less brilliant, surrounded by a nebulosity, which, by condensing on its surface, transforms it into a star. If all the stars are conceived to be similarly formed, we can suppose their anterior state of nebulosity to be preceded by other states, in which the nebulous matter was more or less diffuse, the nucleus being at the same time more or less brilliant. By going back in this manner, we shall arrive at a state of nebulosity so diffuse, that its existence can with difficulty be conceived.

For a considerable time back, the particular arrangement of some stars visible to the naked eye, has engaged the attention of philosophers. Mitchel [John Michell] remarked long since how extremely improbable it was that the stars composing the constellation called the Pleiades, for example, should be confined within the narrow space which contains them, by the sole chance of hazard; from which he inferred that this group of stars, and the similar groups which the heavens present to us, are the effects of a primitive cause, or of a primitive law of nature. These groups are a general result of the condensation of nebulae of several nuclei; for it is evident that the nebulous matter being perpetually attracted by these different nuclei, ought at length to form a group of stars, like to that of the Pleiades. The condensation of nebulae consisting of two nuclei, will in like manner form stars very near to each other, revolving the one about the other like to the double stars, whose respective motions have been already recognized.

But in what manner has the solar atmosphere determined the motions of rotation and revolution of the planets and satellites? If these bodies had penetrated deeply into this atmosphere, its resistance would cause them to fall on the Sun. We may therefore suppose that the planets were formed at its successive limits, by the condensation of zones of vapours, which it must, while it was cooling, have abandoned in the plane of its equator.

Let us resume the results which we have given in the tenth chapter of the preceding book. The Sun's atmosphere cannot extend indefinitely; its limit is the point where the centrifugal force arising from the motion of rotation balances the gravity; but according as the cooling contracts the atmosphere, and condenses the molecules which are near to it, on the surface of the star, the motion of rotation increases; for in virtue of the principle of areas, the sum of the areas described by the radius vector of each particle of the Sun and of its atmosphere, and projected on the plane of its equator, is always the same. Consequently the rotation ought to be quicker, when these particles approach to the centre of the Sun. The centrifugal force arising from this motion becoming thus greater; the point where the gravity is equal to it, is nearer to the centre of the Sun. Supposing therefore, what is natural to admit, that the atmosphere extended at any epoch as far as this limit, it ought, according as it cooled, to abandon the molecules, which are situated at this limit, and at the successive limits produced by the increased rotation of the Sun. These particles, after being abandoned, have continued to circulate about this star, because their centrifugal force was balanced by their gravity. But as this equality does not obtain for those molecules of the atmosphere which are situated on the parallels to the Sun's equator, these have come nearer by their gravity to the atmosphere according as it condensed, and they have not ceased to belong to it, inasmuch as by this motion, they have approached to the plane of this equator.

Let us now consider the zones of vapours, which have been successively abandoned. These zones ought, according to all probability, to form by their condensation, and by the mutual attraction of their particles, several concentrical rings of vapours circulating about the Sun. The mutual friction of the molecules of each ring ought to accelerate some and retard others, until they all had acquired the same angular motion. Consequently the real velocities of the molecules which are farther from the Sun, ought to be greatest. The following cause ought likewise to contribute to this difference of velocities: The most distant particles of the Sun, and which, by the effects of cooling and of condensation, have collected so as to constitute the superior part of the ring, have always described areas proportional to the times, because the central force by which they are actuated has been constantly directed to this star; but this constancy of areas requires an increase of velocity, according as they approach more to each other. It appears that the same cause ought to diminish the velocity of the particles, which, situated near the ring, constitute its inferior part.

If all the particles of a ring of vapours continued to condense without separating, they would at length constitute a solid or a liquid ring. But the regularity which this formation requires in all the parts of the ring, and in their cooling, ought to make this phenomenon very rare. Thus the solar system presents but one example of it; that of the rings of Saturn. Almost always each ring of vapours ought to be divided into several masses, which, being moved with velocities which differ little from each other, should continue to revolve at the same distance about the Sun. These masses should assume a spheroidical form, with a rotatory motion in the direction of that of their revolution, because their inferior particles have a less real velocity than the superior; they have therefore constituted so many planets in a state of vapour. But if one of them was sufficiently powerful, to unite successively by its attraction, all the others about its centre, the ring of vapours would be changed into one sole spheroidical mass, circulating about the

Sun, with a motion of rotation in the same direction with that of revolution. This last case has been the most common; however, the solar system presents to us the first case, in the four small planets which revolve between Mars and Jupiter, at least unless we suppose with [Wilhelm] Olbers, that they originally formed one planet only, which was divided by an explosion into several parts, and actuated by different velocities. Now if we trace the changes which a farther cooling ought to produce in the planets formed of vapours, and of which we have suggested the formation, we shall see to arise in the centre of each of them, a nucleus increasing continually, by the condensation of the atmosphere which environs it. In this state, the planet resembles the Sun in the nebulous state, in which we have first supposed it to be; the cooling should therefore produce at the different limits of its atmosphere, phenomena similar to those which have been described, namely, rings and satellites circulating about its centre in the direction of its motion of rotation, and revolving in the same direction on their axes. The regular distribution of the mass of rings of Saturn about its centre and in the plane of its equator, results naturally from this hypothesis, and, without it, is inexplicable. Those rings appear to me to be existing proofs of the primitive extension of the atmosphere of Saturn, and of its successive condensations. Thus the singular phenomena of the small eccentricities of the orbits of the planets and satellites, of the small inclination of these orbits to the solar equator, and of the identity in the direction of the motions of rotation and revolution and of all those bodies with that of the rotation of the Sun, follow from the hypothesis which has been suggested, and render it extremely probable. If the solar system was formed with perfect regularity, the orbits of the bodies which compose it would be circles, of which the planes, as well as those of the various equators and rings, would coincide with the plane of the solar equator. But we may suppose that the innumerable varieties which must necessarily exist in the temperature and density of different parts of these great masses, ought to produce the eccentricities of their orbits, and the deviations of their motions, from the plane of this equator.

[Laplace goes on to show how his hypothesis explains the origin of comets and the great eccentricity of their orbits, the zodiacal light, the shape of the planets, and the equality between the angular motions of rotation and revolution of the satellites.]

Notes

ABBREVIATIONS USED IN THE REFERENCES

AAAS   American Association for the Advancement of Science
AJS   *American Journal of Science and Arts*
APS   American Philosophical Society
DAB   *Dictionary of American Biography*
SIA   Smithsonian Institution Archives

CHAPTER I

1. William Whiston, "A Discourse Concerning the Nature, Stile, and Extent of the Mosaic History of the Creation," *A New Theory of the Earth, from Its Original to the Consummation of All Things, Wherein the Creation of the World in Six Days, the Universal Deluge, and the General Conflagration, as Laid Down in the Holy Scriptures, Are Shewn to Be Perfectly Agreeable to Reason and Philosophy* (London: Benj. Tooke, 1696), p. 6.

2. On the length of the days of creation, see ibid., p. 51.

3. John C. Greene develops this thesis in *The Death of Adam: Evolution and Its Impact on Western Thought* (Ames: Iowa State University Press, 1959).

4. René Descartes, *Principia Philosophiae*, in Charles Adam and Paul Tannery, eds., *Oeuvres de Descartes* (Paris: Léopold Cerf, 1897-1910), vol. 8, pt. 1, pp. 99-100; Descartes, *Le Monde, ou Traité de la Lumière*, ibid., 10:31-36.

5. Blaise Pascal, *Pensées and The Provincial Letters* (New York: Modern Library, 1941), p. 29.

6. Isaac Newton, *Mathematical Principles of Natural Philosophy and His System of the World*, trans. Andrew Motte, revised by Florian Cajori (Berkeley: University of California Press, 1960), pp. 543-44. For statements

that the solar system could not have been produced by natural causes alone, see *Isaac Newton's Papers and Letters on Natural Philosophy and Related Documents*, ed. I. Bernard Cohen (Cambridge: University Press, 1958), p. 282; and Isaac Newton, *Opticks* (New York: Dover Publications, 1952), p. 402.

7. Newton to Thomas Burnet, January 1680/1, *The Correspondence of Isaac Newton*, ed. H. W. Turnbull (Cambridge: University Press, 1960), 2:334.

8. Ibid., pp. 331-34. For an excellent discussion of Newton's cosmogony, see David Kubrin, "Newton and the Cyclical Cosmos: Providence and the Mechanical Philosophy," *Journal of the History of Ideas* 28 (July-September 1967): 325-46.

9. On the cosmogonies of Burnet and Whiston, see David C. Kubrin, "Providence and the Mechanical Philosophy: The Creation and Dissolution of the World in Newtonian Thought. A Study of the Relations of Science and Religion in Seventeenth Century England" (Ph.D. diss., Cornell University, 1969), chaps. 5 and 10.

10. Ibid., p. 335.

11. Burnet to Newton, 13 January 1680/1, *The Correspondence of Isaac Newton*, 2:325.

12. Immanuel Kant, *Universal Natural History and Theory of the Heavens*, in *Kant's Cosmogony*, ed. and trans. W. Hastie (Glasgow: James Maclehose & Sons, 1900), p. 72.

13. Georges Louis Leclerc, comte de Buffon, *Natural History: General and Particular*, trans. William Smellie (London: W. Strahan & T. Cadell, 1781), 1:63, 34. A discussion of the background and development of Buffon's cosmogonical ideas can be found in Jacques Roger's introduction to Buffon, *Les Époques de la nature* ("Mémoires du Muséum National d'Histoire Naturelle," series C: Sciences de la Terre, vol. 10) (Paris: Editions du Muséum, 1962). See also Roger's biographical sketch of Buffon in the *Dictionary of Scientific Biography*, 2:576-82.

14. Buffon, *Natural History*, 1:63.

15. Ibid., pp. 65-66.

16. Ibid., p. 66.

17. Ibid., p. 77.

18. Ibid., pp. 80-81. Roger has called attention to the fact that Buffon initially attributed the comet's motion to "the hand of God," which was an obvious violation of his own scientific standards. He later corrected this egregious error by suggesting that comets were perhaps nothing more than the debris of an exploded sun. Roger, introduction to Buffon's *Les Époques de la nature*, p. xlvi.

19. Buffon, *Natural History*, 1:82.

20. Quoted in Aram Vartanian, *Diderot and Descartes: A Study of Scientific Naturalism in the Enlightenment* (Princeton, N.J.: Princeton University Press, 1953), p. 126.

21. Ibid., p. 111.

22. The Swiss mathematician Leonhard Euler raised several scientific objections to Buffon's cosmogony: "According to the laws of mechanics, the material torn from the sun should have fallen back into it after the first revolution; the densest planets should be farthest away from the sun; and the planetary orbits should always coincide at the point of initial impact." Also, "as early as 1770, it became apparent that comets had a very low density, which destroyed the impact hypothesis." Roger, *Dictionary of Scientific Biography*, 2:578.

23. This connection was suggested to me by Professor Roger Hahn. Bailly's comments on Buffon's cosmogony are in his *Histoire de l'astronomie moderne: Depuis la fondation de l'École d'Alexandria, jusqu'à l'époque de MDCCXXX* (new ed.; Paris, 1785), 2:718-32.

24. Roger Hahn, *Laplace as a Newtonian Scientist* (Los Angeles: William Andrews Clark Memorial Library, 1967), p. 8.

25. The most pertinent parts of this note as it appeared in the 1830 English translation are reprinted in Appendix 2.

26. Pierre Simon Laplace, *The System of the World*, trans. J. Pond (London: Richard Phillips, 1809), 2:360. This translation is based on the first French edition, 1796.

27. Ibid., pp. 360-62.

28. Ibid., pp. 357-58.

29. Ibid., pp. 358-59.

30. Ibid., pp. 363-65.

31. Pierre Simon Laplace, *The System of the World*, trans. Henry H. Harte (Dublin: University Press, 1830), 2:358-59. This translation is based on the fifth French edition, 1824. See Charles A. Whitney, *The Discovery of Our Galaxy* (New York: Alfred A. Knopf, 1971), pp. 137-53, for a variorum translation of the passage relating to the nebular hypothesis.

32. Laplace, *The System of the World* (1830), 2:360-61.

33. William Herschel, "On Nebulous Stars, Properly So Called," *The Scientific Papers of Sir William Herschel* (London: The Royal Society and the Royal Astronomical Society, 1912), 1:415-16, 423. This article was published originally in the *Philosophical Transactions* 81 (1791): 71-88. See also Bernhard Sticker's two recent articles on Herschel's views: " 'Artificial' and 'Natural' Classifications of Celestial Bodies in the Work of William Herschel," Tenth International Congress of the History of Science, *Proceedings* (1962), 2:729-31; and "Herschel's Cosmology," *History of Science* 3 (1964): 91-101.

34. William Herschel, "Astronomical Observations Relating to the Construction of the Heavens, Arranged for the Purpose of a Critical Examination, the Result of Which Appears to Throw Some New Light upon the Organization of the Celestial Bodies," *The Scientific Papers of Sir William Herschel*, 2:494-95; published originally in the *Philosophical Transactions* (1811), pp. 269-336. See also Herschel, "Astronomical Observations Relating to the Sidereal Part of the Heavens, and Its Connection with the Nebulous Part: Arranged for the Purpose of a Critical Examination," *The Scientific Papers of Sir William Herschel*, 2:520-41; reprinted from the *Philosophical Transactions* (1814), pp. 248-84.

35. Quoted in Constance A. Lubbock, ed., *The Herschel Chronicle: The Life-Story of William Herschel and His Sister Caroline Herschel* (Cambridge: University Press, 1933), p. 310.

36. Laplace, *The System of the World* (1830), 2:336-37.

37. Ibid., p. 328.

38. For example, see Walter F. Cannon, "John Herschel and the Idea of Science," *Journal of the History of Ideas* 22 (April-June 1961): 229.

39. Pierre Simon Laplace, *Traité de mécanique céleste*, vol. 5 of Laplace's *Oeuvres complètes* (Paris: Gauthier-Villars, 1882), pp. 322-23.

40. Olbers to Bessel, 4 June 1812, *Briefwechsel zwischen W. Olbers and F. W. Bessel*, ed. Adolph Erman (Leipzig: Avenarius & Mendelssohn, 1852), 1:337.

41. Katharine Brownell Collier, *Cosmogonies of Our Fathers: Some Theories of the Seventeenth and Eighteenth Centuries* (1934; reprint ed., New York: Octagon Books, 1968), p. 283.

42. Kant, *Universal Natural History*, pt. 2.

43. Ibid., pp. lxvi-lxvii, in the introduction by W. Hastie.

CHAPTER II

1. Samuel Miller, *A Brief Retrospect of the Eighteenth Century* (New York: T. & J. Swords, 1803), 1:167.

2. William Paley, *Natural Theology: Or, Evidences of the Existence and Attributes of the Deity, Collected from the Appearances of Nature*, with additional notes, etc., by John Ware (Boston: Gould & Lincoln, 1866), pp. 227-28. By 1866 this work had passed through at least forty editions.

3. Ebenezer Grant Marsh, *An Oration, on the Truth of the Mosaic History of the Creation; Delivered at New-Haven, on the Public Commencement, September, A.D. 1798* (Hartford: Hudson & Goodwin, 1798), pp. 14-15.

4. Daniel J. Boorstin, *The Lost World of Thomas Jefferson* (Boston: Beacon Press, 1960), pp. 29-30. See also John C. Greene, "Some Aspects of American Astronomy, 1750-1815," *Isis* 45 (December 1954): 357.

5. Quoted in Boorstin, *The Lost World of Thomas Jefferson,* p. 31.

6. Benjamin Franklin, "Conjectures concerning the Formation of the Earth, &c. in a Letter from Dr. B. Franklin, to the Abbé Soulavie," APS, *Transactions* 3 (1793): 4-5. This letter also appeared in the *Universal Asylum, and Columbian Magazine* 2 (August 1792): 106-8.

7. Franklin, "Formation of the Earth," pp. 2-3.

8. Isaac Orr, "An Essay on the Formation of the Universe," *AJS* 6 (1823): 129; "Alexander Metcalf Fisher," *Appletons' Cyclopaedia of American Biography,* 2:464; "Isaac Orr," ibid., 4:593. For an account of Orr's work with the American Colonization Society, see P. J. Staudenraus, *The African Colonization Movement, 1816-1865* (New York: Columbia University Press, 1961).

9. Orr, "Formation of the Universe," p. 148.

10. Ibid., p. 129.

11. Ibid., pp. 131-32.

12. Ibid., p. 134.

13. Ibid., p. 143.

14. Ibid., p. 146. Orr's "simultaneous discovery" of the nebular hypothesis suggests an almost causal relationship between the Newtonian world view and such cosmogonies. Wherever the new science penetrated—in Europe, America, and even Asia—it produced virtually the same effect. It hardly comes as a surprise to find that the man who brought modern physics to Japan, Tadao Shizuki of Nagasaki, also proposed a nebular cosmogony, in 1802. For a French translation of Shizuki's theory, see S. Yajima, "Théorie nebulaire de Shizuki (1760-1806)," *Archives internationales d'histoire des sciences* 12 (April-June 1959): 169-73.

15. Orr, "Formation of the Universe," p. 136.

16. Ibid., p. 147.

17. This conclusion is also supported by the absence of any reference to Laplace in Jared Sparks's survey of cosmogonies from antiquity to the nineteenth century or in the discussion of cosmogonies by the anonymous author of an article on the hollow-earth theory of Captain John Cleves Symmes. See [Jared Sparks], "Theories of the Earth," *North American Review* 18 (April 1824): 266-79; and "Symmes' Theory," *American Quarterly Review* 1 (March 1827): 235-37.

18. Orr, "Formation of the Universe," p. 148.

19. [John Playfair], "Laplace's System of the World," *Edinburgh Review* 15 (January 1810): 396-417.

20. [Nathaniel Bowditch], "Modern Astronomy," *North American Review* 20 (April 1825): 354, 339. A search of Bowditch's papers and library in the Rare Book Department of the Boston Public Library uncovered no additional comments on the nebular hypothesis.

21. "Astronomy of Laplace," *American Quarterly Review* 7 (June 1830): 279.

22. [Thomas Cooper ?], "Cuvier's Theory of the Globe," *Southern Review* 8 (November 1831): 72, 84.

23. William Whewell, *Astronomy and General Physics Considered with Reference to Natural Theology* (5th ed.; London: William Pickering, 1836; first published in 1833), p. 181.

24. William Buckland, *Geology and Mineralogy Considered with Reference to Natural Theology* (London: William Pickering, 1836), 1:40.

25. Thomas Chalmers, *On the Power, Wisdom, and Goodness of God as Manifested in the Adaptation of External Nature to the Moral and Intellectual Constitution of Man* (London: William Pickering, 1835), 1:31-32, 42. Chapter VII will be devoted to a discussion of the relationship between the nebular hypothesis and the argument from design.

26. On the sales of the Bridgewater Treatises, see Charles Coulston Gillispie, *Genesis and Geology: A Study in the Relations of Scientific Thought, Natural Theology, and Social Opinion in Great Britain, 1790-1850* (New York: Harper Torchbooks, 1959), p. 294.

27. Review of *Geology and Mineralogy Considered with Reference to Natural Theology*, by William Buckland, *Knickerbocker* 9 (April 1837): 416. Extracts from Whewell's account of the nebular hypothesis appeared in Canada in Henry Taylor's *An Attempt to Form a System of the Creation of Our Globe, of the Planets, and the Sun of Our System* (Toronto: W. J. Coates, 1836), p. 106.

28. J. P. N[ichol], "State of Discovery and Speculation concerning the Nebulae," *Westminster Review* 25 (July 1836): 406.

29. A[gnes] M. C[lerke], "John Pringle Nichol," *Dictionary of National Biography* 14:412-13.

30. J. P. Nichol, *Views of the Architecture of the Heavens* (2nd ed.; New York: Dayton & Newman, 1842), p. 108.

31. Ibid., p. 101.

32. Ibid., pp. 101-2.

33. Ibid., p. 101.

34. Constantine Samuel Rafinesque, *Celestial Wonders and Philosophy; or, The Structure of the Visible Heavens* (Philadelphia: Printed for the Central University of Illinois, 1838), pp. 3, 62, 65.

35. Publisher's preface to the American edition, Nichol, *Views of the Architecture of the Heavens*, pp. iii-iv.

36. Review of *Views of the Architecture of the Heavens*, by J. P. Nichol, *Knickerbocker* 13 (April 1839): 355.

37. Review of *Views of the Architecture of the Heavens*, by J. P. Nichol, *Princeton Review* 13 (January 1841): 154-55.

38. [Alexis Caswell], "Whewell's Astronomy and General Physics," *Christian Review* 1 (June 1836): 215-47; [Caswell], "Architecture of the Heavens," ibid. 6 (December 1841): 595-620. Caswell is identified as the

author of these articles in Walter Cochrane Bronson's biographical sketch of Caswell in the *DAB*, 3:570-71.

39. [Caswell], "Architecture of the Heavens," pp. 615-18.

40. Auguste Comte, *Cours de philosophie positive* (5th ed.; Paris: Schleicher Frères, 1908), 2:195-98; Comte, *Positive Philosophy*, trans. Harriet Martineau (London: John Chapman, 1853), 1:211-12.

41. [David Brewster], review of *Cours de philosophie positive*, by Auguste Comte, *Edinburgh Review* 67 (July 1838): 300; John Stuart Mill, *A System of Logic* (London: John W. Parker, 1843), 2:28.

42. Comte, *Positive Philosophy*, 1:212.

43. [Edward Hitchcock], "The New Theory of the Earth," *North American Review* 28 (April 1829): 281.

44. Gideon Algernon Mantell, *The Wonders of Geology* (3rd ed.; London: Relfe & Fletcher, 1839), 1: 26-29; on de la Beche, see Francis C. Haber, *The Age of the World: Moses to Darwin* (Baltimore, Md.: Johns Hopkins Press, 1959), p. 186.

45. Horsford is here referring to recent work in chemistry on the expansion of bodies when caloric is introduced.

46. Eben N. Horsford, "Theory of the formation of the earth," 8 March 1839 (Eben N. Horsford Papers, Rensselaer Polytechnic Institute Archives, Box 23). On Horsford and his later career, see Samuel Reznick, "The European Education of an American Chemist and Its Influence in 19th-Century America: Eben Norton Horsford," *Technology and Culture* 11 (July 1970): 336-88.

47. Joseph Henry, Geology Course, Lecture 3rd (Joseph Henry Papers, SIA); Henry, "Notes on a series of lectures on geology given at Nassau Hall, Princeton," August 1841, apparently taken by George Musgrave Giger of the class of 1841 (Presbyterian Historical Society, Philadelphia; a copy of the original manuscript is in the Joseph Henry Papers).

48. Joseph Lovering, "On the Application of Mathematical Analysis to Researches in the Physical Sciences," *Cambridge Miscellany of Mathematics, Physics, and Astronomy*, no. 3 (October 1842), pp. 128-29.

49. [Benjamin Peirce], "Bowditch's Translation of the *Mécanique Céleste*," *North American Review* 48 (January 1839): 173-77.

50. O. M. Mitchel, *The Planetary and Stellar Worlds: A Popular Exposition of the Great Discoveries and Theories of Modern Astronomy* (New York: Charles Scribner, 1860), pp. 246-48. This book, first published in 1848, is composed of a series of ten lectures Mitchel delivered in the mid-1840s.

51. Frederick William Conner, *Cosmic Optimism: A Study of the Interpretation of Evolution by American Poets from Emerson to Robinson* (Gainesville: University of Florida Press, 1949), p. 44. Emerson developed his history of nature in the 1830s and 1840s.

52. [Edgar A. Poe], review of *Critical and Miscellaneous Essays*, vol. 3, by T. Babington Macaulay, *Graham's Magazine* 18 (June 1841): 295.

53. Edgar A. Poe, *The Complete Works of Poe*, ed. James A. Harrison, vol. 16: *Marginalia—Eureka* (New York: Thomas Y. Crowell, 1902), p. 252. *Eureka* was not well received. In the words of one reviewer, who was not at all opposed to the nebular hypothesis, Poe's work was "a tissue of the baldest, stupidest, second-hand pantheism" (J[oseph] C[lark], "Eureka," *Mercersburg Review* 4 [January 1852]: 90-91).

54. [Matthew Boyd Hope], "On the Relation between the Holy Scriptures and Some Parts of Geological Science," *Princeton Review* 13 (July 1841): 392-93.

CHAPTER III

1. Milton Millhauser, *Just before Darwin: Robert Chambers and Vestiges* (Middletown, Conn.: Wesleyan University Press, 1959), pp. 87-88.

2. [Robert Chambers], *Vestiges of the Natural History of Creation* (2nd ed., from the 3rd London ed.; New York: Wiley & Putnam, 1845), p. 9.

3. Ibid., pp. 10-11.

4. Ibid., pp. 12-14.

5. Ibid., pp. 19, 279.

6. Agnes M. Clerke, *A Popular History of Astronomy during the Nineteenth Century* (4th ed.; London: Adam and Charles Black, 1902), pp. 114-19; "The Earl of Rosse's Leviathan Telescope," *AJS* 49 (April-June 1845): 222.

7. Earl of Rosse, "Observations on Some of the Nebulae," Royal Society of London, *Philosophical Transactions* 134 (1844): 324.

8. [Robert Chambers], *Explanations: A Sequel to "Vestiges of the Natural History of Creation"* (New York: Wiley & Putnam, 1846), pp. 5-6.

9. Ibid., pp. 10-12; Joseph Plateau, "On the Phaenomena Presented by a Free Liquid Mass Withdrawn from the Action of Gravity," (Taylor's) *Scientific Memoirs*, vol. 4, pt. 13 (1846), pp. 16-43; Plateau, "Experimental and Theoretical Researches on the Figures of Equilibrium of a Liquid Mass Withdrawn from the Action of Gravity, &c.," Smithsonian Institution, *Annual Report*, 1864, pp. 221, 276.

10. [Francis Bowen], "A Theory of Creation," *North American Review* 60 (April 1845): 427, 438, 467, 442.

11. E. B. Hunt to James D. Dana, 31 January 1856 (James Dwight Dana Correspondence, Yale University). Hunt, formerly an assistant professor of engineering at West Point, was serving with the U.S. Coast Survey in Newport, Rhode Island.

12. [Tayler Lewis], review of *Vestiges of the Natural History of Creation*, *American Review* 1 (May 1845): 525-28, 539-42.

13. [Asa Gray], "Explanations of the Vestiges," *North American Review* 62 (April 1846): 466.

14. [William Henry Allen], "Natural History of Creation," *Methodist Quarterly Review* 28 (April 1846): 298-306.

15. [Albert Baldwin Dod], review of *Vestiges of the Natural History of Creation, Princeton Review* 17 (October 1845): 513-14; [David Brewster], review of *Vestiges of the Natural History of Creation, North British Review* 3 (August 1845): 479-80.

16. J[oseph] H[enry] A[llen], "Vestiges of Creation and Sequel," *Christian Examiner* 40 (May 1846): 334-35, 344.

17. Henry Darwin Rogers to William Barton Rogers, 24 January 1845, quoted in George H. Daniels, *American Science in the Age of Jackson* (New York: Columbia University Press, 1968), p. 58.

18. Alexander Winchell, *Sketches of Creation: A Popular View of Some of the Grand Conclusions of the Sciences in References to the History of Matter and of Life* (New York: Harper & Brothers, 1870), p. 46.

19. [James Davenport Whelpley], review of *A Sequel to "Vestiges of the Natural History of Creation," American Review* 3 (April 1846): 395.

20. W. C. Bond to President Everett, 22 September 1847, printed in Astronomical Observatory of Harvard College, *Annals,* vol. 1, pt. 1 (1856), pp. cxxi-cxxii. Printed also in "The New Telescope at Cambridge," *AJS,* 2nd ser., 4 (November 1847): 426-27.

21. Lord Rosse to J. P. Nichol, 19 March 1846, printed in J. P. Nichol, *Thoughts on Some Important Points Relating to the System of the World* (Edinburgh: William Tait, 1846), p. 55.

22. Ibid., pp. 65-66; "Astronomy," *Scientific American* 3 (11 December 1847): 93; O. M. Mitchel's introduction to Pontecoulant, "La Place's Theory of the Formation of the Universe," *Sidereal Messenger* 1 (June 1847): 108.

23. John F. W. Herschel, "Address of the President," British Association for the Advancement of Science, *Report,* 1845, pp. xxxvi-xxxix; extracts from this address were reprinted in the Franklin Institute, *Journal,* 3rd ser., 10 (September 1845): 203-7. Herschel's public opposition to the nebular hypothesis encouraged other critics to voice their objections. See, for example, John Wallis, *A Brief Examination of the Nebulous Hypothesis, with Strictures on a Work Entitled Vestiges of the Natural History of Creation* (London: R. Groombridge & Sons, 1845).

24. [O. M. Mitchel], "Lord Rosse's Discoveries and Their Influence on the Nebular Hypothesis," *Sidereal Messenger* 1 (February 1847): 77-78; Asa Smith, *Smith's Illustrated Astronomy, Designed for the Use of the Public or Common Schools in the United States* (19th ed.; New York: Ivison & Phinney, 1848), p. 58.

25. James M'Cosh and George Dickie, *Typical Forms and Special Ends in Creation* (New York: Robert Carter & Brothers, 1857), p. 400.

26. [George Taylor], "Theories of Creation and the Universe," *De Bow's Commercial Review* 4 (October 1847): 181, 183; [George Taylor], "Nebular Hypothesis," *Knickerbocker* 37 (January 1851): 26, 29. Taylor is probably best known for having served as a representative from New York in the Thirty-fifth Congress, 1857-59.

27. Austin Phelps, "The Oneness of God in Revelation and in Nature," *Bibliotheca Sacra* 16 (October 1859): 849.

28. "The Nebular Hypothesis," *Southern Quarterly Review* 10 (July 1846): 227-30.

29. Peirce to Loomis, 30 January 1846 (Elias Loomis Papers, Yale University).

30. Loomis to Peirce, 2 March 1846 (Benjamin Peirce Papers, Harvard University).

31. Benjamin Peirce, "On the Connection of Comets with the Solar System," AAAS, *Proceedings* 2 (1849): 121.

32. Ibid., pp. 118-22.

CHAPTER IV

1. Minutes of the Section of Mathematics, Physics, and Astronomy, Fifth Day, 18 August 1849, AAAS, *Proceedings* 2 (1849): 217.

2. For biographical information on Kirkwood, see Joseph Swain, "Daniel Kirkwood," Astronomical Society of the Pacific, *Publications* 13 (1 October 1901): 140-47; Raymond S. Dugan, "Daniel Kirkwood," *DAB*, 10:436; Brian G. Marsden, "Daniel Kirkwood," *Dictionary of Scientific Biography*, 7:384-87; and Daniel Kirkwood to Joseph Henry, 25 July 1876 (Official Incoming Correspondence, SIA).

3. Kirkwood to B. A. Gould, 23 January 1850 (James Dwight Dana Correspondence, Yale University); printed in the *AJS*, 2nd ser., 9 (May 1850): 398-99. The source of this statement is not clear. Kirkwood claims to have read it on page 204 of "Young's Mechanics." On page 270 of Thomas Young's *Elementary Illustrations of the Celestial Mechanics of Laplace* (London: John Murray, 1821) this comment appears: "Now if we imagine any one of the planets to be a homogeneous sphere, deriving its rotation and its annual motion round the sun from a single impulse. . . ." The same words appear on page 270 of the 1832 edition.

4. Kirkwood to Gould, 23 January 1850.

5. Ibid. Kirkwood used the term "analogy" only to signify that the ratio n^2/n'^2 is analogous or approximately equivalent to the ratio D^3/D'^3—nothing more. Failure to appreciate this peculiar usage can lead to a serious misunderstanding of what Kirkwood was trying to say; see, for instance, George H. Daniels, *American Science in the Age of Jackson* (New York: Columbia University Press, 1968), p. 175.

6. Kirkwood to Gould, 23 January 1850.

7. Daniel Kirkwood to Edward C. Herrick, 26 September 1848 (Edward C. Herrick Papers, Yale University).

8. Kirkwood to Herrick, 26 March 1849 (ibid.).

9. Kirkwood to Sears C. Walker, 4 July 1849, printed in the AAAS, *Proceedings* 2 (1849): 208-10.

10. AAAS, *Proceedings* 2 (1849): 210.

11. Ibid., pp. 210-11; APS, *Proceedings* 5 (April-September 1849): 97-98.

12. Walker to Kirkwood, 24 July 1849, printed in the AAAS, *Proceedings* 2 (1849): 211.

13. Kirkwood to Herrick, 30 July 1849 (Edward C. Herrick Papers).

14. Kirkwood to Walker, 31 July 1849, printed in the AAAS, *Proceedings* 2 (1849): 211-12.

15. These remarks were made by E. B. Hunt in a "Tribute of Respect to the Memory of Sears C. Walker," minutes of a meeting of the officers and members of the Coast Survey in Washington, D.C., 2 February 1853 (Benjamin Peirce Papers, Harvard University).

16. AAAS, *Proceedings* 2 (1849): 212, 217.

17. Ibid., pp. 217-18.

18. Ibid., pp. 220-21.

19. Ibid., pp. 363-66.

20. Ibid., p. 369.

21. "Kirkwood's Analogy," *Annual of Scientific Discovery*, 1850, p. 338. Parts of this article were reprinted in the *Edinburgh New Philosophical Journal* 49 (July 1850): 165-70.

22. "Kirkwood's Analogy," p. 338.

23. *Daily Evening Traveller* (Boston), 7 and 13 September 1849; T. H. [Thomas Hill], "The Scientific Meeting at Cambridge," *Christian Examiner* 47 (November 1849): 328; J. L. [Joseph Lovering], "Baron Humboldt's Cosmos," ibid. 48 (January 1850): 72; Daniel Kirkwood, "On a New Analogy in the Periods of Rotation of the Primary Planets," *AJS*, 2nd ser., 9 (May 1850): 395-99.

24. Daniel Kirkwood to the Editors of the American Journal [*sic*], 23 March 1850 (James Dwight Dana Correspondence).

25. Adam Sedgwick, *A Discourse on the Studies of the University of Cambridge* (5th ed.; London: John W. Parker, 1850), pp. 182, 220-21.

26. [C. Piazzi Smyth], "On a New Analogy in the Periods of Rotation of the Primary Planets Discovered by Daniel Kirkwood of Pottsville, Pennsylvania," *Edinburgh New Philosophical Journal* 49 (July 1850): 169-70. For an interesting sidelight to Smyth's article, see S. M. Drach's letter to Smyth, ibid. 49 (October 1850): 400, in which Drach claims to have partially anticipated Kirkwood.

27. David Brewster, "Address before the Twentieth Meeting of the British Association at Edinburgh, July 31, 1850," *AJS*, 2nd ser., 10

(November 1850): 308. Brewster's remarks about Kirkwood's analogy were printed also in "Astronomy," *Scientific American* 6 (12 October 1850): 26. On the naming of the broken planet, see AAAS, *Proceedings* 2 (1849): 215.

28. J. P. Nichol, *The Planetary System: Its Order, and Physical Structure* (London: H. Bailliere, 1850), pp. *248-49. See also Nichol's note in Auguste Comte, *Positive Philosophy*, trans. Harriet Martineau (London: John Chapman, 1853), 1:212-13. Sergio Vaghi of the Osservatorio Astronomico di Torino has called my attention to the interest of Karl Marx and Friedrich Engels in Kirkwood's analogy and its connection with the nebular hypothesis. See *Karl Marx-Friedrich Engels Werke* (Berlin: Dietz Verlag, 1965), vol. 31, pp. 143-47; and Engels, *Dialectics of Nature*, trans. Clemens Dutt (New York: International Publishers, 1940), pp. 8-9, 15, 186-87.

29. Sears C. Walker, Letter to the Editor, *Astronomische Nachrichten* 30 (1850): 11-14.

30. New York: Harper & Brothers, 1850.

31. Joseph Henry to Elias Loomis, n.d. (Joseph Henry Papers, SIA).

32. Denison Olmsted to Elias Loomis, 30 September 1850 (Elias Loomis Papers, Yale University).

33. Loomis to Olmsted, 4 October 1850 (ibid.).

34. Olmsted to Loomis, 23 November 1850 (ibid.).

35. Loomis to Herrick, 28 November 1850 (Herrick-Loomis Correspondence, Yale University).

36. Review of *The Recent Progress of Astronomy; Especially in the United States*, by Elias Loomis, *AJS*, 2nd ser., 11 (January 1851): 147.

37. Review of *The Recent Progress of Astronomy; Especially in the United States*, by Elias Loomis, *Literary World* 7 (23 November 1850): 408.

38. Elias Loomis, "On Kirkwood's Law of the Rotation of the Primary Planets," *AJS*, 2nd ser., 11 (March 1851): 217-23.

39. Elias Loomis, "The Zone of Small Planets between Mars and Jupiter," Smithsonian Institution, *Annual Report*, 1854, pp. 137-46; Loomis, "Outline of the Astronomical Lectures in Yale College," ca. 1863, pp. 30-31, the interleaved copy used by Professor Loomis in his lectures, with his own notes (Historical Manuscripts Room, Sterling Library, Yale University).

40. Olmsted to Loomis, 19 March 1851 (Elias Loomis Papers).

41. Olmsted to Loomis, 8 April 1851 (ibid.).

42. Daniel Kirkwood, "On the Law of the Rotation of the Primary Planets," *AJS*, 2nd ser., 11 (May 1851): 397-98.

43. B. A. Gould to Elias Loomis, 28 March 1851 (Elias Loomis Papers).

44. J. Bradford Cherriman, "On Kirkwood's Analogy," *AJS*, 2nd ser., 14 (July 1852): 9-10.

45. "Addresses of Scientific Men in the United States," composed of replies to a circular sent out on November 25, 1852, by Spencer F. Baird,

Permanent Secretary of the AAAS, requesting information about the members of the AAAS (SIA).

46. Chester Dewey to Elias Loomis, 4 January 1851 and 2 April 1851 (Elias Loomis Papers).

47. Swain, Astronomical Society of the Pacific, *Publications* 13 (1 October 1901): 144; C. A. Young, "Pending Problems in Astronomy," AAAS, *Proceedings* 33 (1884): 14.

48. In 1884 Kirkwood was forced to restrict the application of his analogy after discovering that it would not apply in cases where one planet was interior to the asteroids and the other superior. Kirkwood, "The Limits of Stability of Nebulous Planets, and the Consequences Resulting from Their Mutual Relations," APS, *Proceedings* 22 (21 November 1884): 111.

CHAPTER V

1. Joseph Louis Lagrange, "Sur l'origine des comètes," *Oeuvres de Lagrange* (Paris: Gauthier-Villars, 1877), 7:389; David Brewster, "Address before the Twentieth Meeting of the British Association at Edinburgh, July 31, 1850," *AJS*, 2nd ser., 10 (November 1850): 308; Daniel Kirkwood, "On Certain Analogies in the Solar System," ibid. 14 (September 1852): 214.

2. Elias Loomis, "The Zone of Small Planets between Mars and Jupiter," Smithsonian Institution, *Annual Report*, 1854, pp. 141-44. See also his *Recent Progress of Astronomy; Especially in the United States* (3rd ed.; New York: Harper & Brothers, 1856), p. 93.

3. Simon Newcomb, "On the Secular Variations and Mutual Relations of the Orbits of the Asteroids," American Academy of Arts and Sciences, *Memoirs*, new ser., vol. 7, pt. 1 (1861), pp. 123-52. On a draft of this article (in the Simon Newcomb Papers, Library of Congress) Newcomb penciled: "My first paper to the AAAS—1859."

4. Ibid., p. 124.

5. Daniel Kirkwood, "On the Law of the Rotation of the Primary Planets," *AJS*, 2nd ser., 11 (May 1851): 394-98.

6. Joseph Lovering, "On the Application of Mathematical Analysis to Researches in the Physical Sciences," *Cambridge Miscellany of Mathematics, Physics, and Astronomy*, no. 3 (October 1842), p. 129.

7. Daniel Kirkwood, "On Saturn's Ring," *AJS*, 2nd ser., 12 (July 1851): 109-10.

8. [Daniel Kirkwood], "The Nebular Hypothesis," *Presbyterian Quarterly Review*, 2 (March 1854): 532-33, 544.

9. Alexander von Humboldt, *Cosmos: A Survey of the General Physical History of the Universe* (New York: Harper & Brothers, 1845), p. 32. See also the translation of the *Cosmos* by E. C. Otte and Others (New York: Harper & Brothers, 1850), 1:94-95.

10. [Kirkwood], "The Nebular Hypothesis," pp. 537-41.

11. Ibid., pp. 541-42.

12. Ibid., pp. 542-44.

13. Daniel Kirkwood, "On the Nebular Hypothesis," *AJS*, 2nd ser., 30 (September 1860): 168-75.

14. F[rederick] E[dward] B[rasch], "Stephen Alexander," *DAB*, 1:174-75.

15. C. A. Young, "Memoir of Stephen Alexander, 1806-1883," National Academy of Sciences, *Biographical Memoirs* 2 (1886): 256-57.

16. Quoted ibid., p. 258, from an address given at Alexander's funeral by Rev. Horace G. Hinsdale. The lecture described was apparently given in the late 1840s or early 1850s.

17. Stephen Alexander to Joseph Henry, 22 December 1847 (Joseph Henry Papers, SIA); Alexander, "On the Origin of the Forms and Present State of Some of the Clusters of Stars, and Resolvable Nebulae," AAAS, *Proceedings* 6 (1851): 128-29; Alexander, "On the Origin of the Forms and the Present Condition of Some of the Clusters of Stars, and Several of the Nebulae," *Astronomical Journal* 2 (1852): 95-96, 97-103, 105-11, 113-15, 126-28, 140-42, 148-52, 158-60.

18. Alexander, "On the Origin of the Forms and the Present Condition of Some of the Clusters of Stars," pp. 97-99.

19. Alexander, "On the Origin of the Forms and Present State of Some of the Clusters of Stars," pp. 128-29; Alexander, "On the Similarity of Arrangement of the Asteroids and the Comets of Short Period, and the Possibility of Their Common Origin," *Astronomical Journal* 1 (14 March 1851): 181-84. The common origin of the asteroids and the comets of short periods is the subject of two letters from Stephen Alexander to Joseph Henry, 16 and 31 January 1851 (Joseph Henry Papers).

20. Alexander, "On the Origin of the Forms and the Present Condition of Some of the Clusters of Stars," p. 160.

21. Alexander to Henry, 26 May 1848 and 25 July 1850 (Joseph Henry Papers); Young, "Memoir of Stephen Alexander," p. 256; Alexander, "On the Origin of the Forms and Present State of Some of the Clusters of Stars," p. 128. Alexander's 1850 paper did not appear in the *Proceedings* of the AAAS.

22. See Alexander to Henry, 23 May 1851; 24 November 1852 (two letters); and 26 November 1852 (Joseph Henry Papers).

23. B. A. Gould to W. C. Bond, 9 December 1849 (William Cranch Bond Papers, Harvard University Archives); Alexander to Henry, 29 November 1852 (Joseph Henry Papers).

24. Henry to Alexander, 4 July 1857 (Joseph Henry Papers); Alexander, "Statement and Exposition of Certain Harmonies of the Solar System," *Smithsonian Contributions to Knowledge* 21 (March 1875): 1-95. See also

Henry to Alexander, 26 August 1875 (Joseph Henry Papers), regarding the reception of Alexander's work.

25. "The Nebular Hypothesis," *Southern Quarterly Review*, new ser., 1 (April 1856): 96-97, 111.

26. Notably absent from this list of astronomers are William Cranch Bond and his son, George Phillips Bond, the two directors of the Harvard College Observatory in the 1850s, whose views on the nebular hypothesis we have been unable to determine. It is simply not true, as Charles Clayton Wylie maintained, that "astronomers following Laplace were not greatly interested [in the nebular hypothesis] before the publication of Darwin's book." Wylie, "The Nebular Hypothesis in the Nineteenth Century," *Scientific Monthly* 27 (September 1928): 262.

27. Denison Olmsted, "Notes and other material relating to his Lectures in Yale College on Natural Philosophy, Astronomy and Meteorology," 1843-59, pp. 121-23 (Beinecke Library, Yale University).

28. Ibid., pp. 123-24. For Olmsted's views on William Herschel's speculations, see his *Compendium of Astronomy* (stereotype ed.; New York: Robert B. Collins, 1852), pp. 248-49.

29. AAAS, *Proceedings* 6 (1851): 129.

30. Alexander Wilcocks, "Reflections upon the Nature of the Temporary Star of the Year 1572: An Application of the Nebular Hypothesis," Academy of Natural Sciences of Philadelphia, *Journal*, 2nd ser., 4 (March 1860): 316.

31. [William Whewell], *The Plurality of Worlds*, with an introduction by Edward Hitchcock (new ed.; Boston: Gould & Lincoln, 1855), pp. xii-xiii; David Brewster, *More Worlds Than One: The Creed of the Philosopher and the Hope of the Christian* (New York: Robert Carter & Brothers, 1854), pp. 45-46; John F. W. Herschel, *Outlines of Astronomy* (new ed.; Philadelphia: Blanchard & Lea, 1855), p. 504; [Herbert Spencer], "Recent Astronomy, and the Nebular Hypothesis," *Westminster Review* 70 (July 1858): 185-225; [Henry Holland], "The Progress and Spirit of Physical Science," *Edinburgh Review*, 108 (July 1858): 90. Both Spencer's and Holland's articles were reprinted in America in vol. 45 of the *Eclectic Magazine*.

CHAPTER VI

1. William Huggins, "On the Spectra of Some of the Nebulae," *AJS*, 2nd ser., 40 (July 1865): 77-81; from a paper presented to the Royal Society of London, 8 September 1864. See also Huggins, "On the Results of Spectrum Analysis as Applied to the Heavenly Bodies," British Association for the Advancement of Science, *Report*, 1868, pp. 147-51.

2. In 1847 the American chemist, John William Draper, had noted the distinctive continuous spectra of incandescent solids. After Huggins used this information to identify true nebulae, Draper proudly took credit for

having discovered a means of testing the nebular hypothesis. See Draper, *History of the Conflict between Religion and Science* (5th ed.; New York: D. Appleton, 1875), p. 241; Draper, *Scientific Memoirs: Being Experimental Contributions to a Knowledge of Radiant Energy* (New York: Harper & Brothers, 1878), pp. 31-32; and Daniel Norman, "John William Draper's Contributions to Astronomy," *Telescope* 5 (January-February 1938): 13.

3. William Huggins, "The New Astronomy: A Personal Retrospect," *Nineteenth Century* 41 (June 1897): 917.

4. Huggins, "On the Results of Spectrum Analysis," p. 150.

5. [Rush Emery], "Spectrum Analysis," *Methodist Quarterly Review* 53 (April 1871): 213-14. See also Emery, "The Nebular Theory," *Appletons' Journal* 8 (26 October 1872): 460-61; and Daniel Kirkwood, "On the Testimony of the Spectroscope to the Truth of the Nebular Hypothesis," *AJS*, 3rd ser., 2 (September 1871): 155-56, reprinted in the *Philosophical Magazine*, 4th ser., 42 (November 1871): 399-400.

6. Emery, "The Nebular Theory," p. 461. The spectroscopic confirmation of the nebular hypothesis had come as a surprise. Only a year or so prior to Huggins' discovery Lewis M. Rutherfurd, an American pioneer in astronomical spectroscopy, had suggested that spectroscopic research was undermining the hypothesis. See Rutherfurd, "Astronomical Observations with the Spectroscope," *AJS*, 2nd ser., 35 (January 1863): 77.

7. See, for example, [S. D. Hillman], "Recent Astronomy and the Mosaic Record," *Methodist Quarterly Review* 50 (October 1868): 532-52; William C. Richards, "Spectrum Analysis," *Baptist Quarterly* 4 (January 1870): 37; and "Proof of the Nebular Hypothesis by the Spectroscope," *Harper's New Monthly Magazine* 44 (January 1872): 305.

8. Alexander Winchell, "The Geology of the Stars," *Half-Hour Recreations in Popular Science: First Series*, ed. Dana Estes (Boston: Estes & Lauriat, 1874), pp. 260-61.

9. [George W. Eveleth], "Provings of Current Theories in Science," *American Monthly* 45 (March 1865): 207 and *passim*. In 1852 Eveleth had tried without success to get Harvard to invite him to lecture on the falsity of the nebular hypothesis and the theory of gravitation; G. W. Eveleth to W. C. Bond, 12 November 1852 (William Cranch Bond Papers, Harvard University Archives).

10. Asaph Hall, Address, AAAS, *Proceedings* 29 (1880): 113-14. Hall himself did not feel competent to test the nebular hypothesis; Hall to Spencer F. Baird, 19 March 1881 (Official Incoming Correspondence, SIA).

11. For biographical sketches of Hinrichs, see *Appletons' Cyclopaedia of American Biography*, 3:215; and Carl A. Zapffe, "Gustavus Hinrichs, Precursor of Mendeleev," *Isis* 60 (Winter 1969): 462-64. In 1875 Trowbridge listed his occupation as "Teacher & Mechanic" in a questionnaire sent out by the Smithsonian Institution ("Answers to Circulars: Smithsonian

Correspondents: Subjects in Which Interested," SIA); on his work and education, see Trowbridge to Joseph Henry, 28 July 1861, and Trowbridge to Spencer F. Baird, 17 June 1881 (Official Incoming Correspondence, SIA). Ennis had formerly taught science in the United States Military Academy, and in the 1870s he tried unsuccessfully to obtain a position at the Naval Observatory in Washington. See Ennis to Simon Newcomb, 12 February 1878 (Simon Newcomb Papers, Library of Congress). On Chase, see Marjory Hendricks Davis' article in the *DAB*, 4:27.

12. Jacob Ennis, *The Origin of the Stars, and the Causes of Their Motions and Their Light* (New York: D. Appleton, 1867), pts. 3-4; Ennis, "The Necessity and Velocity of Nebular Rotation," Academy of Natural Sciences of Philadelphia, *Proceedings*, 1867, pp. 87-93; Ennis, "The Discovery of the Force Which Originally Imparted All Their Motions to All the Stars," AAAS, *Proceedings* 19 (1870): 25-39; Ennis, "The Velocity of Nebular Rotation," ibid., pp. 40-47; Ennis, "The Four Great Eras of Modern Astronomy," ibid. 20 (1871): 103-21; Ennis, "Physical and Mathematical Principles of the Nebular Theory," *Philosophical Magazine*, 5th ser., 3 (April 1877): 262-71; Ennis, "The Origin of the Power Which Causes the Stellar Radiations," ibid. 6 (September 1878): 216-25. Ennis' work was generally not well received; see [Chauncey Wright], "Ennis on the Origin of the Stars," *Nation* 4 (21 March 1867): 231-32; [Wright], "Ennis's *Origin of the Stars*," *North American Review* 104 (April 1867): 618-26; and Stephen Alexander to Spencer F. Baird, [1881], with a note by Charles A. Young (Official Incoming Correspondence, SIA).

13. Daniel Kirkwood, "On Certain Harmonies of the Solar System," *AJS*, 2nd ser., 38 (July 1864): 2; Kirkwood, "On the Nebular Hypothesis, and the Approximate Commensurability of the Planetary Periods," Royal Astronomical Society, *Monthly Notices* 29 (8 January 1869): 96-97.

14. Simon Newcomb, *Popular Astronomy* (New York: Harper & Brothers, 1878), p. 498.

15. Daniel Kirkwood, "On the Theory of Meteors," AAAS, *Proceedings* 15 (1866): 13-14; Kirkwood, "On the Nebular Hypothesis," pp. 96-102; Kirkwood, "On the Mass of Asteroids between Mars and Jupiter," APS, *Proceedings* 11 (19 August 1870): 498, reprinted in the *AJS*, 3rd ser., 1 (January 1871): 71; Kirkwood, "De l'hypothèse des nébuleuses et de la commensurabilité approximative des périodes planétaires," *Les Mondes* 25 (10 August 1871): 118-26; Kirkwood, "On the Distribution of the Asteroids," AAAS, *Proceedings* 24 (1875): 74-77; Kirkwood, "The Asteroids between Mars and Jupiter," Smithsonian Institution, *Annual Report*, 1876, pp. 368-71; Kirkwood, "The Zone of Asteroids and the Ring of Saturn," APS, *Proceedings* 21 (5 October 1883): 263-66; Kirkwood, *The Asteroids, or Minor Planets between Mars and Jupiter* (Philadelphia: J. B. Lippincott, 1888), pp. 41-46. See also Richard A. Proctor, "The Asteroids and the Nebular Hypothesis," *Student and Intellectual Observer* 4 (1870): 14-25.

16. Jacques Babinet, "Note sur un point de la Cosmogonie de Laplace," Académie des Sciences, *Comptes rendus* 52 (1861): 481-84.

17. Daniel Kirkwood, "The Cosmogony of Laplace," APS, *Proceedings* 18 (19 September 1879): 326; reprinted in the *Observatory* 3 (1 May 1880): 409-12.

18. David Trowbridge, "On the Nebular Hypothesis," *AJS*, 2nd ser., 38 (November 1864): 353.

19. Pierre Simon Laplace, *The System of the World*, trans. Henry H. Harte (Dublin: University Press, 1830), 2:357.

20. Kirkwood, "The Cosmogony of Laplace," p. 326.

21. Newcomb, *Popular Astronomy*, p. 515.

22. Ibid., p. 496; Davidson's copy is in the main library of the University of California, Berkeley.

23. Kirkwood, "The Cosmogony of Laplace," pp. 324-26.

24. Daniel Kirkwood, "On the Origin of Planets," APS, *Proceedings* 19 (2 April 1880): 15, reprinted in the *Observatory* 3 (1 June 1880): 446-47; Kirkwood, "The Limits of Stability of Nebulous Planets, and the Consequences Resulting from Their Mutual Relations," APS, *Proceedings* 22 (21 November 1884): 108. See also John N. Stockwell, "Theory of the Mutual Perturbations of Planets Moving at the Same Mean Distance from the Sun, and Its Bearing on the Constitution of Saturn's Ring and the Cosmogony of Laplace," *Astronomical Journal* 24 (4 March 1904): 38.

25. Kirkwood, "On Certain Harmonies of the Solar System," p. 3; Gustavus Hinrichs, "The Density, Rotation and Relative Age of the Planets," *AJS*, 2nd ser., 37 (January 1864): 48-56; David Trowbridge, "On the Nebular Hypothesis," ibid., 39 (January 1865): 25-27. See also William H. Pickering, "The Nebular Hypothesis," *Encyclopedia Americana* (New York: Americana Co., 1904), vol. 11 (no pagination).

26. Daniel Kirkwood, "On the Nebular Hypothesis," *AJS*, 2nd ser., 30 (September 1860): 177-78; Hinrichs, "The Density, Rotation and Relative Age of the Planets," p. 52; Trowbridge, "On the Nebular Hypothesis," pp. 40-41. See also Elias Loomis, *A Treatise on Astronomy* (New York: Harper & Brothers, 1865), p. 315.

27. Pliny Earle Chase, "Criteria of the Nebular Hypothesis," APS, *Proceedings* 17 (1 March 1878): 342-44; Chase, "On the Nebular Hypothesis," *Philosophical Magazine*, 5th ser., 5 (May 1878): 362-63; Chase, "The Moons of Mars, and the Nebular Hypothesis," *Analyst* 8 (March 1881): 56-57; Daniel Kirkwood, "Does the Motion of the Inner Satellite of Mars Disprove the Nebular Hypothesis?" *AJS*, 3rd ser., 14 (October 1877): 327-28; Kirkwood, "The Satellites of Mars and the Nebular Hypothesis," *Observatory* 1 (1 January 1878): 280-82. See also Pickering, "The Nebular Hypothesis"; and G. H. Darwin, "The Evolution of Satellites," *Atlantic Monthly* 81 (April 1898): 452-53.

28. For historical accounts of the criticisms and modifications of the nebular hypothesis, see Agnes M. Clerke, *Modern Cosmogonies* (London: Adam and Charles Black, 1905), chaps. 3-4; Clerke, *A Popular History of Astronomy during the Nineteenth Century* (4th ed.; London: Adam and Charles Black, 1902), chap. 9; and J. Ellard Gore, *The Visible Universe: Chapters on the Origin and Construction of the Universe* (London: Crosby Lockwood & Son, 1893), chap. 1. The last account is based on C. Wolf, *Les Hypothèses cosmogoniques: Examen des théories scientifiques modernes sur l'origine des mondes, suivi de la traduction de la théorie du ciel de Kant* (Paris: Gauthier-Villars, 1886), chaps. 3-4.

29. Extract from a letter lost in a fire from Simon Newcomb to T. J. J. See, 1889 (T. J. J. See Papers, Library of Congress). See also See to Newcomb, 2 December 1889 (Simon Newcomb Papers, Library of Congress); and Newcomb, "Meteoric Showers," *North American Review* 107 (July 1868): 50.

30. Clerke, *Popular History of Astronomy*, pp. 310-11.

31. Ibid., pp. 310-12; J. Ellard Gore, "The Meteoritic Hypothesis," *Popular Science Monthly* 39 (July 1891): 344-48.

32. J. Homer Lane, "On the Theoretical Temperature of the Sun; under the Hypothesis of a Gaseous Mass Maintaining Its Volume by Its Internal Heat, and Depending on the Laws of Gases as Known to Terrestrial Experiment," *AJS*, 2nd ser., 50 (July 1870): 57-74; read before the National Academy of Sciences in April 1869. As Cleveland Abbe pointed out, Lane apparently failed to see the implications of his discovery; see Abbe, "Memoir of Jonathan Homer Lane, 1819-1880," National Academy of Sciences, *Biographical Memoirs* 3 (1895): 260. See also A. Pannekoek, *A History of Astronomy* (New York: Interscience Publishers, 1961), pp. 397-98.

33. Chauncey Wright to Mrs. J. P. Lesley, 22 March 1870, *Letters of Chauncey Wright*, ed. James Bradley Thayer (Cambridge: John Wilson & Son, 1878), p. 176.

34. [Chauncey Wright], "A Physical Theory of the Universe," *North American Review* 99 (July 1864): 1-33; reprinted in Wright, *Philosophical Discussions* (New York: Henry Holt, 1878), pp. 1-34. See also [Wright], "The Philosophy of Herbert Spencer," *North American Review* 100 (April 1865): 423-76, reprinted in *Philosophical Discussions*, pp. 43-96; [Wright], "Ennis on the Origin of the Stars," pp. 231-32; and [Wright], "Ennis's *Origin of the Stars*," pp. 618-26. For comments on Wright's attitude toward the nebular hypothesis, see John Fiske, *Darwinism and Other Essays* (London: Macmillan, 1879), pp. 96-99; Edward H. Madden, *Chauncey Wright and the Foundations of Pragmatism* (Seattle: University of Washington Press, 1963), pp. 87-90; Madden, *Chauncey Wright* (New York: Washington Square Press, 1964), pp. 34-38; and Philip P. Wiener,

Evolution and the Founders of Pragmatism (New York: Harper Torchbooks, 1965), p. 62.

35. J. B. Stallo, *The Concepts and Theories of Modern Physics*, ed. Percy W. Bridgman (Cambridge: Belknap Press of Harvard University Press, 1960), pp. 285-300; reproduced from the 3rd American ed., 1888. For another instance of a favorable American response to the meteoric cosmogony, see [James Davenport Whelpley], "Birth of the Solar System: A New Theory," *Atlantic Monthly* 23 (February 1869): 221-28.

36. T. C. Chamberlin, "A Group of Hypotheses Bearing on Climatic Changes," *Journal of Geology* 5 (October-November 1897): 653-83; Chamberlin, "An Attempt to Test the Nebular Hypothesis by the Relations of Masses and Momenta," ibid. 8 (January-February 1900): 58-73; F. R. Moulton, "An Attempt to Test the Nebular Hypothesis by an Appeal to the Laws of Dynamics," *Astrophysical Journal* 11 (March 1900): 103-30; Chamberlin and Moulton, "Certain Recent Attempts to Test the Nebular Hypothesis," *Science*, new ser., 12 (10 August 1900): 201-8; Chamberlin and Moulton, "The Development of the Planetesimal Hypothesis," ibid., new ser., 30 (5 November 1909): 642-45. Susan Schultz's recently completed dissertation on Chamberlin (University of Wisconsin) devotes a chapter to the development of his cosmogony.

37. Chamberlin and Moulton, "Certain Recent Attempts to Test the Nebular Hypothesis," p. 207; Chamberlin, "Fundamental Problems of Geology," Carnegie Institution of Washington, *Year Book*, 3 (1904): 195-258; Moulton, "On the Evolution of the Solar System," *Astrophysical Journal* 22 (October 1905): 165-81; Chamberlin and Moulton, "The Planetesimal Hypothesis," 642-45; Chamberlin and Others, *Contributions to Cosmogony and the Fundamental Problems of Geology: The Tidal and Other Problems*, Carnegie Institution of Washington, Publication no. 107 (Washington: Carnegie Institution of Washington, 1909).

38. Pannekoek, *History of Astronomy*, p. 401; Robert Jastrow and A. G. W. Cameron, eds., *Origin of the Solar System* (New York: Academic Press, 1963), p. vii. T. J. J. See, an astronomer at the United States Naval Observatory on Mare Island, California, championed a somewhat different hypothesis of the origin of the solar system from a spiral nebula, which he labeled the "capture theory." See T. J. J. See, "On the Cause of the Remarkable Circularity of the Orbits of the Planets and Satellites and on the Origin of the Planetary System," *Astronomische Nachrichten* 180 (1909): 185-94, reprinted in *Popular Astronomy* 17 (May 1909): 263-72; See, "The Laws of Cosmical Evolution and the Extension of the Solar System beyond Neptune," Astronomical Society of the Pacific, *Publications* 21 (10 April 1909): 60-71; See, "The Past History of the Earth as Inferred from the Mode of Formation of the Solar System," APS, *Proceedings* 48 (January-April 1909): 119-25; See, "Results of Recent Researches in Cosmical Evolution,"

ibid. 49 (July 1910): 207-21; and See, "The New Cosmogony," ibid. 50 (May-August 1911): 261-65.

39. J. H. Jeans, *The Nebular Hypothesis and Modern Cosmogony* (Oxford: Clarendon Press, 1923), pp. 26-27. See also Jeans, "Present Position of the Nebular Hypothesis," *Scientific American Supplement* 88 (11 October 1919): 215.

40. See H. P. Berlage, *The Origin of the Solar System,* Pergamon International Popular Science Series (Oxford: Pergamon Press, 1968), p. 65. Gerard P. Kuiper, "The Formation of the Planets," Royal Astronomical Society of Canada, *Journal* 50 (March-April 1956): 57-68; (May-June 1956): 105-21; (July-August 1956): 158-76. Gerald James Whitrow, "The Nebular Hypothesis of Kant and Laplace," 12th Congrès International d'Histoire des Sciences, *Actes* (Paris, 1968), III B, 175-80. Among the objections to encounter theories were "that 99% of the mass drawn from the sun would fall back into it as the intruding star receded," and "that the line of droplets of protoplanetary material drawn out of tidal attractions, when captured by the sun, will be in elongated orbits of large eccentricity" (Jastrow and Cameron, *Origin of the Solar System,* p. vii).

CHAPTER VII

1. In my discussion of American theology in the early nineteenth century I have benefited greatly from the chapter on "The Religious Mind and Science" in John Arlo De Jong, "American Attitudes toward Evolution before Darwin" (Ph.D. diss., State University of Iowa, 1962).

2. See Stow Persons, "Evolution and Theology in America," *Evolutionary Thought in America,* ed. Stow Persons (New York: George Braziller, 1956), pp. 422-23; and George H. Daniels, *American Science in the Age of Jackson* (New York: Columbia University Press, 1968), p. 53.

3. William Whewell, *Astronomy and General Physics Considered with Reference to Natural Theology* (5th ed.; London: William Pickering, 1836), pp. 184, 189-91. These comments on the nebular hypothesis were reprinted in Whewell's *Indications of the Creator* (London: John W. Parker, 1845), pp. 9-19.

4. William Buckland, *Geology and Mineralogy Considered with Reference to Natural Theology* (London: William Pickering, 1836), 1:40.

5. Thomas Chalmers, *On the Power, Wisdom, and Goodness of God as Manifested in the Adaptation of External Nature to the Moral and Intellectual Constitution of Man* (London: William Pickering, 1835), 1:30-32.

6. J. P. N[ichol], "State of Discovery and Speculation concerning the Nebulae," *Westminster Review* 25 (July 1836): 406-8.

7. J. P. Nichol, *Views of the Architecture of the Heavens* (2nd ed.; New York: Dayton & Newman, 1842), pp. 103-5.

8. John Le Conte, "The Nebular Hypothesis," *Popular Science Monthly* 2 (April 1873): 655.

9. "The Nebular Hypothesis," *Southern Quarterly Review* 10 (July 1846): 228. See also [J. E. Ford], "The Nebular Theory," *Williams Monthly Miscellany* 1 (1844):14-15.

10. "The Nebular Hypothesis," *Southern Quarterly Review*, new ser., 1 (April 1856): 110-11.

11. [Daniel Kirkwood], "The Nebular Hypothesis," *Presbyterian Quarterly Review*, 2 (March 1854): 544.

12. "The Nebular Hypothesis," *Southern Quarterly Review* (1856), pp. 115-16.

13. [O. M. Mitchel], "Lord Rosse's Discoveries and Their Influence on the Nebular Hypothesis," *Sidereal Messenger* 1 (February 1847): 76; Mitchel, *The Astronomy of the Bible* (New York: Blakeman & Mason, 1863), pp. 135, 159.

14. "The Nebular Hypothesis," *Southern Quarterly Review* (1846), p. 240.

15. [Alexis Caswell], "Architecture of the Heavens," *Christian Review* 6 (December 1841): 620.

16. Edward Hitchcock, *Religious Truth, Illustrated from Science, in Addresses and Sermons on Special Occasions* (Boston: Phillips, Sampson, 1857), p. 33; Hitchcock, *The Religion of Geology and Its Connected Sciences* (Boston: Phillips, Sampson, 1857), pp. 286-88, 293-95, 301.

17. [Benjamin Peirce], "Bowditch's Translation of the *Mécanique Céleste*," *North American Review* 48 (January 1839): 174.

18. Benjamin Peirce to James D. Dana, n.d. [1851] (James Dwight Dana Correspondence, Yale University). This statement was printed in Peirce, "On the Constitution of Saturn's Ring," *AJS*, 2nd ser., 12 (July 1851): 106-8, but not in the same article published in the AAAS, *Proceedings* 5 (1851): 18-22.

19. Benjamin Peirce, "On the Constitution of Saturn's Ring," *Astronomical Journal* 2 (16 June 1851): 19.

20. Benjamin Peirce, *Ideality in the Physical Sciences* (Boston: Little, Brown, 1881), pp. 53-54. Peirce first delivered these lectures at the Lowell Institute in Boston in February and March 1879; he repeated them in January and February of the following year at the Peabody Institute in Baltimore.

21. Ibid., pp. 70-71.

22. George Taylor, *The Indications of the Creator; or, The Natural Evidences of Final Cause* (New York: Charles Scribner, 1851), pts. 1-2 and *passim*. For biographical information, see "George Taylor," *Dictionary of the United States Congress*, ed. Charles Lanman (Philadelphia: J. B. Lippincott, 1859), p. 466.

23. Review of *The Indications of the Creator; or, The Natural Evidences of Final Cause*, by George Taylor, *Princeton Review* 24 (January 1852): 143-44.

24. [Kirkwood], "The Nebular Hypothesis," pp. 544-46.

25. "The Logical Relations of Religion and Natural Science," *Princeton Review* 32 (October 1860): 579.

26. [Stephen Alexander], "On the Nebular Hypothesis," *Annual of Scientific Discovery*, 1857, pp. 374-75. This paper was read at the 1856 meetings of the AAAS in Albany, but did not appear in the *Proceedings* of those meetings.

CHAPTER VIII

1. Matthew F. Maury to the Reverend Mr. Field, 22 January 1855 (Records of the Naval Observatory, Letters Sent, vol. 11). Maury had no difficulty accepting the nebular hypothesis. He treated it favorably in an unpublished work on "Astronomy" begun in 1866, of which the galley proofs are extant (Matthew F. Maury Papers, Library of Congress).

2. John Arlo De Jong, "American Attitudes toward Evolution before Darwin" (Ph.D. diss., State University of Iowa, 1962), p. 53. On the harmonization of science and the Bible, see ibid., pp. 47-53.

3. Charles Woodruff Shields, *Philosophia Ultima: Or Science of the Sciences*, vol. 1 (3rd ed.; New York: Charles Scribner's Sons, 1888), p. 138. Shields himself was a harmonizer of some note. In 1865 Princeton had named him "professor of the harmony of science and revealed religion," one of the first such appointments in an American college.

4. William B. Hayden, *Science and Revelation; or, The Bearing of Modern Scientific Developments upon the Interpretation of the First Eleven Chapters of Genesis* (Boston: Otis Clapp, 1852), p. 77. On American attitudes toward developments in geology in the first half of the nineteenth century, see Conrad Wright, "The Religion of Geology," *New England Quarterly* 14 (June 1941): 335-58; and the section on "Mosaic Geology in America" in Francis C. Haber, *The Age of the World: Moses to Darwin* (Baltimore, Md.: Johns Hopkins Press, 1959), pp. 250-64.

5. See Thomas Chalmers, "Remarks on Cuvier's Theory of the Earth; in extracts from a review of that theory which was contributed to 'The Christian Instructor' in 1814," *The Select Works of Thomas Chalmers* (New York: Robert Carter & Brothers, 1850), 1:180-93; Chalmers, *On the Miraculous and Internal Evidences of the Christian Revelation and the Authority of Its Records* (New York: Robert Carter & Brothers, 1859), 1:298-310; William Buckland, *Vindiciae Geologicae; or the Connexion of Geology with Religion Explained*, an inaugural lecture delivered before the University of Oxford, 15 May 1819 (Oxford: University Press, 1820), pp.

31-33; Buckland, *Geology and Mineralogy Considered with Reference to Natural Theology* (London: William Pickering, 1836), 1:8-33; Edward Hitchcock, "The Connection between Geology and the Mosaic History of the Creation," *Biblical Repository and Quarterly Observer* 5 (April 1835): 439-51; Hitchcock, *Elementary Geology* (8th ed.; New York: Mark H. Newman, 1847; first published in 1840), pp. 284-302; and Hitchcock, *The Religion of Geology and Its Connected Sciences* (Boston: Phillips, Sampson, 1857; first published in 1851), pp. 33-70. For an excellent study of the development of Hitchcock's views on Genesis, see Stanley M. Guralnick, "Geology and Religion before Darwin: The Case of Edward Hitchcock, Theologian and Geologist (1793-1864)," *Isis* 63 (December 1972): 529-43. As Guralnick points out, Hitchcock did not insist that the days of creation week necessarily be twenty-four hours long.

6. Hitchcock, *Elementary Geology*, p. 296.

7. The preference of concerned individuals for Chalmers' method of harmonizing geology and revelation over all others is frequently mentioned in contemporary literature. See Hayden, *Science and Revelation*, p. 80; and Michael Jacobs, "The Consistency of the Discoveries of Geology with the Teachings of Revelation," *Evangelical Review* 1 (January 1850): 375. Even Hugh Miller, who championed a different method, conceded that Chalmers' theory "may, indeed, still be regarded as the most popular of the various existing schemes"; Miller, *The Testimony of the Rocks; or, Geology in Its Bearings on the Two Theologies, Natural and Revealed* (Boston: Gould & Lincoln, 1857), p. 143.

8. John Pye Smith, *On the Relation between the Holy Scriptures and Some Parts of Geological Science* (New York: D. Appleton, 1840), pp. 233-35. The first English edition of this book was published in 1839.

9. See Benjamin Silliman, "Suggestions Relative to the Philosophy of Geology as Deduced from the Facts and to the Consistency of Both the Facts and Theory of This Science with Sacred History," an appendix to Robert Bakewell, *An Introduction to Geology* (3rd American ed.; New Haven, Conn.: B. and W. Noyes, 1839), pp. 461-579. Silliman's views can also be found in his supplement to the second American edition of Bakewell (1833). Silliman was greatly influenced by the writings of the Scottish geologist, Robert Jameson; see [Robert Jameson], "Remarks on some of Baron Cuvier's Lectures on the History of the Natural Sciences, in reference to the Scientific Knowledge of the Egyptians; of the source from whence Moses derived his Cosmogony, and the general agreement of that Cosmogony with Modern Geology," *Edinburgh New Philosophical Journal* 13 (July 1832): 41-75; reprinted in part in *AJS* 25 (January 1834): 26-41. For a good account of Hugh Miller's ideas on the harmony of Genesis and geology, see his last work, *The Testimony of the Rocks*, pp. 141-78. See also J[oseph] C[lark], "Hugh Miller as a Geologist," *Mercersburg Review* 9 (October 1857): 601-32.

10. Silliman, "Suggestions Relative to the Philosophy of Geology," pp. 536-39, 566-73.

11. At least one partisan of this theory, a former student of Silliman's at Yale, claimed that it was "the most generally received" method of reconciling science and the Bible, but he was apparently exaggerating. See W. F., "Geology and Scripture," *Universalist Quarterly and General Review* 2 (October 1845): 375.

12. James D. Dana, "Memoir of Arnold Guyot, 1807-1884," National Academy of Sciences, *Biographical Memoirs*, 2 (1886): 309-47.

13. Ibid., pp. 314-15, 326; see especially Guyot's account of the origin of his views in a letter to Dana, 6 December 1856, ibid., pp. 327-28. See also Arnold Guyot, *The Earth and Man: Lectures on Comparative Physical Geography, in Its Relation to the History of Mankind*, trans. C. C. Felton (Boston: Gould, Kendall, & Lincoln, 1849), p. 93.

14. Arnold Guyot, *Creation: or, The Biblical Cosmogony in the Light of Modern Science* (Edinburgh: T. and T. Clark, [1883]), p. vii.

15. Ibid., p. 135 and *passim*.

16. Ibid., pp. viii-x; Arnold Guyot, "The Mosaic Cosmogony and Modern Science Reconciled," *Evening Post* (New York), 6, 12, 15, and 23 March 1852 (no pagination); John O. Means, "The Narrative of the Creation in Genesis," *Bibliotheca Sacra* 12 (January 1855): 83-130 and (April 1855): 323-38; Guyot, "Cosmogony and the Bible; or, The Biblical Account of Creation in the Light of Modern Science," *History, Essays, Orations, and Other Documents of the Sixth General Conference of the Evangelical Alliance, Held in New York, October 2-12, 1873* (New York: Harper & Brothers, 1874), pp. 276-87, 319.

17. Guyot to Dana, 15 November 1858 (James Dwight Dana Correspondence, Yale University).

18. Guyot to Dana, 4 February 1881 (ibid.).

19. James D. Dana, "Creation; or the Biblical Cosmogony in the Light of Modern Science," *Bibliotheca Sacra* 42 (April 1885): 204, 221.

20. James D. Dana to Arnold Guyot, 30 January 1851, quoted in Daniel C. Gilman, *The Life of James Dwight Dana* (New York: Harper & Brothers, 1899), pp. 326-27. Dana's "Professor Mitchell" was the Cincinnati astronomer, Ormsby MacKnight Mitchel, who, for almost two decades prior to the outbreak of the Civil War, toured the country lecturing on astronomy. In one of his lectures, entitled "The Mosaic Account of Creation Compared with the Cosmogony of the Universe as Revealed in the Actual Condition of Astronomy," he proposed an interpretation of Genesis very similar to Guyot's, and, like it, based largely on the nebular hypothesis. See O. M. Mitchel, *The Astronomy of the Bible* (New York: Blakeman & Mason, 1863), pp. 173-211.

21. For recent discussions of the Lewis-Dana debate, see Morgan B. Sherwood, "Genesis, Evolution, and Geology in America before Darwin:

The Dana-Lewis Controversy, 1856-1857," in *Toward a History of Geology*, ed. Cecil J. Schneer (Cambridge, Mass.: M.I.T. Press, 1969), pp. 305-16; Franklin D. Steen, "Tayler Lewis on Scripture: A Defense of Revelation and Creation in Nineteenth Century America" (Ph.D. diss., Westminster Theological Seminary, 1971); and John C. Greene, "Science and Religion," in *The Rise of Adventism*, ed. Edwin S. Gaustad (New York: Harper & Row, 1974), pp. 50-69.

22. Tayler Lewis, *The Six Days of Creation; or, The Scriptural Cosmology, with the Ancient Idea of Time-Worlds, in Distinction from Worlds in Space* (Schenectady, N.Y.: G. Y. Van Debogert, 1855), pp. 1-11.

23. Ibid., pp. 60, 140.

24. Ibid., pp. 146-47.

25. James D. Dana, "Science and the Bible," *Bibliotheca Sacra* 13 (January 1856): 89, 110, 116, and *passim*.

26. Bond to Dana, 18 March 1856 (James Dwight Dana Correspondence).

27. Richard S. McCulloh to Dana, 11 February 1856 (James Dwight Dana Correspondence). McCulloh was professor of natural and experimental philosophy and chemistry in Columbia College.

28. Joy to Dana, 18 February 1856 (James Dwight Dana Correspondence).

29. James D. Dana, "Science and the Bible: Number II," *Bibliotheca Sacra* 13 (July 1856): 631-56; Dana to Peirce, 4 July 1856 (Benjamin Peirce Papers, Harvard University).

30. Tayler Lewis, *The Bible and Science; or, The World-Problem* (Schenectady, N.Y.: G. Y. Van Debogert, 1856), p. iii.

31. Dana to Peirce, 20 July 1856 (Benjamin Peirce Papers).

32. Lewis, *The Bible and Science*, pp. iv, 215-17.

33. Ibid., pp. 251-58, 267.

34. James D. Dana, "Science and the Bible: Number III," *Bibliotheca Sacra* 14 (April 1857): 388-413 and (July 1857): 461-524.

35. Ibid., pp. 476-77, 521-22.

36. Lewis was not, however, without his supporters. The *Mercersburg Review*, a publication of the German Reformed church, had nothing but praise for his writings on Genesis and for his scholarly ability. "In patient and laborious scholarship, in profound and comprehensive thought, in honest and intense earnestness, in intelligent and vigorous grasp of any subject germaine to his mind, Prof. Lewis has few equals and perhaps no superior in this country." C[lark], "Hugh Miller as a Geologist," pp. 621-22.

37. Lewis to Dana, 13 March 1871 (James Dwight Dana Correspondence). In this reply to a letter from Dana, Lewis says: "Your letter is conciliatory. It is such as one professed Christian should write to another, and I am willing to meet it in the same spirit. The feeling which I had before

had grown weaker in time. It was almost gone; and your letter, I think, has wholly extinguished it." See also Dana's letter to Guyot, 30 January 1875, telling his old friend that he has now adopted "essentially the view [of Genesis] taken by Professor Tayler Lewis of Schenectady, whom I once criticised on account of it." Gilman, *Life of James Dwight Dana*, pp. 330-31.

38. Dawson to Dana, 17 March 1856 (James Dwight Dana Correspondence).

39. J. W. Dawson, *Archaia; or, Studies of the Cosmogony and Natural History of the Hebrew Scriptures* (Montreal: B. Dawson & Son, 1860), pp. 89-96. See also Charles F. O'Brien's recent biography of Dawson, *Sir William Dawson: A Life in Science and Religion* (Philadelphia: American Philosophical Society, 1971), which does not, however, mention the influence of Guyot and Dana on Dawson's view of Genesis.

40. James D. Dana, *Manual of Geology* (rev. ed.; Philadelphia: Theodore Bliss, 1865), pp. 741-44. The first edition appeared in 1863.

41. Joseph P. Thompson, *Man in Genesis and in Geology; or, The Biblical Account of Man's Creation, Tested by Scientific Theories of His Origin and Antiquity* (New York: Samuel R. Wells, 1870), p. vi. Though Thompson speaks favorably of the nebular hypothesis in this volume (pp. 15-16), he had earlier treated it less kindly; see his "The Permanence of Christianity in the Intention of Its Founder," *Bibliotheca Sacra* 22 (April 1865): 239.

42. James McCosh, *Development: What It Can Do and What It Cannot Do* (New York: Charles Scribner's Sons, 1883), pp. 33-34.

43. E. P. Barrows, "The Mosaic Six Days and Geology," *Bibliotheca Sacra* 14 (January 1857): 93-97. The same argument was made by one of Tayler Lewis' disciples, Francis W. Upham, who maintained that Guyot's interpretation of Genesis, though "brilliant . . . in itself," could not "be made philologically to coincide with the Mosaic history"; [Francis W. Upham], *The Debate between the Church and Science; or, The Ancient Hebraic Idea of the Six Days of Creation*, with an essay on the literary character of Tayler Lewis (Andover, Mass.: Warren F. Draper, 1860), p. 81. For later criticism of Guyot's loose translations, see the anonymous review of *Creation; or, The Biblical Cosmogony in the Light of Modern Science*, by Arnold Guyot, *New Englander* 43 (July 1884): 591-94; and S. R. Driver, "The Cosmogony of Genesis," *Andover Review* 8 (December 1887): 639-49.

44. Thomas A. Davies, *Cosmogony, or the Mysteries of Creation* (New York: Rudd & Carleton, 1857), pp. 9, 305-6, 311. For biographical information on Davies, who served as a Union general in the Civil War, see the *National Cyclopaedia of American Biography*, 3:26-27. For Dana's reaction to Davies' book, see [James D. Dana], "The Mosaic Cosmogony," *New Englander* 16 (February 1858): 79.

45. Hiram Mattison, *High-School Astronomy* (New York: Mason Brothers, 1858), pp. 157-58. This book, first published in 1853, was a revision of Mattison's earlier *Elementary Astronomy* (1847). See James R. Joy's biographical sketch of Mattison in the *DAB*, 12:423.

46. C. W. Goodwin, "The Mosaic Cosmogony," *Recent Inquiries in Theology, by Eminent English Churchmen; Being "Essays and Reviews,"* with an introduction by Frederick H. Hedge (Boston: Walker, Wise, 1860), p. 238.

47. [E. A. Walker], "The First Document of Genesis," *New Englander* 19 (July 1861): 542. See also the reply to Goodwin by G. Rorison, "The Creative Week," *Replies to "Essays and Reviews"* (Oxford and London: John Henry and James Parker, 1862), pp. 277-345.

48. T[homas] H[ill], "The First Chapter of Genesis," *Christian Examiner* 59 (November 1855): 387, 392-93. This exposition of Peirce's views on Genesis was published with Peirce's permission. See also Benjamin Peirce, *Ideality in the Physical Sciences* (Boston: Little, Brown, 1881), pp. 46, 50. For Gray's views on science and revelation, see his review of *Manual of Geology*, by James D. Dana, *North American Review* 97 (October 1863): 375; and A. Hunter Dupree, *Asa Gray, 1810-1888* (Cambridge, Mass.: Harvard University Press, 1959), p. 136.

49. "The Logical Relations of Religion and Natural Science," *Princeton Review* 32 (October 1860): 579.

50. Eli Bowen, *The Physical History of the Creation of the Earth and Its Inhabitants; or, A Vindication of the Cosmogony of the Bible from the Assaults of Modern Science* (Philadelphia: W. S. Laird, 1861), p. 38.

51. "The Nebular Hypothesis," *Southern Quarterly Review* 10 (July 1846): 242. Paul A. Chadbourne, of Williams College, made a similar remark in a lecture at the Lowell Institute in 1855. *Lectures on Natural Theology; or, Nature and the Bible from the Same Author* (New York: G. P. Putnam & Sons, 1871), pp. 304-5.

52. "The Mosaic Account of Creation, Scientific," *Presbyterian Quarterly Review* 7 (July 1858): 140-41. Some persons went so far as to argue that if the Mosaic account of creation were not true, then the nebular hypothesis must necessarily be false. See Charles B. Warring, *The Mosaic Account of Creation, the Miracle of To-Day; or, New Witnesses to the Oneness of Genesis and Science* (New York: J. W. Schermerhorn, 1875), pp. 115, 244.

53. Andrew D. White, *A History of the Warfare of Science with Theology in Christendom* (New York: George Braziller, 1955), 1:18-19.

54. This statement holds despite occasional allusions to the contrary made in the post-Darwinian period. See, for example, Benjamin A. Gould, "Address of the President," *AAAS, Proceedings* 18 (1869): 20-21; Asa Gray, *Natural Science and Religion* (New York: Charles Scribner's Sons, 1880), pp. 6-7; and White, *Warfare of Science with Theology*, 1:17.

CHAPTER IX

1. Charles Darwin, *On the Origin of Species,* a facsimile of the first edition with an introduction by Ernst Mayr (Cambridge, Mass.: Harvard University Press, 1966).

2. E. D. Cope, *The Origin of the Fittest: Essays on Evolution* (New York: D. Appleton, 1887), p. 2, from an article entitled "Evolution and Its Consequences," first published in the *Penn Monthly Magazine,* May 1872.

3. Louis Agassiz, "Evolution and the Permanence of Type," *Atlantic Monthly* 33 (January 1874): 95.

4. [William Hayes Ward], "Do Our Colleges Teach Evolution?" *Independent* 31 (18 December 1879): 14-15; Ward, "Evolution and Christianity," ibid. 32 (29 January 1880): 4. The three naturalists named by the *Observer* as not believing in evolution were A. S. Packard, Asa Gray, and James Dwight Dana, all of whom by this time acknowledged some form of evolution. It should be noted that the teaching of evolution was not limited to the North. In a speech before the Presbyterian Synod of South Carolina in October 1884, Dr. James Woodrow mentioned a number of Southern schools where evolution was being taught: the University of Virginia, Davidson College in North Carolina, Wofford College in South Carolina, the University of Georgia, Southwestern Presbyterian University in Tennessee, Central University in Kentucky, and the University of North Carolina. Woodrow, "Speech before the Synod of South Carolina," in *Dr. James Woodrow As Seen by His Friends,* ed. Marion W. Woodrow (Columbia, S.C.: R. L. Bryan Co., 1909), pp. 752-54. See also William H. Brewer's letter to Woodrow, 21 October 1884, ibid., pp. 789-91, in which the Yale professor discusses the popularity of evolution among American naturalists.

5. George Daniels, ed., *Darwinism Comes to America* (Waltham, Mass.: Blaisdell Publishing Co., 1968), p. 75. On the American Neo-Lamarckians, see also Edward J. Pfeifer, "The Reception of Darwinism in the United States, 1859-1880" (Ph.D. diss., Brown University, 1957), pp. 160-76.

6. Daniels, *Darwinism Comes to America,* p. 95.

7. Michael McGiffert, "Christian Darwinism: The Partnership of Asa Gray and George Frederick Wright, 1874-1881" (Ph.D. diss., Yale University, 1958), p. 3. According to Edward J. Pfeifer, the process of incorporating organic evolution into "traditional patterns of thought" took only about twenty years ("The Reception of Darwinism in the United States," p. 192).

8. William G. McLoughlin, Jr., *Billy Sunday Was His Real Name* (Chicago: University of Chicago Press, 1955), p. 119.

9. In his influential pioneering study of "The Impact of the Doctrine of Evolution on American Thought" (Ph.D. diss., Harvard University, 1934), p. 271, Bert James Loewenberg explains the initial "denunciation and rejection" of Darwinism as resulting from the fact that "evolution was so

alien an idea and so at variance with the accepted formulas in science, philosophy and theology that an immediate acceptance could not be expected." The evidence, as I see it, does not support this explanation. See also Loewenberg's three published articles on Darwinism in America: "The Reaction of American Scientists to Darwinism," *American Historical Review* 38 (July 1933): 687-701; "The Controversy over Evolution in New England, 1859-1873," *New England Quarterly* 8 (June 1935): 232-57; and "Darwinism Comes to America, 1859-1900," *Mississippi Valley Historical Review* 28 (December 1941): 339-68.

10. Stephen Toulmin and June Goodfield, *The Discovery of Time* (New York: Harper & Row, 1965), p. 141 and *passim.* On pre-Darwinian discussions of the origin of races, see William Stanton, *The Leopard's Spots: Scientific Attitudes toward Race in America, 1815-59* (Chicago: University of Chicago Press, 1960). John Arlo De Jong has shown that geological discussions about the earth's history and anthropological arguments over the origin of races had familiarized an important segment of American society with the concept of development prior to the coming of Darwinism; "American Attitudes toward Evolution before Darwin" (Ph.D. diss., State University of Iowa, 1962).

11. George Frederick Wright, "Recent Works Bearing on the Relation of Science to Religion: No. II," *Bibliotheca Sacra* 33 (July 1876): 480. For a similar statement, see [William North Rice], "The Darwinian Theory of the Origin of Species," *New Englander* 26 (October 1867): 608-9.

12. Quoted in A. C. Crombie, *Medieval and Early Modern Science* (Garden City, N.Y.: Doubleday Anchor Books, 1959), 1:26.

13. S. R. Calthrop, "Religion and Evolution," *Religious Magazine and Monthly Review* 50 (September 1873): 205.

14. Francis E. Abbot, "Philosophical Biology," *North American Review* 107 (October 1868): 391.

15. F. R. Moulton, "Influence of Astronomy on Science," *Scientific Monthly* 47 (October 1938): 306. Others who have recognized the importance of the nebular hypothesis in preparing the way for Darwinism are Milton Millhauser, *Just before Darwin: Robert Chambers and Vestiges* (Middletown, Conn.: Wesleyan University Press, 1959), p. 79; John C. Greene, *The Death of Adam: Evolution and Its Impact on Western Thought* (Ames: Iowa State University Press, 1959), chap. 2; and Walter F. Cannon, "John Herschel and the Idea of Science," *Journal of the History of Ideas* 22 (April-June 1961): 239.

Cannon, however, attaches more importance to the speculations of William Herschel than to Laplace's cosmogony. "Herschelian astronomy," he says, "first made the English public, and English scientists, evolution-conscious at a serious intellectual level." In *Darwin's Century: Evolution and the Men Who Discovered It* (Garden City, N.Y.: Doubleday Anchor

Books, 1958), p. 330, Loren Eisely questions the significance of the nebular hypothesis to the Darwinian revolution, as Simon Newcomb did eighty years earlier in "Evolution and Theology: A Rejoinder," *North American Review* 28 (June 1879): 659.

16. A. S. Packard, Jr., "The Law of Evolution," *Independent* 32 (5 February 1880): 10.

17. J. S. Stahr, "Evolution Theories and Theology," *Mercersburg Review* 19 (July 1872): 440. See also George W. Samson, "Modern Evolution Theories," *Baptist Quarterly* 10 (October 1876): 503-4; and John Pindar Bland, "Some Implications of the Philosophy of Evolution," *Unitarian Review* 3 (June 1875): 577-78.

18. [Henry Ware Holland], "Gray's Darwiniana," *Nation* 23 (14 December 1876): 358.

19. Clarence King, "Catastrophism and Evolutionism," *American Naturalist* 11 (August 1877): 466. A connection between Darwinism and the nebular hypothesis was commonly seen in the nineteenth century; see Benjamin Peirce, "The Conflict between Science and Religion," *Unitarian Review* 7 (June 1877): 622; and Cope, *The Origin of the Fittest*, p. 1. Dr. John Harvey Kellogg, of cornflake fame, looked upon Darwinism "as a sort of supplement to the 'nebular hypothesis.'" [J. H. Kellogg], "Darwinism," *Health Reformer* 8 (December 1873): 381.

20. E. O. Haven, "Darwinism and Christianity," *Lakeside Monthly* 7 (April 1872): 308.

21. Daniel S. Martin, *The Relation of Christian Educators to the Modern Phases of Science* (Albany, N.Y.: Proceedings of the University Convocation, 29-31 July 1873), p. 17.

22. Conrad Wright discusses the effect of geology on views of the Mosaic record in "The Religion of Geology," *New England Quarterly* 14 (June 1941): 335-58.

23. Loewenberg's contention that Biblical arguments were a major reason for the rejection of Darwinism during the period from 1859 to 1873 is belied by his own statements. "A large proportion of the religiously minded public," he wrote, was impressed by the argument "that the flexibility of language in the Holy Word rendered any discovery ultimately reconcilable with it." For these persons, "the Biblical rendition of the origin of the world apparently did not deny an evolutionary development but confirmed it." Loewenberg, "The Controversy over Evolution in New England," pp. 254-55.

24. See, for example, C. Nisbet, "Darwinism," *Baptist Quarterly* 7 (January 1873): 77; the editor's introduction to R. P. Stebbins, "Darwinism, or Evolution," *Religious Magazine and Monthly Review* 50 (December 1873): 496; and Frederick Gardiner, "Darwinism," *Bibliotheca Sacra* 29 (April 1872): 262.

25. Andrew P. Peabody, "The Bearing of Modern Scientific Theories on the Fundamental Truths of Religion," *Bibliotheca Sacra* 21 (October 1864): 716-17.

26. [Rice], "The Darwinian Theory," pp. 609, 634-35.

27. [William Hayes Ward], "Deliver Us from Our Friends," *Independent* 31 (4 December 1879): 14.

28. Theophilus Parsons, "On the Origin of Species," *AJS*, 2nd ser., 30 (July 1860): 11.

29. James Woodrow, Address before the Alumni Association of the Columbia Theological Seminary, 7 May 1884, in M. W. Woodrow, ed., *Dr. James Woodrow*, pp. 628-29. On the controversy over Woodrow's evolutionary beliefs, see Clement Eaton, "Professor James Woodrow and the Freedom of Teaching in the South," in *The Pursuit of Southern History*, ed. George Brown Tindall (Baton Rouge: Louisiana State University Press, 1964), pp. 438-50.

30. Among those who have made this point are A. Hunter Dupree, *Asa Gray, 1810-1888* (Cambridge, Mass.: Harvard University Press, 1959), pp. 266-69; and R. J. Wilson, *Darwinism and the American Intellectual* (Homewood, Ill.: Dorsey Press, 1967), pp. 3-4, 39-40.

31. [Oliver Wendell Holmes], "Mechanisms of Vital Actions," *North American Review* 85 (July 1857): 77.

32. John Fiske, "The Triumph of Darwinism," *North American Review* 124 (January 1877): 92.

33. Charles Hitchcock, "The Relations of Geology to Theology," *Bibliotheca Sacra* 24 (April 1867): 371.

34. James McCosh, "Is the Development Hypothesis Sufficient?" *Popular Science Monthly* 10 (November 1876): 96. For the views of those who saw Darwinism in opposition to natural theology, see Francis Bowen's articles, "Darwin on the Origin of Species," *North American Review* 90 (April 1860): 474-506; and "Remarks on the Latest Form of the Development Theory," American Academy of Arts and Sciences, *Memoirs* 8 (1861): 97-122; and Charles Hodge's *What Is Darwinism?* (New York: Scribner, Armstrong, 1874).

35. George Frederick Wright, "Recent Works Bearing on the Relation of Science to Religion: No. IV," *Bibliotheca Sacra* 34 (April 1877): 363; Paul A. Chadbourne, "Design in Nature," *Princeton Review*, 4th ser., 1 (March 1878): 303; and [Samuel Atkins Eliot], "The Origin of Species," *North American Review* 91 (October 1860): 529. See also [H. S. Stanley], "Evolution as Bearing on Method in Teleology," *New Englander* 42 (September 1883): 579-97.

36. See A. Hunter Dupree's introduction to Asa Gray, *Darwiniana: Essays and Reviews Pertaining to Darwinism* (Cambridge, Mass.: Harvard

University Press, 1963), pp. ix-xxiii; and Dupree, *Asa Gray*, pp. 136, 266-69, 382. The following discussion is based upon three of the essays that compose *Darwiniana:* "The Origin of Species by Means of Natural Selection," originally published in the *AJS* (March 1860); "Darwin on the Origin of Species," which first appeared in two parts in the *Atlantic Monthly* (July and August 1860); and "Darwin and His Reviewers," also printed in the *Atlantic Monthly* (October 1860). The last two essays appear together in *Darwiniana* under the heading "Natural Selection Not Inconsistent with Natural Theology."

37. Gray, *Darwiniana*, p. 45.

38. Ibid., pp. 43-44.

39. Ibid., p. 127. Here Gray is referring to Agassiz' argument in his *Contributions to the Natural History of the United States* that the physical and biological worlds give evidence of having been designed by the same mind. In one passage Agassiz cites approvingly Benjamin Peirce's discovery that the law of phyllotaxis, according to which the arrangements of leaves on plants may be expressed by a simple series of fractions, also holds for the successive periods of revolution of the planets. This discovery was meaningful only to those who believed that the planets were genetically related like leaves on a plant or, in other words, to those who accepted the nebular hypothesis. Agassiz, *Essay on Classification*, ed. Edward Lurie (Cambridge, Mass.: Harvard University Press, 1962), pp. 127-32. This *Essay* forms the greater portion of volume 1 of *Contributions to the Natural History of the United States of America*, first published in 1857. See also Agassiz' views on the origin of the earth in his "Contemplations of God in the Kosmos," *Christian Examiner* 50 (January 1851): 1-17.

40. Gray, *Darwiniana*, pp. 45, 88-89, 111.

41. Ibid., pp. 78-79.

42. Ibid., pp. 112-13.

43. Ibid., p. 118.

44. Dupree, *Asa Gray*, pp. 296-301, 339-41. I am indebted to Professor Dupree for pointing out the significance of this decision.

45. "Darwinism," *Southern Review* 12 (April 1873): 422. George B. Cheever argued that "the watch supposed by Huxley is far more impossible than that supposed by Paley, and instead of the demonstration of design being weakened, it is forcibly strengthened." "The Philosophy of Evolution," *Presbyterian Quarterly and Princeton Review*, n.s., 4 (January 1875): 143.

46. Joseph Le Conte, "Evolution in Relation to Materialism," *Princeton Review*, 4th ser., 7 (March 1881): 153.

47. Richard A. Proctor, *Our Place among Infinities* (New York: Longmans, Green, 1901), p. 23. From a lecture delivered in New York on 3 April 1874.

48. [Uriah Smith], "Giving Way," *Advent Review and Sabbath Herald* 60 (23 October 1883): 664. Princeton's John T. Duffield saw "a *polar* opposition" between Darwinism and the Biblical record. "Evolutionism Respecting Man, and the Bible," *Princeton Review*, 4th ser., 1 (January 1878): 153.

49. [John Amory Lowell], "Darwin's Origin of Species," *Christian Examiner* 68 (May 1860): 449. E. D. Cope saw this repugnance as arising from two considerations: "first, that the human species is certainly involved, and man's descent from an ape asserted; and, secondly, that the scheme in general seems to conflict with that presented by the Mosaic account of the Creation, which is regarded as communicated to its author by an infallible inspiration." *The Origin of the Fittest*, p. 128.

50. P. R. Russel, "Darwinism Examined," *Advent Review and Sabbath Herald* 47 (18 May 1876): 153.

51. On Gray's lack of influence among the materialists, see Dupree, *Asa Gray*, pp. 377-82.

APPENDIX 1

1. Scholarly opinion is divided on the Presbyterian response to evolution. Windsor Hall Roberts states that in spite of the "liberalizing influence" of President James McCosh, of Princeton, the Presbyterians "put up the most stubborn, the most persistent and no doubt the ablest fight against evolution" (*The Reaction of American Protestant Churches to the Darwinian Philosophy, 1860-1900* [private ed.; Chicago: distributed by the University of Chicago Libraries, 1938], p. 40). Herbert W. Schneider, on the other hand, maintains that "the Presbyterians found Darwinism congenial" ("The Influence of Darwin and Spencer on American Philosophical Theology," *Journal of the History of Ideas* 6 [January 1945]: 5). Edward J. Pfeifer finds that although the Presbyterians were "particularly sensitive about the Biblical account of creation," by the late 1860s they were beginning to concede the possibility of reconciling their theology with Darwinism ("The Reception of Darwinism in the United States, 1859-1880" [Ph.D. diss., Brown University, 1957], pp. 44-45, 78). On the Unitarians and the Congregationalists, see Roberts, p. 40, and Pfeifer, p. 78.

2. Information regarding the various periodicals is based on Frank Luther Mott, *A History of American Magazines* (4 vols.; Cambridge, Mass.: Harvard University Press, 1930-57).

3. Editor's introduction to R. P. Stebbins, "Darwinism, or Evolution," *Religious Magazine and Monthly Review* 50 (December 1873): 496.

4. See J[oseph] H[enry] A[llen], "Vestiges of Creation and Sequel," *Christian Examiner* 40 (May 1846): 335; J[oseph] L[overing], "Baron Humboldt's Cosmos," ibid. 48 (January 1850): 57; T[homas] H[ill], "The First

Chapter of Genesis," ibid. 59 (November 1855): 392; John Pindar Bland, "Some Implications of the Philosophy of Evolution," *Unitarian Review* 3 (June 1875): 576-87; and Benjamin Peirce, "The Conflict between Science and Religion," ibid. 7 (June 1877): 662-66.

5. See [E. A. Walker], "The First Document of Genesis," *New Englander* 19 (July 1861): 585-90; [William North Rice], "The Darwinian Theory of the Origin of Species," ibid. 26 (October 1867): 609; [Burritt A. Smith], "Evolutionism *Versus* Theism," ibid. 33 (January 1874): 76-88; and [H. S. Stanley], "Evolution as Bearing on Method in Teleology," ibid. 42 (September 1883): 583.

John O. Means, "The Narrative of the Creation in Genesis," *Bibliotheca Sacra* 12 (January 1855): 128-29 and 12 (April 1855): 327-28; James D. Dana, "Science and the Bible," ibid. 14 (July 1857): 477, 480; E. P. Barrows, "The Mosaic Six Days and Geology," ibid. 14 (January 1857): 94-97; Andrew P. Peabody, "The Bearing of Modern Scientific Theories on the Fundamental Truths of Religion," ibid. 21 (October 1864): 712, 717; Charles Hitchcock, "The Relations of Geology to Theology," ibid. 24 (April 1867): 371, 438; Samuel Hopkins, "An Exposition of the Original Text of Genesis I. and II.," ibid. 33 (July 1876): 510-11; and James D. Dana, "Creation; or, the Biblical Cosmogony in the Light of Modern Science," ibid. 42 (April 1885): 220.

H. M. Lyman, "The Nebular Hypothesis," *Congregational Review* 11 (November 1871): 537-48.

6. Samuel Harris, "The Harmony of Natural Science and Theology," *New Englander* 10 (February 1852): 10; Austin Phelps, "The Oneness of God in Revelation and in Nature," *Bibliotheca Sacra* 16 (October 1859): 849; and Joseph P. Thompson, "The Permanence of Christianity in the Intention of Its Founder," *Bibliotheca Sacra* 22 (April 1865): 239. Five years later Thompson endorsed the nebular hypothesis in *Man in Genesis and in Geology: or, The Biblical Account of Man's Creation, Tested by Scientific Theories of His Origin and Antiquity* (New York: Samuel R. Wells, 1870), pp. 13-16.

7. E. F. Burr, *Pater Mundi; or, Doctrine of Evolution: Second Series* (Boston: Noyes, Holmes, 1873), pp. 201-38; [Smith], "Evolutionism," pp. 75-106. See also Burr, *The Stars of God* (Hartford, Conn.: Student Publishing Co., 1896); and Abraham G. Jennings, *The Earth and the World: How Formed?* (New York: Fleming H. Revell Co., 1900). Burr was a sometime lecturer in Amherst College on the scientific evidences of religion; Jennings was a New York businessman and a disciple of Burr's.

8. See the review of *Views of the Architecture of the Heavens*, by J. P. Nichol, *Princeton Review* 13 (January 1841): 155; [Albert Baldwin Dod], review of *Vestiges of the Natural History of Creation*, ibid. 17 (October 1845): 513-14, 536-38; review of *The Indications of the Creator; or, The Natural Evidences of Final Cause*, by George Taylor, ibid. 24 (January

1852): 144; [Daniel Kirkwood], "The Nebular Hypothesis," *Presbyterian Quarterly Review* 2 (March 1854): 529-46; "Professor Lewis' View of the 'Days' of Creation," ibid. 4 (December 1855): 480-81; "The Mosaic Account of Creation, Scientific," ibid. 7 (July 1858): 140-41; and John Bascom, "Evolution, as Advocated by Herbert Spencer," *Presbyterian Quarterly and Princeton Review*, new ser., 1 (July 1872): 504-5.

9. "The Logical Relations of Religion and Natural Science," *Princeton Review* 32 (October 1860): 579; [Matthew Boyd Hope], "On the Relation between the Holy Scriptures and Some Parts of Geological Science," ibid. 13 (July 1841): 392-93.

10. Other prominent Presbyterians who advocated the nebular hypothesis were the philosophers James McCosh and Laurens P. Hickok. See McCosh, *Christianity and Positivism: A Series of Lectures to the Times on Natural Theology and Apologetics* (London: Macmillan, 1875), pp. 16-17; McCosh, "Is the Development Hypothesis Sufficient?" *Popular Science Monthly* 10 (November 1876): 92; McCosh, *Development: What It Can Do and What It Cannot Do* (New York: Charles Scribner's Sons, 1883), pp. 34-35; McCosh, *The Religious Aspect of Evolution* (New York: G. P. Putnam's Sons, 1888), pp. 29, 73; and Hickok, *Rational Cosmology: Or the Eternal Principles and the Necessary Laws of the Universe* (New York: D. Appleton, 1858), pp. 186-202, 322-45.

11. Roberts, *Reaction of American Protestant Churches*, pp. 40-41.

12. [W. H. Allen], "Natural History of Creation," *Methodist Quarterly Review* 28 (April 1846): 299. The effect of the resolutions of nebulae on the nebular hypothesis is briefly mentioned in [C. Hackley], "The Present State of Astronomy," ibid. 33 (January 1851): 63.

13. The four favorable articles were [S. D. Hillman], "Recent Astronomy and the Mosaic Record," ibid. 50 (October 1868): 532-52; [Rush Emery], "Spectrum Analysis," ibid. 53 (April 1871): 213-14; [Alexander Winchell], "The Unity of the Physical World," ibid. 56 (January 1874): 71-75; and [J. T. Crane], "Popular Astronomy," ibid. 61 (April 1879): 270-71. The unfavorable one was [S. Parsons], "The Nebular Hypothesis and Modern Genesis," ibid. 59 (January 1877): 127-57. Paradoxically, Parsons was most critical of another opponent of the nebular hypothesis, W. B. Slaughter, author of *The Modern Genesis* (New York: Nelson & Phillips, 1876).

14. "Modern Atheism," *Southern Review* 10 (January 1872): 129-39.

15. [Alexis Caswell], "Architecture of the Heavens," *Christian Review* 6 (December 1841): 595-620. Caswell also mentioned the nebular hypothesis in his review of *Astronomy and General Physics Considered with Reference to Natural Theology*, by William Whewell, ibid. 1 (June 1836): 237.

16. For the nebular hypothesis were Heman Lincoln, "Development versus Creation," *Baptist Quarterly* 2 (July 1868): 257-58; and William C. Richards, "Spectrum Analysis," ibid. 4 (January 1870): 37. Opposed to it

were M. B. Anderson, "Growth and Relation of the Sciences," *Christian Review* 27 (April 1862): 209; and Charles E. Hamlin, "The Attitude of the Christian Teacher in Respect to Science," *Baptist Quarterly* 6 (January 1872): 26-27. George W. Samson, "Modern Evolution Theories," ibid. 10 (October 1876): 503-4, discusses the nebular hypothesis but does not commit himself.

17. Roberts, *Reaction of American Protestant Churches*, p. 41.

18. J[oseph] C[lark], "Eureka," *Mercersburg Review* 4 (January 1852): 90. See also J[oseph] C[lark], "Hugh Miller as a Geologist," ibid. 9 (October 1857): 609; Theodore Appel, "Man and the Cosmos," ibid. 14 (April 1867): 299; and J. S. Stahr, "Evolution Theories and Theology," ibid. 19 (July 1872): 440.

19. See Tayler Lewis, *The Six Days of Creation; or, The Scriptural Cosmology, with the Ancient Idea of Time-Worlds, in Distinction from Worlds in Space* (Schenectady, N.Y.: G. Y. Van Debogert, 1855), pp. 146-47; and Lewis, *The Bible and Science; or, The World-Problem* (Schenectady, N.Y.: G. Y. Van Debogert, 1856), p. 251. Lewis was less kind toward the nebular hypothesis in his earlier review of *Vestiges of the Natural History of Creation* in *American Review* 1 (May 1845): 542.

20. Roberts, *Reaction of American Protestant Churches*, pp. 41-42.

21. H. I. Schmidt, "Infidelity: Its Metamorphoses, and Its Present Aspects," *Evangelical Review* 5 (January 1854): 412; L. Sternberg, "Geology and Moses," *Evangelical Quarterly Review* 19 (January 1868): 138-39; W. E. Parson, "Evolution—Shall It Be Atheistic?" *Lutheran Quarterly* 9 (April 1879): 182; D. R. Malone, "The Ages of Nature and the Mosaic Account," *Christian Quarterly* 8 (January 1876): 18; M. H. Slosson, "Involution before Evolution," ibid. 8 (July 1876): 332, 341-42; "Herbert Spencer's 'First Principles' and 'Illustrations of Progress,'" *American Quarterly and Church Review* 16 (October 1864): 434.

22. Martyn Paine, *Physiology of the Soul and Instinct, as Distinguished from Materialism* (New York: Harper & Brothers, 1872), pp. 363, 554, 592-93. In the preface to this work (p. ix) Paine states: "The Narratives of Creation and of the Flood will be shown, demonstratively, to be literally direct revelations by the Creator, and that they were intended to be received in their obvious sense."

23. See A[dolphus] Smith, "Science, Falsely so Called," *Advent Review and Sabbath Herald* 42 (8 July 1873): 31; and the book by the Adventist physician, John Harvey Kellogg, *Harmony of Science and the Bible on the Nature of the Soul and the Doctrine of the Resurrection* (Battle Creek, Mich.: Review and Herald Publishing Association, 1879), pp. 20-21. The Adventists continued to oppose the nebular hypothesis well into the twentieth century. See George McCready Price, *A History of Some Scientific Blunders* (New York: Fleming H. Revell Co., 1930), chap. 3. See also

Ronald L. Numbers, "Science Falsely So-Called: Evolution and Adventists in the Nineteenth Century," *Journal of the American Scientific Affiliation* 27 (March 1975): 18-23.

24. Ernest R. Sandeen, in his recent study of *The Roots of Fundamentalism: British and American Millenarianism 1800-1930* (Chicago: University of Chicago Press, 1970), p. 267, points out that "antagonism toward evolution did not follow the same denominational demarcations as millenarianism. . . . There does not seem to be any justification for arguing that millenarians were more ready than other conservative Christians of the [nineteen-] twenties to join the crusade against evolution."

25. John L. Morrison, "A History of American Catholic Opinion on the Theory of Evolution, 1859-1950" (Ph.D. diss., University of Missouri, 1951), pp. 2-3, 8,12.

26. [Orestes A. Brownson], "The Conflict of Science and Religion," *Brownson's Quarterly Review*, last ser., 3 (April 1875): 168. [W. R. Thompson], "Evolution," *Catholic World* 34 (February 1882): 684.

27. Pope Pius IX to the Archbishop of Munich, 21 December 1863, quoted in Morrison, "American Catholic Opinion," p. 33.

28. Ibid., pp. 11-12. See also John Gmeiner, "The Liberty of Catholics in Scientific Matters," *Catholic World* 48 (November 1888): 145-50.

29. [Augustine F. Hewit], "Scriptural Questions," ibid. 40 (November 1884): 150; [Hewit], "Scriptural Questions: Second Series," ibid. 44 (January 1887): 450-52.

Bibliographic Note

Since the most useful documents relating to the nebular hypothesis in America are cited in the references accompanying the text, it is unnecessary to mention them again. However, a brief word about my experiences in locating the periodical and manuscript sources upon which this study is primarily based might be of some interest. When I first set out to discover the significance of Laplace's cosmogony in nineteenth-century American thought, I had no established landmarks to go by. No previous study existed, and no guide provided more than a handful of references. It was thus necessary to search volume by volume through approximately one hundred periodicals—scientific, religious, and general—even to identify the leading participants and issues in the American discussions of the nebular hypothesis. The periodicals systematically searched are listed below, but this list does not take into account the journals, including British publications, in which I happened across additional articles of importance. From this survey of the nineteenth-century periodical literature I was able to single out those individuals who played significant roles in the history of the nebular hypothesis in America, and I then began exploring manuscript collections for the unpublished papers of these persons. My successes and failures are described below in the section on manuscripts.

PERIODICALS

SCIENTIFIC

Academy of Science of Saint Louis, *Transactions*, 1856-1910.
Albany Institute, *Transactions*, 1830-93.
American Academy of Arts and Sciences, *Memoirs* (Boston), 1785-1924.
American Academy of Arts and Sciences, *Proceedings* (Boston), 1848-1911.

American Association for the Advancement of Science, *Proceedings*, 1848-
    1910.
American Journal of Science and Arts (New Haven), 1818-1910.
American Philosophical Society, *Proceedings* (Philadelphia), 1838-1940.
American Philosophical Society, *Transactions* (Philadelphia), 1769-1940.
Analyst: A Journal of Pure and Applied Mathematics (Des Moines), 1874-
    83.
Annual of Scientific Discovery (Boston), 1850-71.
Astronomical Journal (Cambridge and Albany), 1849-61, 1886-1944.
Astronomical Notices (Ann Arbor), 1858-62.
Astronomical Society of the Pacific, *Publications* (San Francisco), 1889-
    1913.
Astronomy and Astro-Physics (Northfield, Minn.), 1892-94.
Astrophysical Journal (Chicago), 1895-1910.
Boston Journal of Philosophy and the Arts, 1823-25.
California Academy of Sciences, *Bulletin* (San Francisco), 1884-87.
California Academy of Sciences, *Proceedings* (San Francisco), 1854-1913.
Cambridge Miscellany of Mathematics, Physics, and Astronomy, 1842-43.
Connecticut Academy of Arts and Sciences, *Transactions* (New Haven),
    1866-1909.
Franklin Journal (later, *Journal of the Franklin Institute*) (Philadelphia),
    1826-1905.
Literary and Philosophical Society of New York, *Transactions*, 1815.
Mathematical Miscellany (Flushing, Long Island), 1836-38.
Mathematical Monthly (Cambridge and New York), 1858-61.
National Academy of Sciences, *Memoirs* (Washington, D.C.), 1866-1915.
Popular Astronomy (Northfield, Minn.), 1893-1910.
Popular Science Monthly (New York), 1872-92.
Science (Cambridge and New York), 1883-1905.
Science Observer (Boston), 1878-81.
Scientific American (New York), 1845-1905.
Sidereal Messenger (Cincinnati), 1846-48.
Sidereal Messenger (Northfield, Minn.), 1882-91.
Smithsonian Contributions to Knowledge (Washington, D.C.), 1848-1916.
Smithsonian Institution, *Annual Report* (Washington, D.C.), 1854-1910.
Smithsonian Miscellaneous Collections (Washington, D.C.), 1862-1907.

RELIGIOUS

Advent Review and Sabbath Herald (Battle Creek, Mich.), 1850-90.
    Seventh-day Adventist.
American Presbyterian Review (New York), 1863-71.
Baptist Quarterly (Philadelphia), 1867-77.

Biblical Repertory (later, *Biblical Repertory and Princeton Review*) (Princeton and Philadelphia), 1825-68. Presbyterian.

Biblical Repository (also, *American Biblical Repository*) (Andover, Mass.), 1831-50. Congregational.

Bibliotheca Sacra (Andover, Mass., and Oberlin, Ohio), 1844-94. Congregational.

Brownson's Quarterly Review (Boston and New York), 1844-75. Roman Catholic.

Catholic World (New York), 1865-96. Roman Catholic.

Christian Disciple (Boston), 1813-16, 1819-21. Unitarian.

Christian Examiner (Boston), 1824-69. Unitarian.

Christian Observer (Boston and New York), 1802-33. Anglican.

Christian Quarterly (Cincinnati), 1869-76. Disciples of Christ.

Christian Review (Boston, New York, and Baltimore), 1836-63. Baptist.

Christian's Magazine (New York), 1808-1911.

Christian Spectator (later, *Quarterly Christian Spectator*) (New Haven), 1823-38. Congregational.

Church Review (later, *American Quarterly Church Review*) (New Haven and New York), 1848-71. Protestant Episcopal.

Congregational Quarterly (Boston), 1859-78.

Evangelical Review (Gettysburg, Penn.), 1849-70. Evangelical Lutheran.

General Repository and Review (Cambridge), 1812-13. Unitarian.

Mercersburg Review (Mercersburg, Penn.), 1849-73. German Reformed.

Methodist Magazine (later, *Methodist Quarterly Review* and *Methodist Review*) (New York), 1818-1900.

New Englander (later, *New Englander and Yale Review*) (New Haven), 1843-92. Quasi-Congregational.

Presbyterian Magazine (Philadelphia), 1851-59.

Presbyterian Quarterly Review (Philadelphia), 1852-62.

Presbyterian Review (New York), 1880-89.

Religious Magazine (Philadelphia), 1828-30.

Southern Review (Baltimore and Saint Louis), 1867-78. Southern Methodist Episcopal.

Theological and Literary Journal (New York), 1852-59. Nondenominational.

Unitarian Review and Religious Magazine (Boston), 1874-85. Unitarian.

GENERAL

American Monthly Magazine (Boston), 1829-31.

American Monthly Magazine (New York), 1836-38.

American Monthly Magazine and Critical Review (New York), 1817-19.

American Monthly Review (Cambridge), 1832-33.

American Quarterly Observer (Boston), 1833-34.

American Quarterly Review (Philadelphia), 1827-37.
American Repertory of Arts, Sciences, and Manufactures (New York), 1840-42.
American Review: A Whig Journal of Politics, Literature, Art and Science (New York), 1845-47.
Analetic Magazine (later, *Literary Gazette*) (Philadelphia), 1813-21.
Appleton's Journal of Literature, Science, and Art (New York), 1869-76.
Atheneum (Boston), 1817-31.
Atlantic Magazine (New York), 1824-25.
Atlantic Monthly (Boston), 1857-1901.
Boston Quarterly Review, 1838-42.
Dial (Boston), 1840-44.
Harper's New Monthly Magazine (New York), 1850-75.
International Review (New York), 1874-83.
Knickerbocker (New York), 1833-65.
Lippincott's Magazine (Philadelphia), 1868-85.
Literary Miscellany (Cambridge), 1805-6.
Massachusetts Quarterly Review (Boston), 1847-48.
Metropolitan Magazine (New Haven), 1833-35.
Monthly Anthology and Boston Review, 1805-11.
Monthly Chronical (Boston), 1840-42.
Nation (New York), 1865-80.
New-England Magazine (Boston), 1831-34.
New York Review, 1837-42.
North American Review (Boston and New York), 1815-1900.
Philadelphia Register and National Recorder (later, *Saturday Magazine*), 1819-22.
Putnam's Monthly Magazine (later, *Putnam's Magazine*) (New York), 1853-57, 1868-70.
Select Reviews and Spirit of Foreign Magazines (Philadelphia), 1809-12.
Southern Literary Messenger (Richmond), 1834-54.
Southern Quarterly Review (New Orleans and Charleston), 1842-56.
Southern Review (Charleston), 1828-32.
United States Review and Literary Gazette (Boston), 1826-27.

MANUSCRIPTS

AMERICAN PHILOSOPHICAL SOCIETY LIBRARY

John Warner Papers. Among these papers are twenty-three letters from Daniel Kirkwood to his friend Warner, most discussing Warner's controversy with Benjamin Peirce over phyllotaxis. None touches on the nebular hypothesis.

Minutes of the A.P.S. The minutes of the meeting held 20 July 1849 record Sears C. Walker's communication to the society on Kirkwood's analogy.

BOSTON PUBLIC LIBRARY

Nathaniel Bowditch Correspondence. None of the correspondence preserved mentions the nebular hypothesis. The only allusion to the origin of the solar system is in a letter from Thomas Jefferson to Bowditch (1818). In Bowditch's personal copy of Laplace's *Système du monde* (4th ed., 1813) there is only one notation, concerning the origin of the asteroids, in the section on the nebular hypothesis.

HARVARD UNIVERSITY ARCHIVES

William Cranch Bond Papers. Nothing in these papers reveals Bond's attitude toward the Laplacian cosmogony. The only items of interest to us are a letter from Benjamin A. Gould (1849) requesting a check of one of Stephen Alexander's predictions and a plea from G. W. Eveleth (1852) to lecture at Harvard on the falsity of the nebular hypothesis and the theory of gravitation.

HARVARD UNIVERSITY, HOUGHTON LIBRARY

Benjamin Peirce Papers. Among the letters received by Peirce are Elias Loomis' reply to his request to solve some problems raised by the nebular hypothesis (1846), two notes from James Dwight Dana concerning his debate with Tayler Lewis (1856), and Stephen Alexander's criticism of a statement on the nebular hypothesis attributed to Peirce (1874). Also in this collection is a copy of the "Tribute of Respect to the Memory of Sears C. Walker" by the officers and members of the Coast Survey (1853), in which E. B. Hunt comments on Walker's early relationship with Daniel Kirkwood.

INDIANA UNIVERSITY, LILLY LIBRARY

Daniel Kirkwood Papers. Unfortunately, most of Kirkwood's papers were destroyed on the night of 12 July 1883, when lightning struck Science Hall at Indiana University. All that remains today are forty-six pages of Kirkwood material, little of which relates to his analogy and the nebular hypothesis.

LIBRARY OF CONGRESS

Cleveland Abbe Papers. In the draft of an undated autobiographical memoir entitled "What I Remember about My Friends and Myself," Abbe describes the meetings of a regular Wednesday-afternoon mathematical club that met in the early 1860s in the rooms of Benjamin Peirce at Cambridge. The nebular hypothesis was one of the topics discussed. Abbe also tells about a series of lectures by Peirce on the nebular hypothesis and theories of creation, given in the autumn of 1861.

Matthew F. Maury Papers. In 1866 Maury began writing an elementary textbook on astronomy that never got published. An undated galley proof of this work survived and is with Maury's papers in the Library of Congress. Chapter 18 is devoted to the nebular hypothesis.

Simon Newcomb Papers. In this collection are drafts of Newcomb's 1859 paper on the origin of the asteroids and an undated paper defining the nebular hypothesis and other scientific terms; letters from T. J. J. See expressing his intention to pursue studies in cosmogony (1889) and defending his personal reputation (1898); and interesting personal correspondence from Jacob Ennis (1878) and David Trowbridge (1882), both of whom devoted much of their lives to solving problems associated with the origin of the solar system.

T. J. J. See Papers. See was a Berlin-trained cosmogonist who showed great promise as a young man but later turned into something of an eccentric. Much of the material in this massive and unexplored collection deals with cosmogonical issues. Of particular interest is Simon Newcomb's letter (1889) discouraging young See from wasting his life on the history of the heavenly bodies.

NATIONAL ARCHIVES

Records of the Naval Observatory (Record Group 78). The only relevant document found either in these records or in the records of the Hydrographic Office was a letter from Matthew F. Maury to the Reverend Mr. Field of New York City (1855) discussing the harmony of science and revelation.

RENSSELAER POLYTECHNIC INSTITUTE ARCHIVES

Eben N. Horsford Papers. In the R. P. I. Archives is Horsford's lecture on the "Theory of the Formation of the Earth," a discussion of the nebular hypothesis with which he began a course on geology, 8 March 1839.

SMITHSONIAN INSTITUTION ARCHIVES

Joseph Henry Papers. Henry's correspondence includes at least ten letters (1847-52) from his brother-in-law, Stephen Alexander, reporting his investigations of the "harmonies of the solar system," together with a letter from Henry (1857) encouraging Alexander in his endeavors.

Among Henry's other papers are several drafts of lectures on the nebular hypothesis, the most significant being his lecture on Laplace's theory given at Princeton from 1841 through 1847 as part of his geology course. The Smithsonian also possesses a copy of George Musgrave Giger's student "Notes on a series of lectures on geology given at Nassau Hall, Princeton," August 1841, the original of which is at the Presbyterian Historical Society in Philadelphia.

Official Incoming Correspondence. This large collection contains a number of letters to the secretary of the Smithsonian Institution from individuals working on the nebular hypothesis. Of use to us were Daniel Kirkwood's biographical sketch furnished at Henry's request (1876), David Trowbridge's revelations about himself (1861-81), Gustavus Hinrichs' comments on his planetary investigations (1864), Pliny Earle Chase's remarks on popular ignorance regarding the nebular hypothesis, and the series of letters on the cosmogonical work of Jacob Ennis (1881-82) written by Asaph Hall, Stephen Alexander, Charles A. Young, and Ennis himself.

YALE UNIVERSITY, BEINECKE LIBRARY

James Dwight Dana Correspondence. Dana's correspondence includes two letters from Daniel Kirkwood (1850), one to Benjamin A. Gould giving a brief history of the discovery of his analogy, the other to the editors of the *American Journal of Science* regarding the publication of his work; some remarks by Benjamin Peirce on the probability of the nebular hypothesis (1851); many congratulatory messages from scientists throughout the country complimenting Dana on his reply to Tayler Lewis' *Six Days of Creation* (1856); Tayler Lewis' answer to Dana's earlier letter of reconciliation, in which Lewis discusses the current relationship between religion and science; and two notes from Arnold Guyot (1858, 1881) complaining about his own tendency to put off publishing his views on Genesis.

Edward C. Herrick Papers. Daniel Kirkwood wrote about his recently discovered analogy in three letters to Herrick (1848-49).

Herrick-Loomis Correspondence. In 1850 Elias Loomis asked Herrick to mention in the *American Journal of Science* the omission of Kirkwood's analogy from his *Recent Progress of Astronomy.*

Elias Loomis Papers. Among these papers are a request from Benjamin Peirce to solve some problems related to the nebular hypothesis (1846), and letters from Denison Olmsted, Benjamin A. Gould, and Chester Dewey (1850-51) commenting on the omission of Kirkwood's analogy from Loomis' *Recent Progress of Astronomy.*

Denison Olmsted's Notes. A lecture on the nebular hypothesis is contained in Olmsted's "Notes and Other Material Relating to His Lectures in Yale

College on Natural Philosophy, Astronomy and Meteorology," 1843-59, pp. 121-24. On pp. 389-400 Olmsted gives an English translation of Laplace's note on the nebular hypothesis.

YALE UNIVERSITY, STERLING LIBRARY

Elias Loomis' Lectures. The Historical Manuscripts Room has Loomis' interleaved copy of his "Outline of the Astronomical Lectures in Yale College," ca. 1863, which includes his lecture on the nebular hypothesis, pp. 30-31.

The following manuscript collections yielded little or nothing of interest:

The Stephen Alexander letters and the Arnold Guyot papers and correspondence in the Princeton University Library.

The George Davidson papers in the Bancroft Library of the University of California, Berkeley.

The William Dawson papers in the McLennan Library of McGill University.

The Chester Dewey papers in the Rush Rhees Library of the University of Rochester.

The O. M. Mitchel papers in the Cincinnati Historical Society.

The Rhees and Kane collections in the Huntington Library, San Marino, California.

Index*

*Prepared with the assistance of
Lawrence D. Lynch